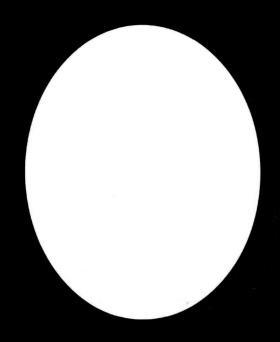

JENNIE WOOD'S

flutter

Flutter is dedicated to anyone who has ever felt uncomfortable in his or her own skin.

Jennie would like to thank:

A very special thank you to Jeff McComsey for helping to make the Flutter dream come true.

Thanks
to the following for their support and inspiration:
Natalie Baumgardner, Anne Calcagno,
Andrew DelQuadro, Michael Easton, The Fictory,
Kelly Ford, Grub Street, Joseph Krzemienski, 215 Ink,
Jorge Vega, Rowena Yow, John Yuskaitis and in
memory of Matthew J. Robinson.

Jeff would like to thank:

A very special thank you to Jennie Wood for trusting me to bring FLUTTER into this world. Her patience, enthusiasm and talent just might very well be limitless.

Thanks to Jorge Vega for saying nice things about me to strangers.

Thanks to Samantha Halsey for her love, support and for keeping me on point.

Thanks
to the following for their support and inspiration:
Andrew DelQuadro, Mike Perkins, Dominic Vivona,
Steve Becker, Jim McMunn, Joseph Krzemienski,
and Bill, Debbie and Elle McComsey.

Flutter Volume 1, first printing, 2013. Published by 215 Ink.

WRITTEN AND CREATED BY:
JENNIE WOOD

ART AND LETTERS BY:
JEFF MCCOMSEY

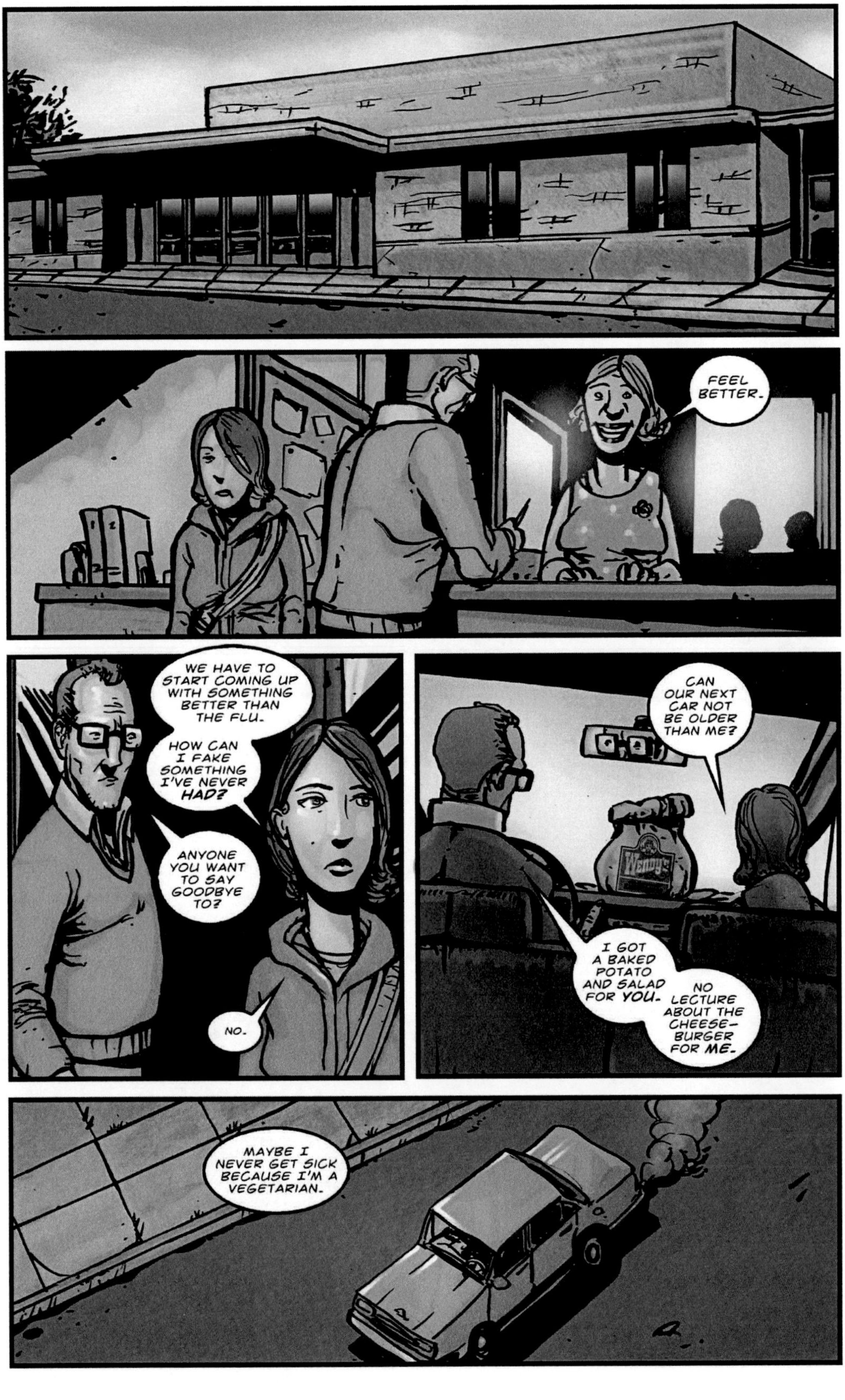
FEEL BETTER.
WE HAVE TO START COMING UP WITH SOMETHING BETTER THAN THE FLU.
HOW CAN I FAKE SOMETHING I'VE NEVER **HAD?**
ANYONE YOU WANT TO SAY GOODBYE TO?
NO.
CAN OUR NEXT CAR NOT BE OLDER THAN ME?
I GOT A BAKED POTATO AND SALAD FOR **YOU.**
NO LECTURE ABOUT THE CHEESE-BURGER FOR **ME.**
MAYBE I NEVER GET SICK BECAUSE I'M A VEGETARIAN.

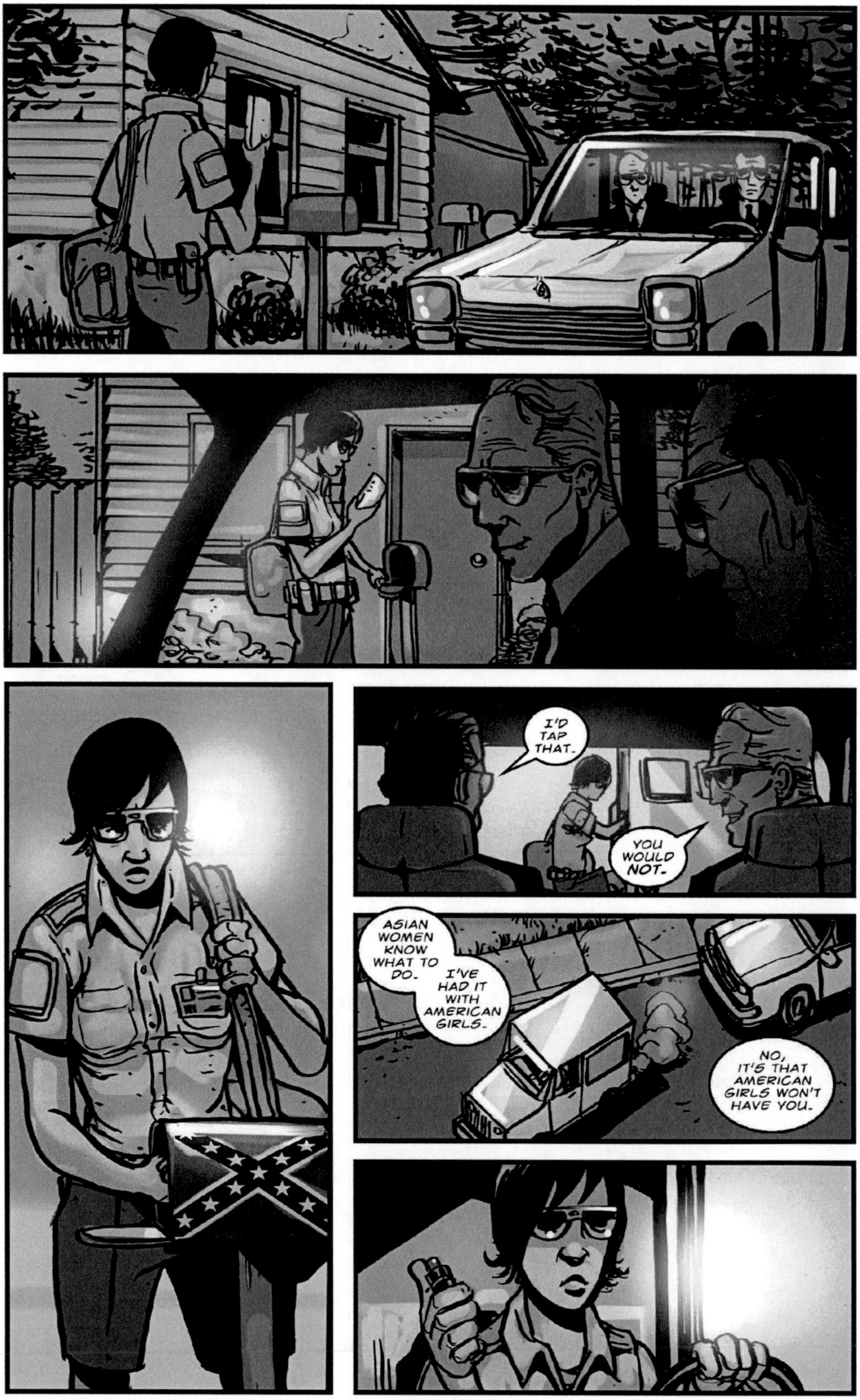

I'D TAP THAT.
YOU WOULD NOT.
ASIAN WOMEN KNOW WHAT TO DO.
I'VE HAD IT WITH AMERICAN GIRLS.
NO, IT'S THAT AMERICAN GIRLS WON'T HAVE YOU.

flutter
Story by: Jennie Wood Art by: Jeff McComsey
WHAM!
CHAPTER ONE:
HELL CAN WAIT...

MARRIAGE MUST REMAIN A SACRED UNION BETWEEN A MAN AND A WOMAN.
WE ARE THE PARTY PUSHING FOR A GAY MARRIAGE BAN ON BALLOTS IN ALL FIFTY STATES.
WE ARE THE PARTY PROTECTING YOUR VALUES, BUT WE CANNOT DO IT WITHOUT YOUR GENEROUS CONTRIBUTIONS.
ANOTHER ROUND OF APPLAUSE FOR GOVERNOR HAMILTON!
♪
YES?
A CIVIL WAR COLLECTOR IN NORTH CAROLINA HAD A SOUVENIR CANNONBALL DELIVERED TO HIS HOME AND IT BLEW UP.
TELL JEFFERSON DAVIS NOT TO WAIT SO LONG TO MOVE NEXT TIME.

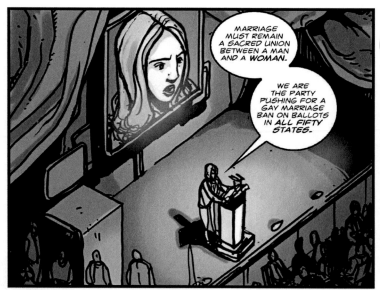

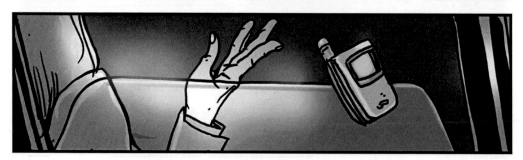

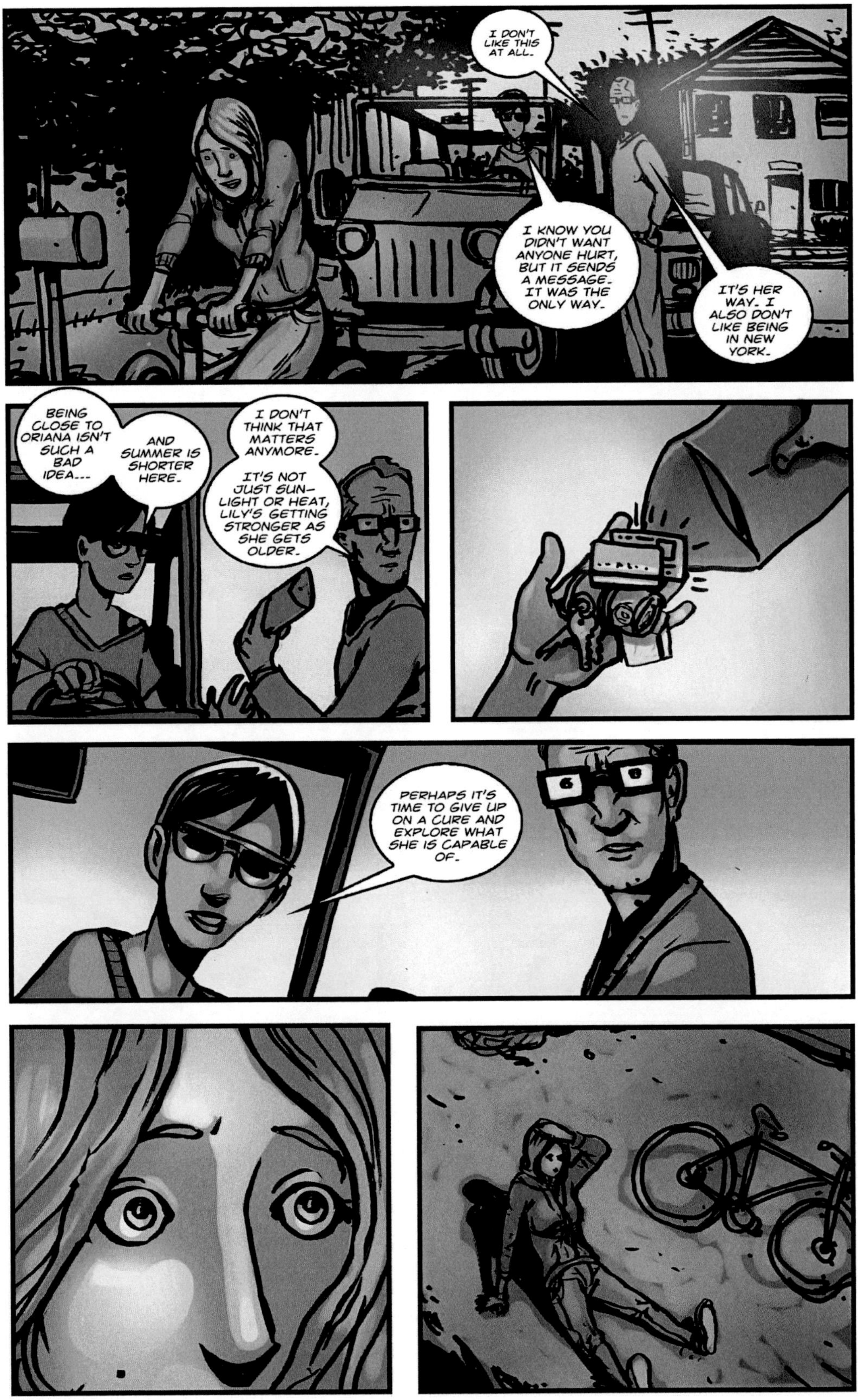
I DON'T LIKE THIS AT ALL.
I KNOW YOU DIDN'T WANT ANYONE HURT, BUT IT SENDS A MESSAGE. IT WAS THE ONLY WAY.
IT'S HER WAY. I ALSO DON'T LIKE BEING IN NEW YORK.
BEING CLOSE TO ORIANA ISN'T SUCH A BAD IDEA...
AND SUMMER IS SHORTER HERE.
I DON'T THINK THAT MATTERS ANYMORE.
IT'S NOT JUST SUN-LIGHT OR HEAT, LILY'S GETTING STRONGER AS SHE GETS OLDER.
PERHAPS IT'S TIME TO GIVE UP ON A CURE AND EXPLORE WHAT SHE IS CAPABLE OF.

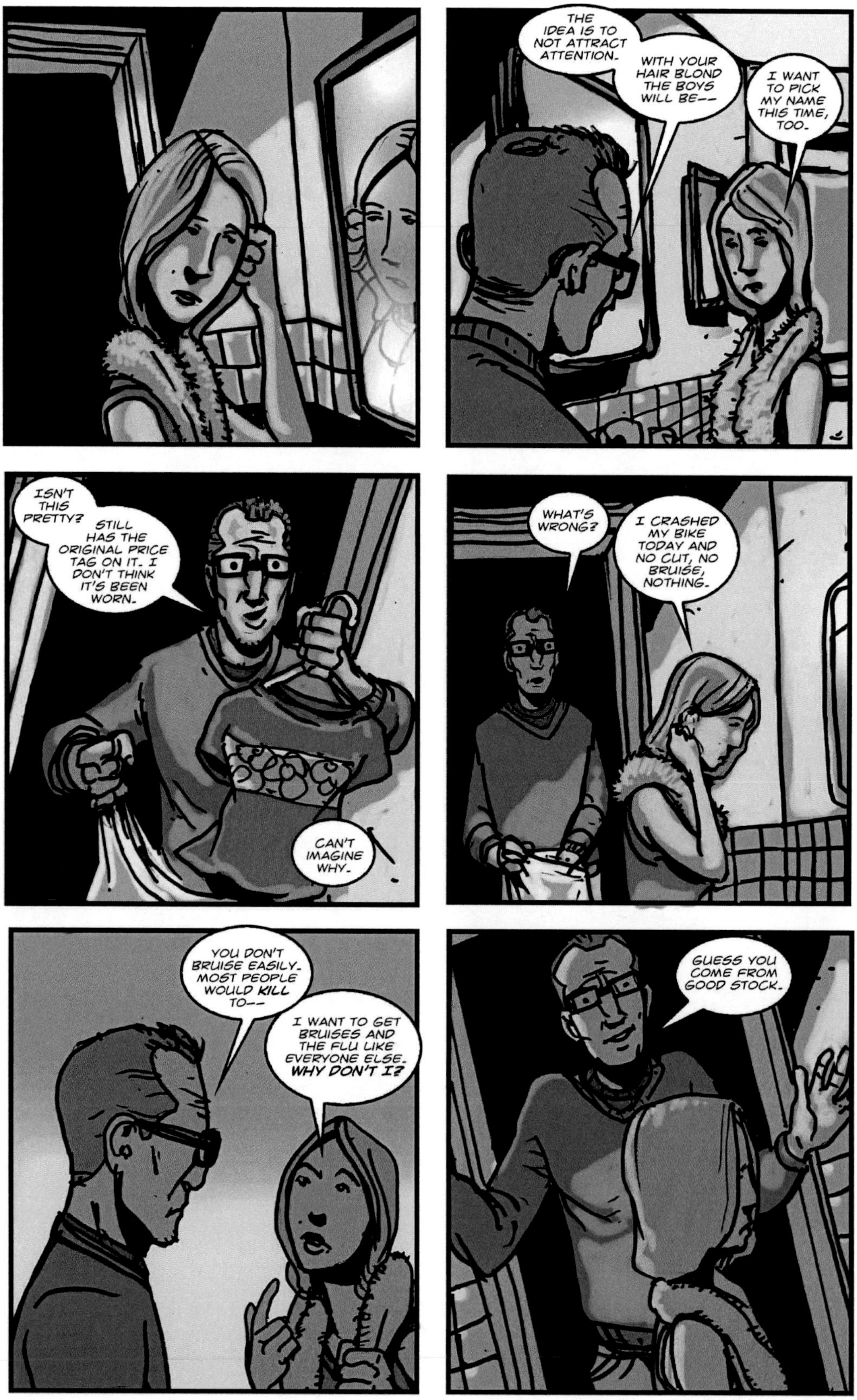
THE IDEA IS TO NOT ATTRACT ATTENTION.
WITH YOUR HAIR BLOND THE BOYS WILL BE--
I WANT TO PICK MY NAME THIS TIME, TOO.
ISN'T THIS PRETTY?
STILL HAS THE ORIGINAL PRICE TAG ON IT. I DON'T THINK IT'S BEEN WORN.
CAN'T IMAGINE WHY.
WHAT'S WRONG?
I CRASHED MY BIKE TODAY AND NO CUT, NO BRUISE, NOTHING.
YOU DON'T BRUISE EASILY. MOST PEOPLE WOULD **KILL** TO--
I WANT TO GET BRUISES AND THE FLU LIKE EVERYONE ELSE. ***WHY DON'T I?***
GUESS YOU COME FROM GOOD STOCK.

I'M OFF TO WORK. IT'S A BEAUTIFUL SUMMER DAY — YOU SHOULD GO OUTSIDE, ENJOY IT.

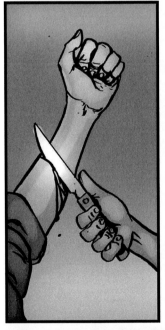

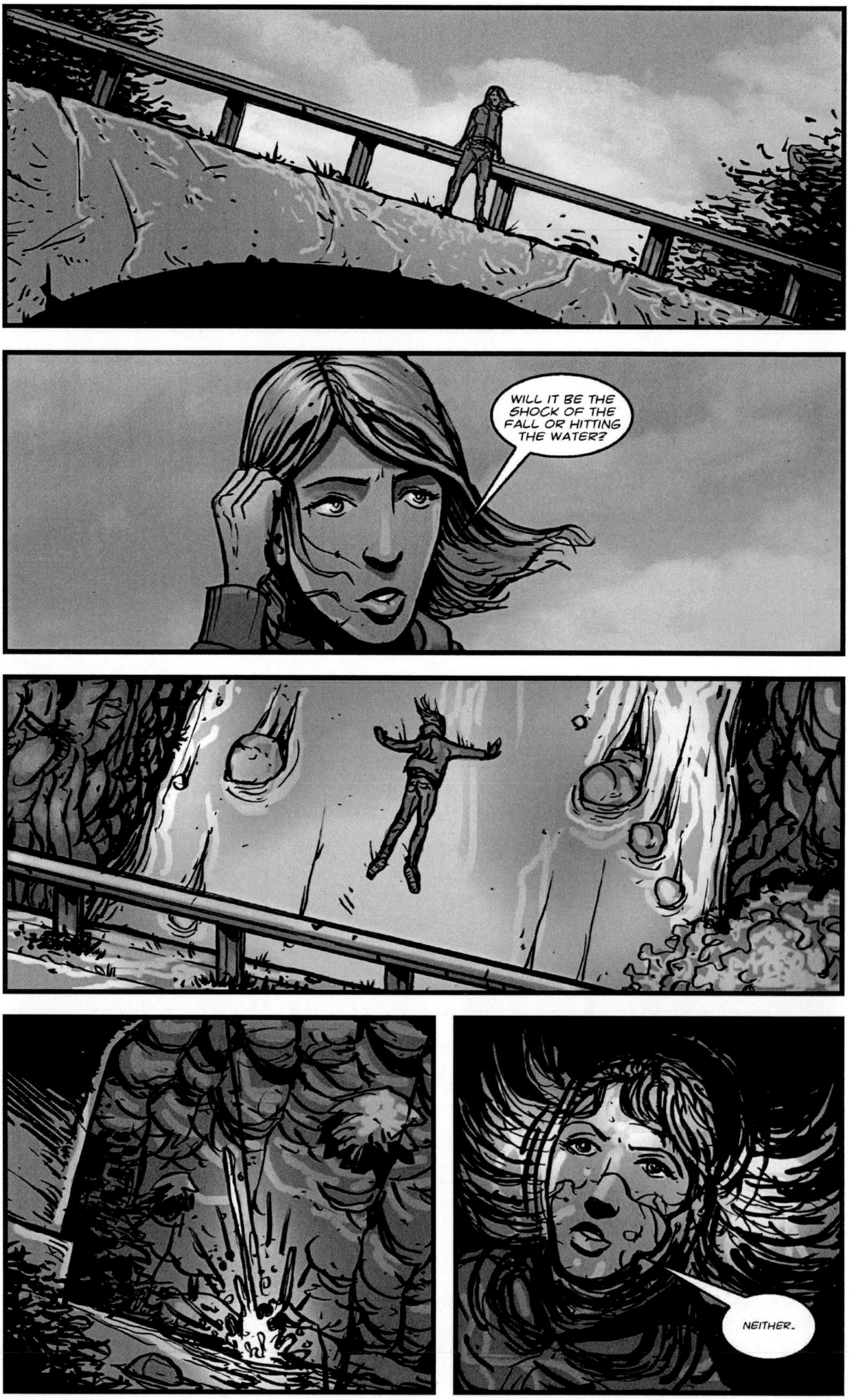
WILL IT BE THE SHOCK OF THE FALL OR HITTING THE WATER?
NEITHER.

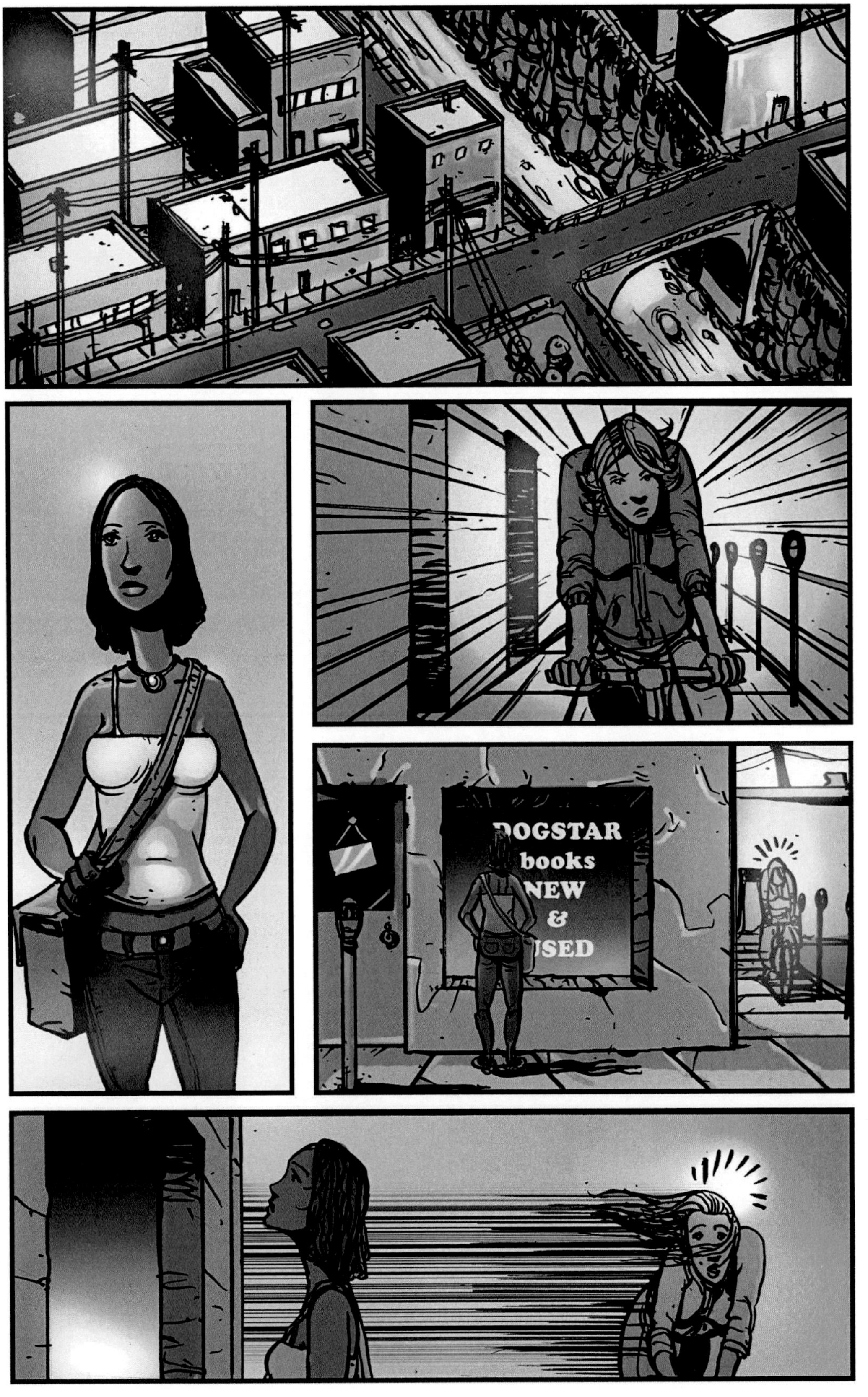
DOGSTAR
books
NEW
&
USED

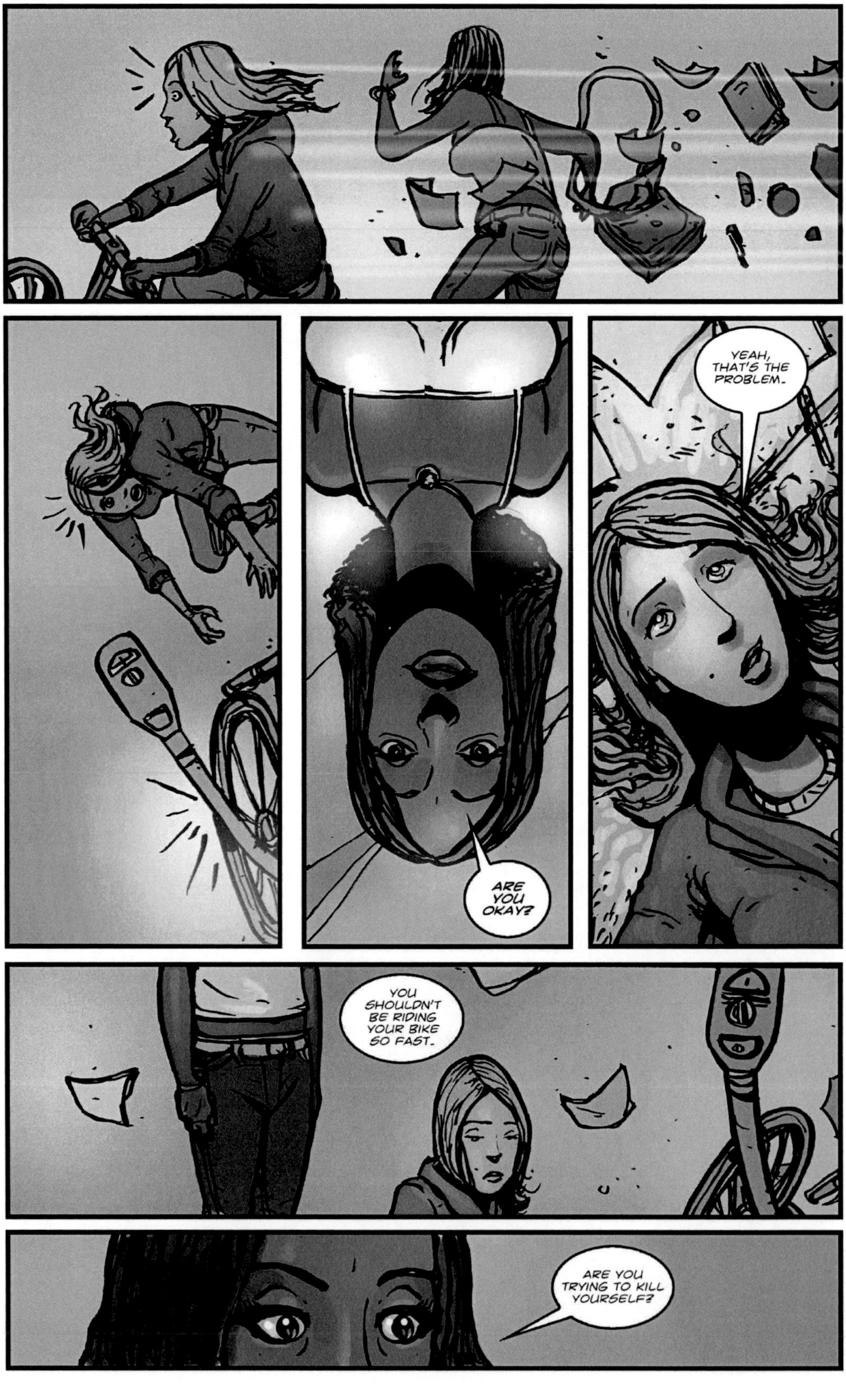
ARE YOU OKAY?
YEAH, THAT'S THE PROBLEM.
YOU SHOULDN'T BE RIDING YOUR BIKE SO FAST.
ARE YOU TRYING TO KILL YOURSELF?

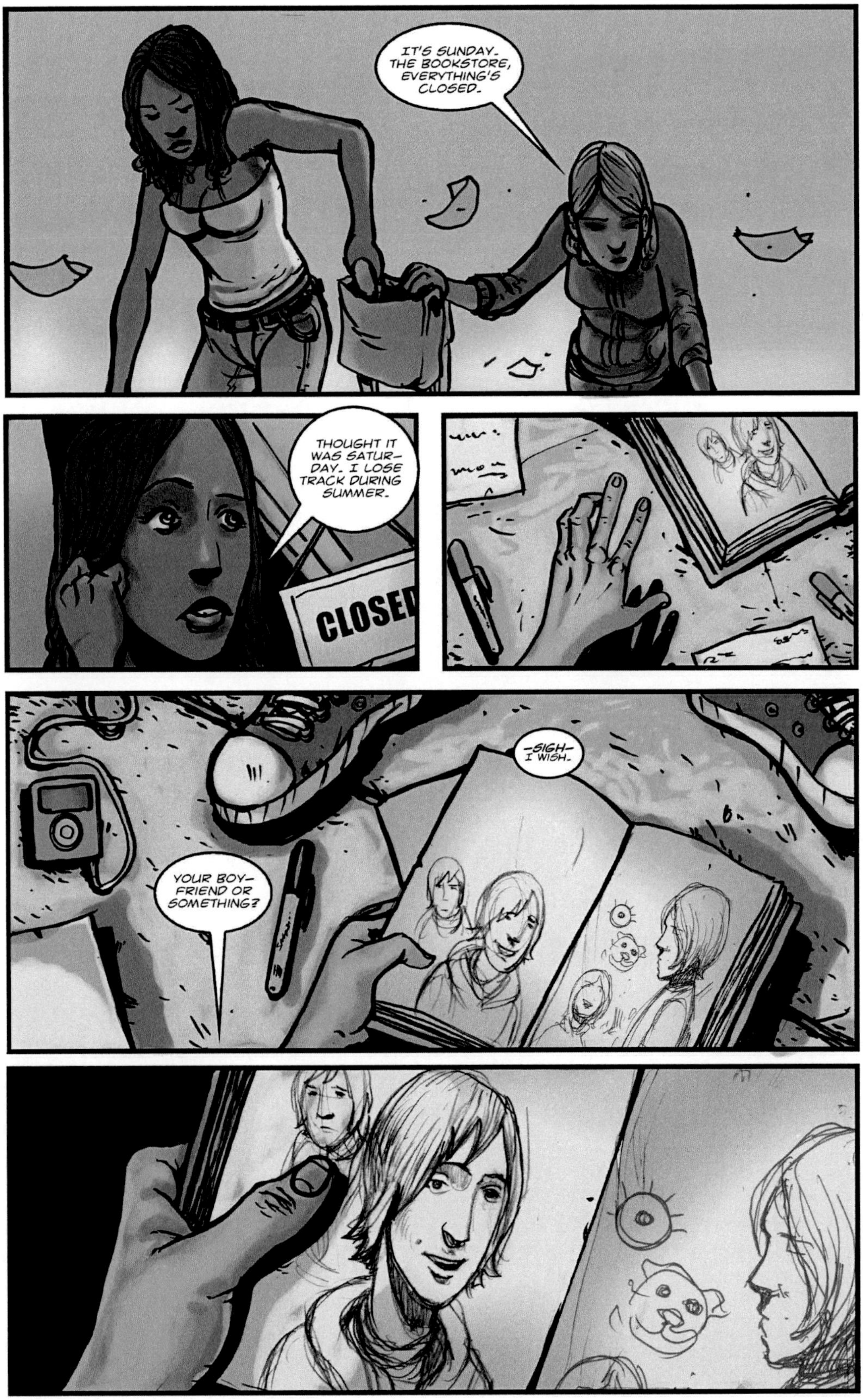
IT'S SUNDAY. THE BOOKSTORE, EVERYTHING'S CLOSED.
THOUGHT IT WAS SATURDAY. I LOSE TRACK DURING SUMMER.
CLOSED
-SIGH- I WISH.
YOUR BOYFRIEND OR SOMETHING?

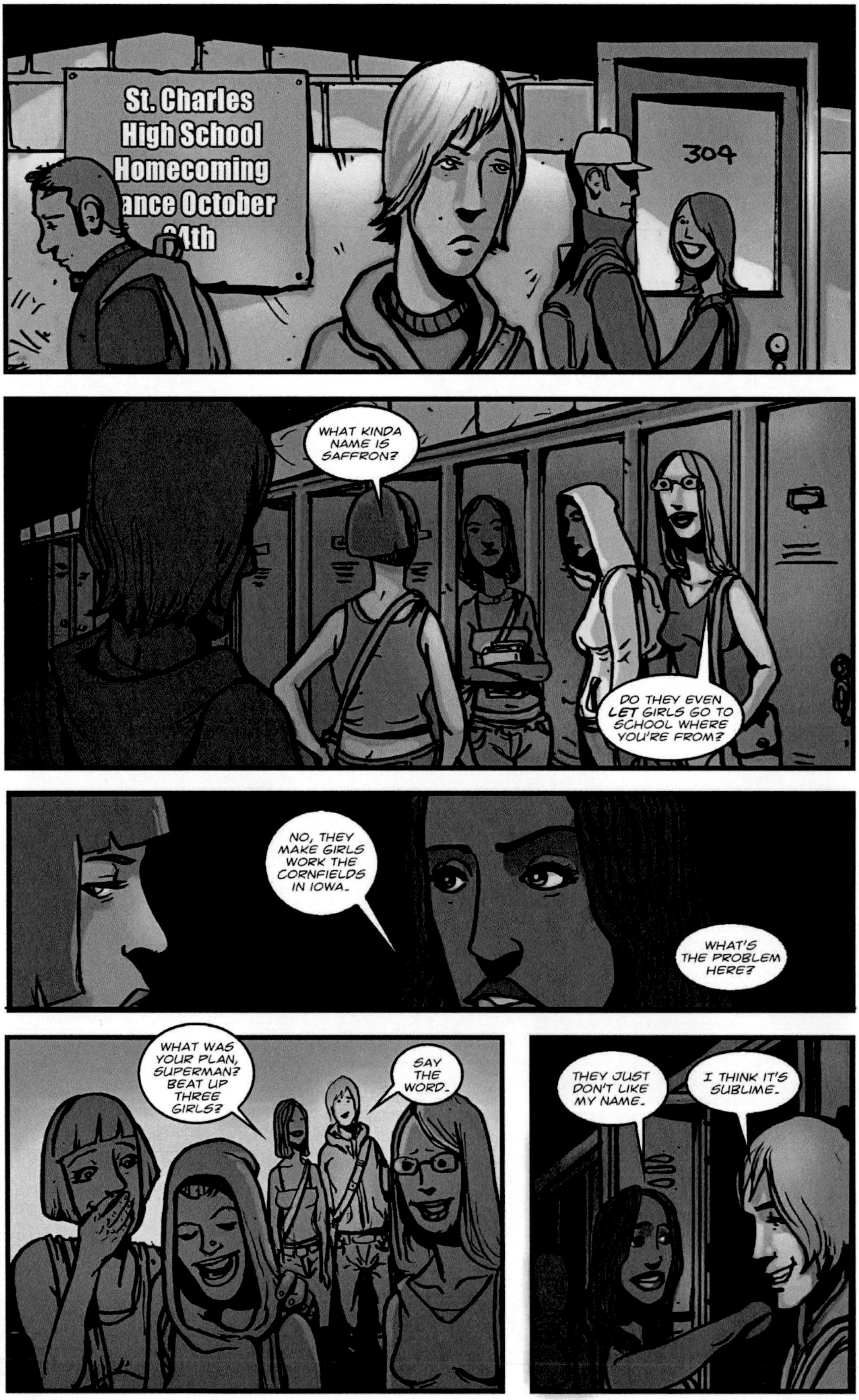
St. Charles
High School
Homecoming
ance October
4th
304
WHAT KINDA NAME IS SAFFRON?
DO THEY EVEN LET GIRLS GO TO SCHOOL WHERE YOU'RE FROM?
NO, THEY MAKE GIRLS WORK THE CORNFIELDS IN IOWA.
WHAT'S THE PROBLEM HERE?
WHAT WAS YOUR PLAN, SUPERMAN? BEAT UP THREE GIRLS?
SAY THE WORD.
THEY JUST DON'T LIKE MY NAME.
I THINK IT'S SUBLIME.

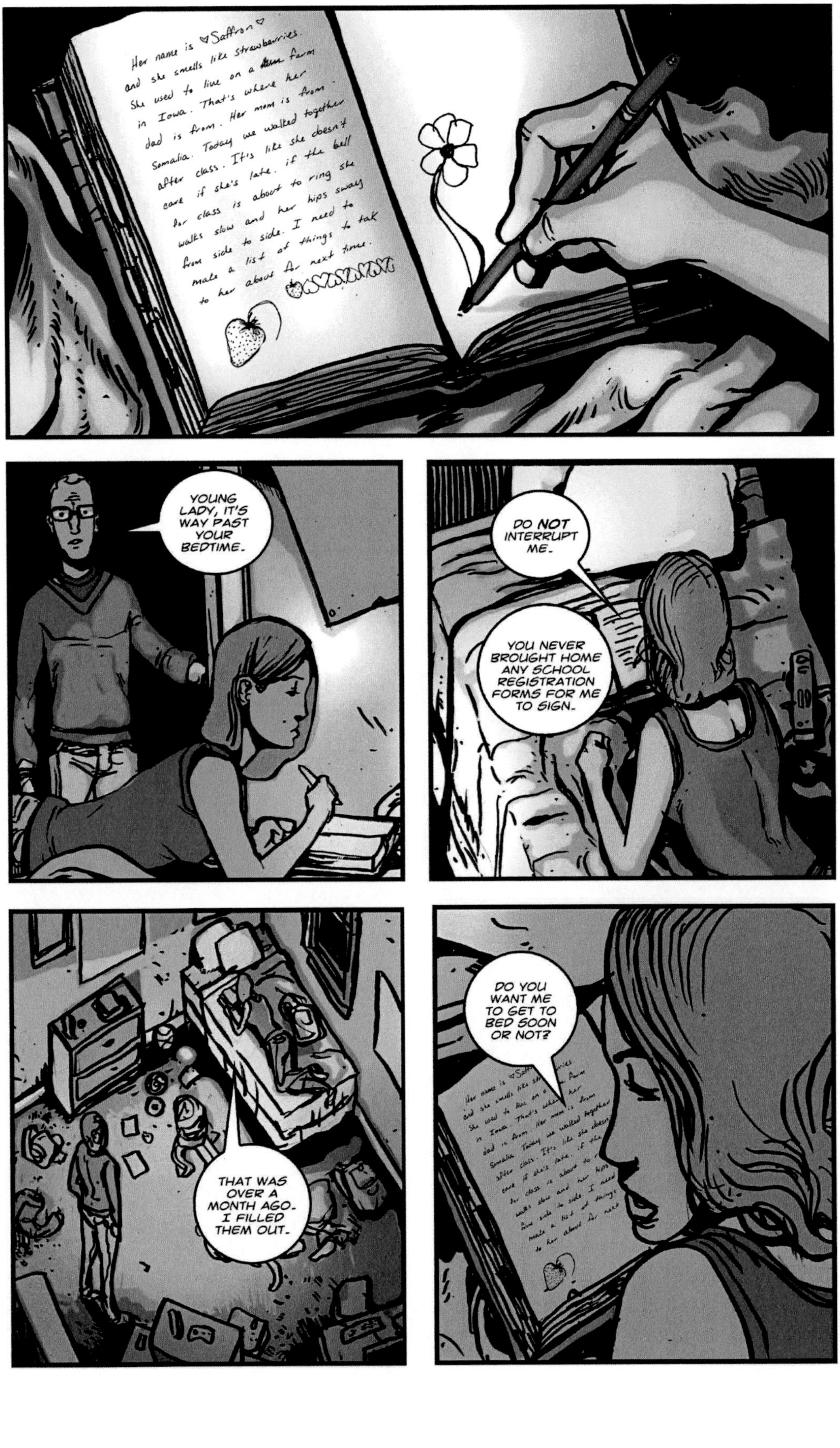
Her name is ♡Saffron♡ and she smells like strawberries. She used to live on a farm in Iowa. That's where her dad is from. Her mom is from Somalia. Today we walked together after class. It's like she doesn't care if she's late. if the bell for class is about to ring she walks slow and her hips sway from side to side. I need to make a list of things to tak to her about fr. next time.
YOUNG LADY, IT'S WAY PAST YOUR BEDTIME.
DO NOT INTERRUPT ME.
YOU NEVER BROUGHT HOME ANY SCHOOL REGISTRATION FORMS FOR ME TO SIGN.
THAT WAS OVER A MONTH AGO. I FILLED THEM OUT.
DO YOU WANT ME TO GET TO BED SOON OR NOT?

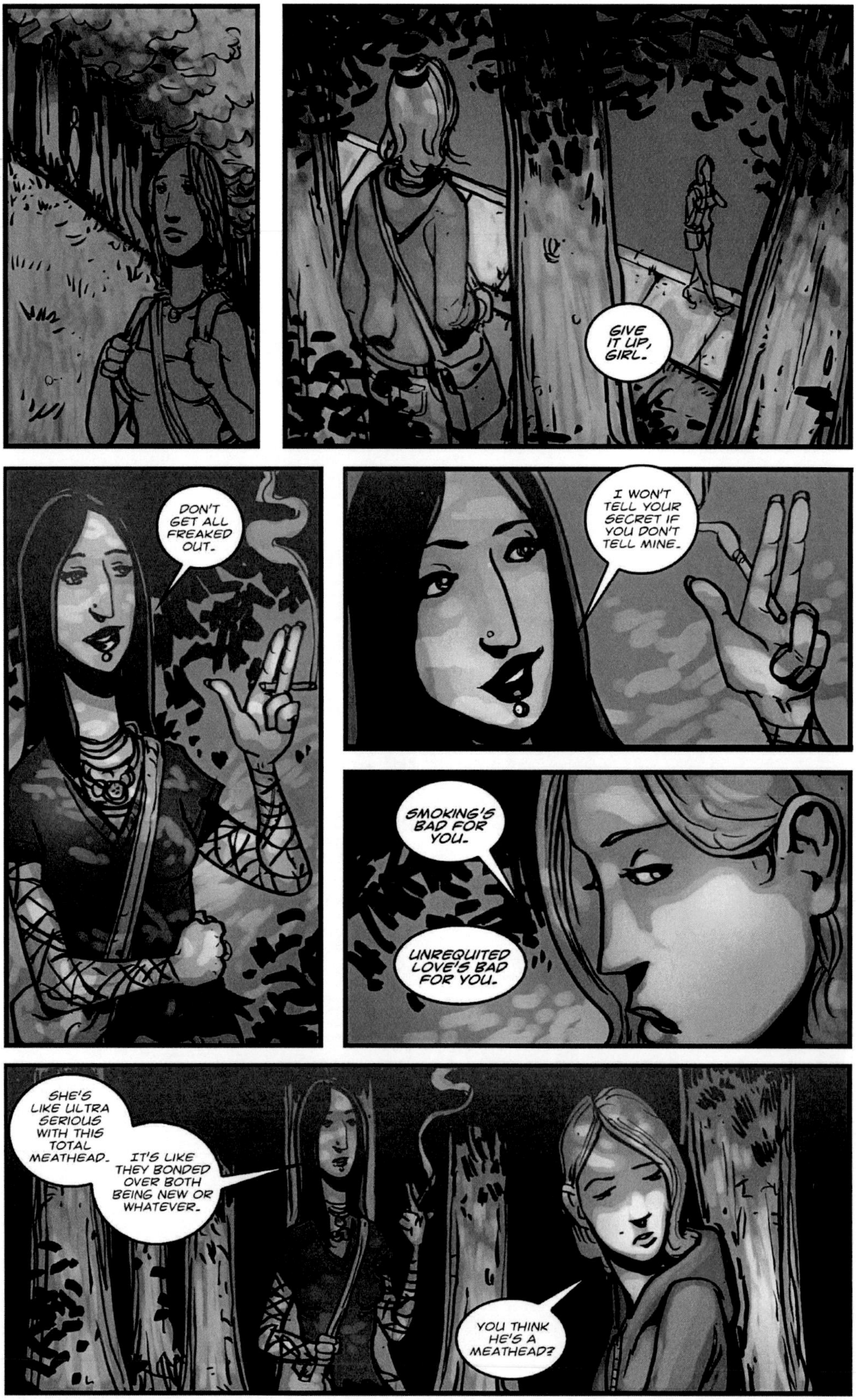
GIVE IT UP, GIRL.
DON'T GET ALL FREAKED OUT.
I WON'T TELL YOUR SECRET IF YOU DON'T TELL MINE.
SMOKING'S BAD FOR YOU.
UNREQUITED LOVE'S BAD FOR YOU.
SHE'S LIKE ULTRA SERIOUS WITH THIS TOTAL MEATHEAD.
IT'S LIKE THEY BONDED OVER BOTH BEING NEW OR WHATEVER.
YOU THINK HE'S A MEATHEAD?

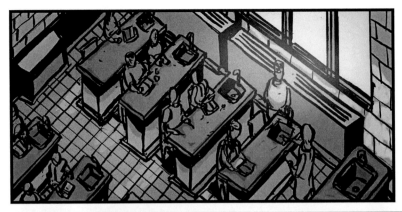

YOU'RE JOKING RIGHT?

MAN, SERIOUSLY? THE *LEZZY?* OVER *ME?*

THE CORRECT TERM IS LESBIAN AND BOYS LIKE YOU MAKE ME WISH I *WAS* ONE.

YOU A GUY THEN? HARD TO TELL IN ALL THOSE CLOTHES.

SHUT UP, *MEATHEAD.*

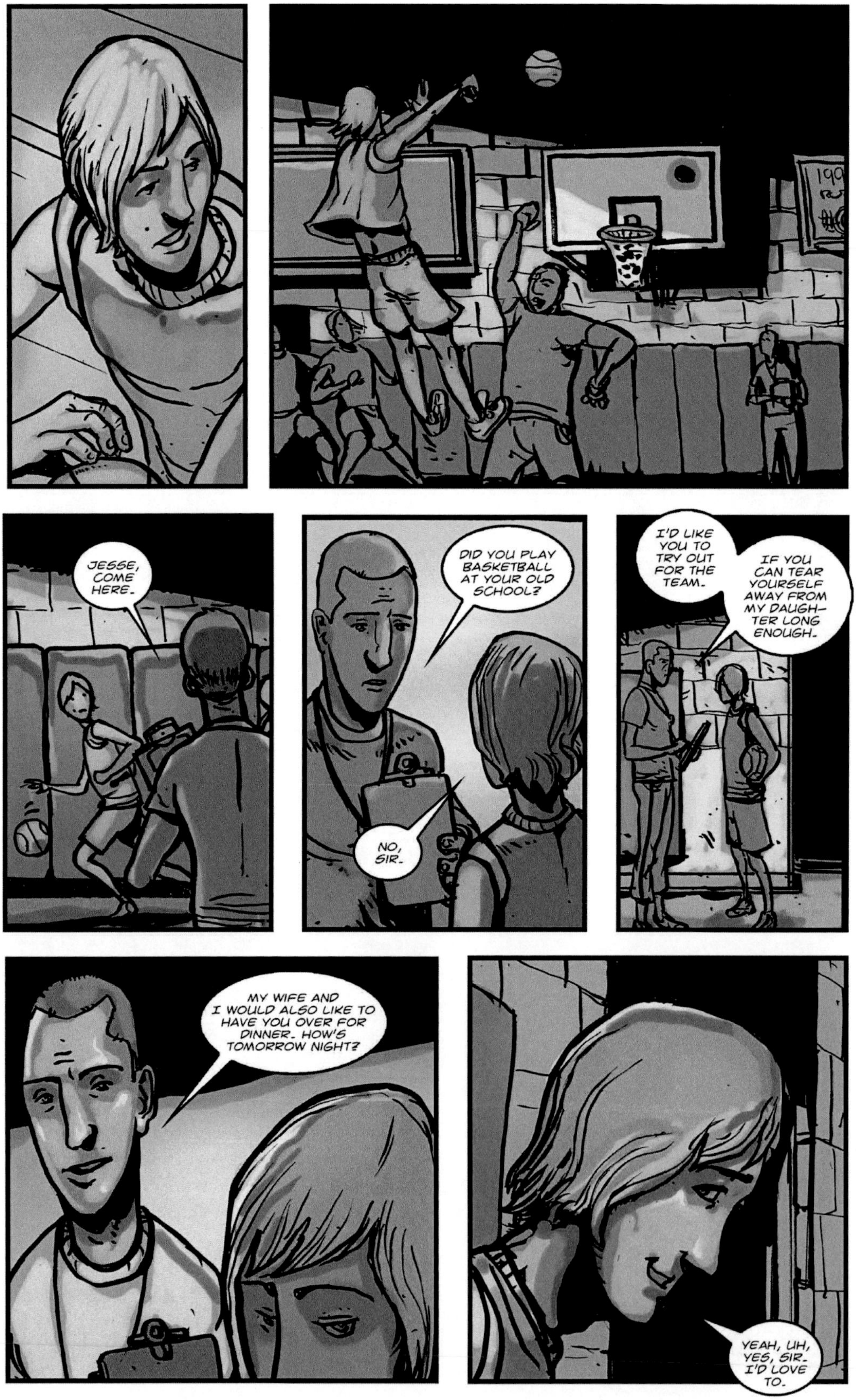
JESSE, COME HERE.
DID YOU PLAY BASKETBALL AT YOUR OLD SCHOOL?
NO, SIR.
I'D LIKE YOU TO TRY OUT FOR THE TEAM.
IF YOU CAN TEAR YOURSELF AWAY FROM MY DAUGHTER LONG ENOUGH.
MY WIFE AND I WOULD ALSO LIKE TO HAVE YOU OVER FOR DINNER. HOW'S TOMORROW NIGHT?
YEAH, UH, YES, SIR. I'D LOVE TO.

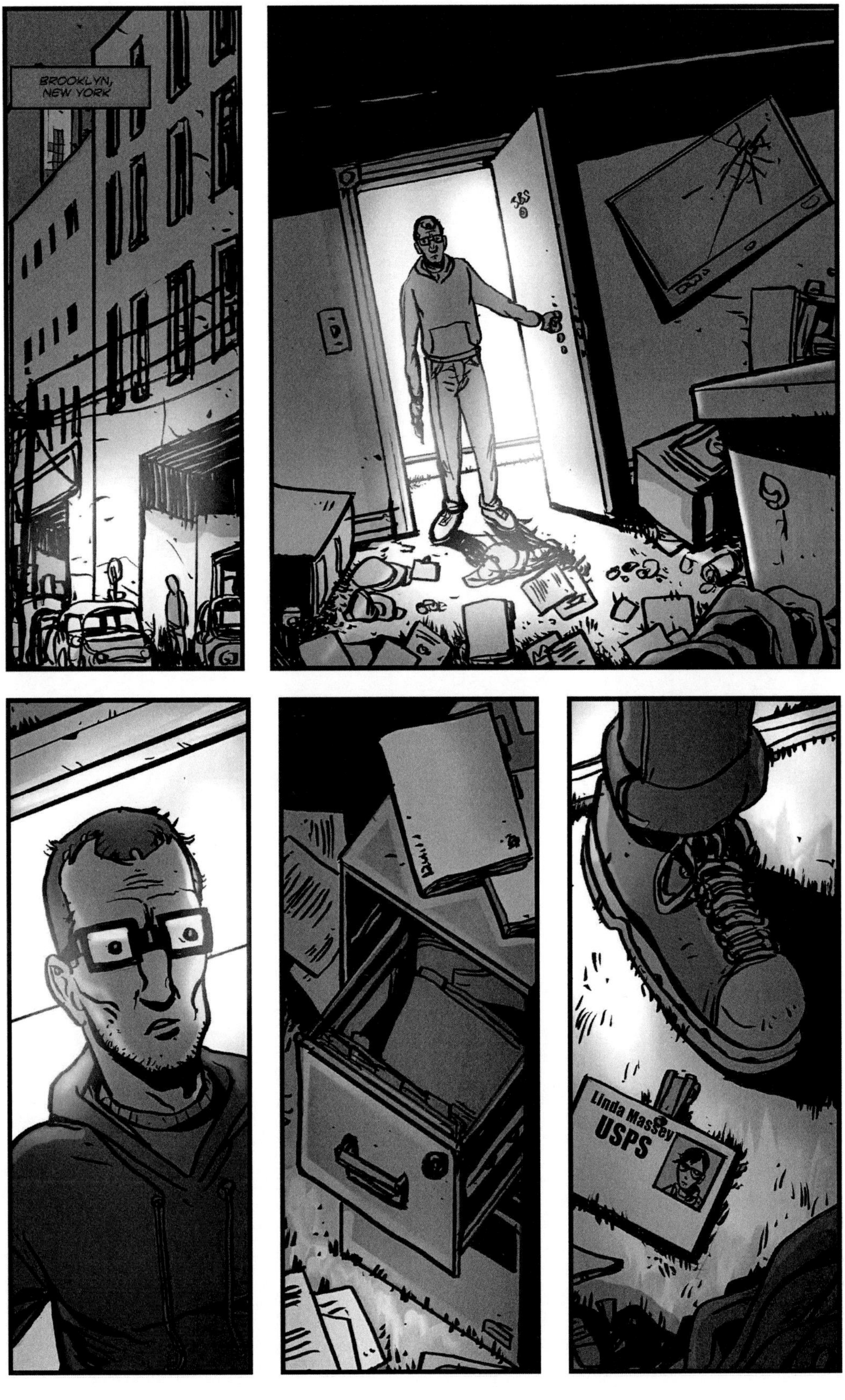
BROOKLYN, NEW YORK
Linda Massey
USPS

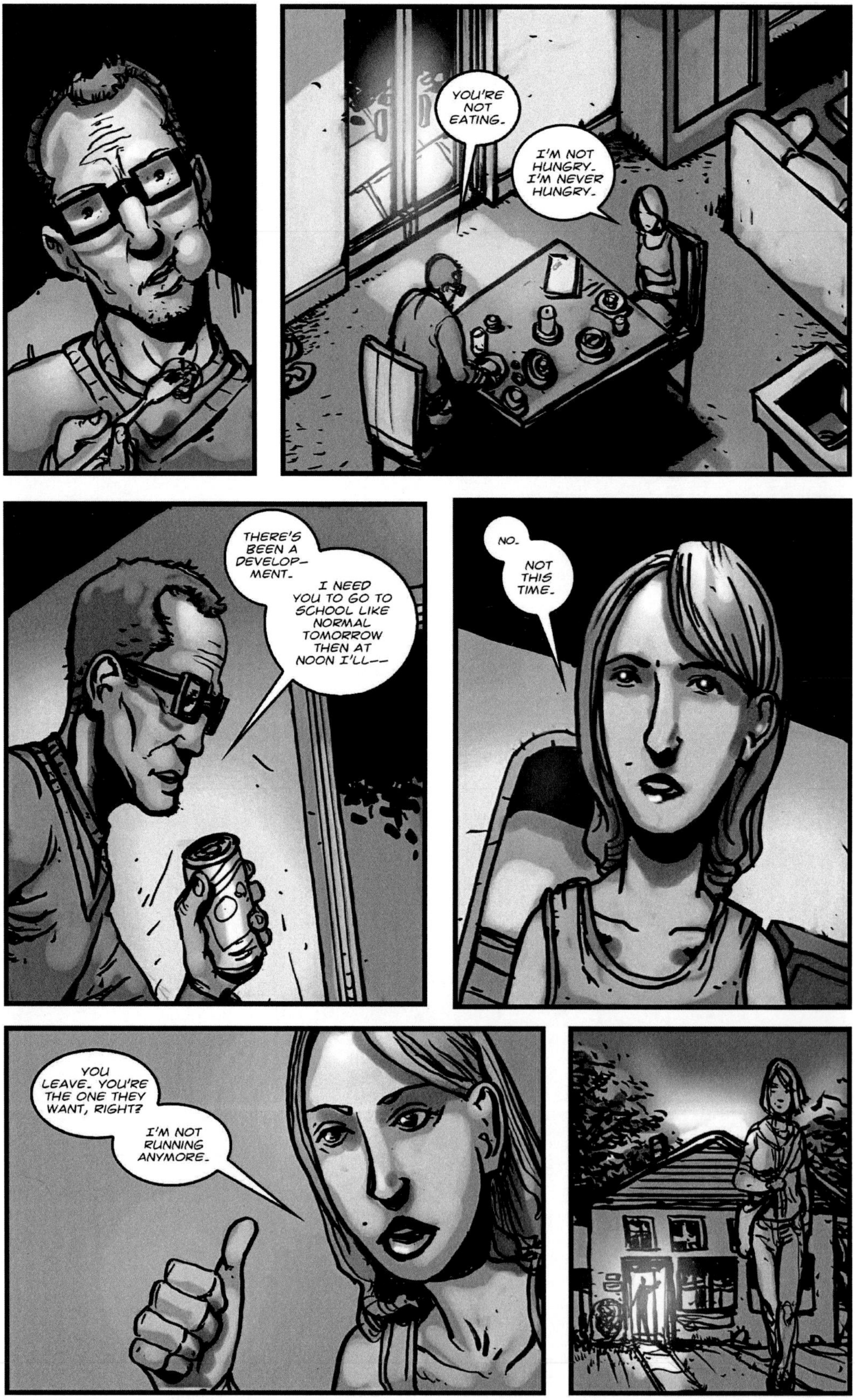
YOU'RE NOT EATING.
I'M NOT HUNGRY. I'M NEVER HUNGRY.
THERE'S BEEN A DEVELOP-MENT.
I NEED YOU TO GO TO SCHOOL LIKE NORMAL TOMORROW THEN AT NOON I'LL--
NO.
NOT THIS TIME.
YOU LEAVE. YOU'RE THE ONE THEY WANT, RIGHT?
I'M NOT RUNNING ANYMORE.

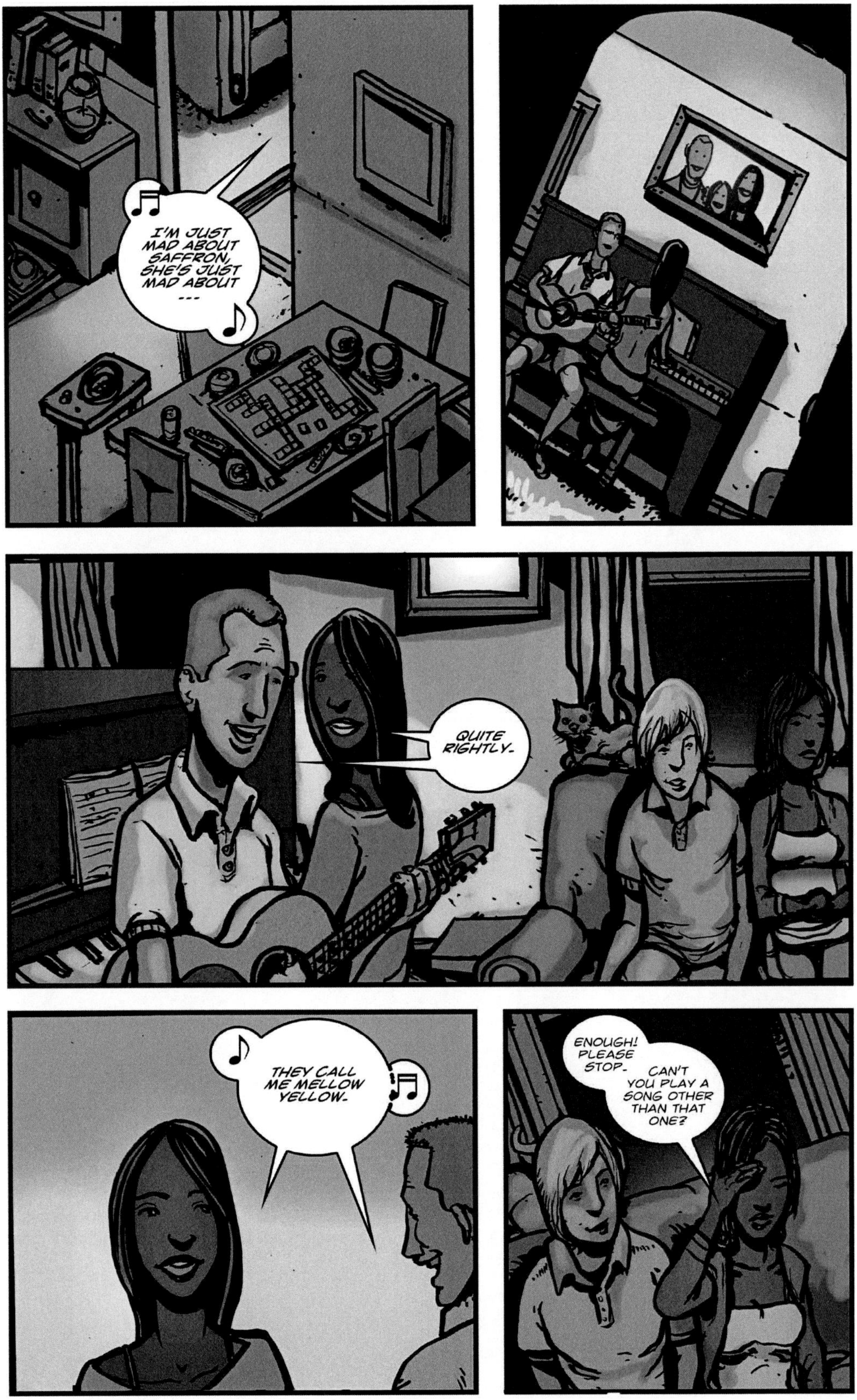
I'M JUST MAD ABOUT SAFFRON, SHE'S JUST MAD ABOUT ...
QUITE RIGHTLY.
THEY CALL ME MELLOW YELLOW.
ENOUGH! PLEASE STOP.
CAN'T YOU PLAY A SONG OTHER THAN THAT ONE?

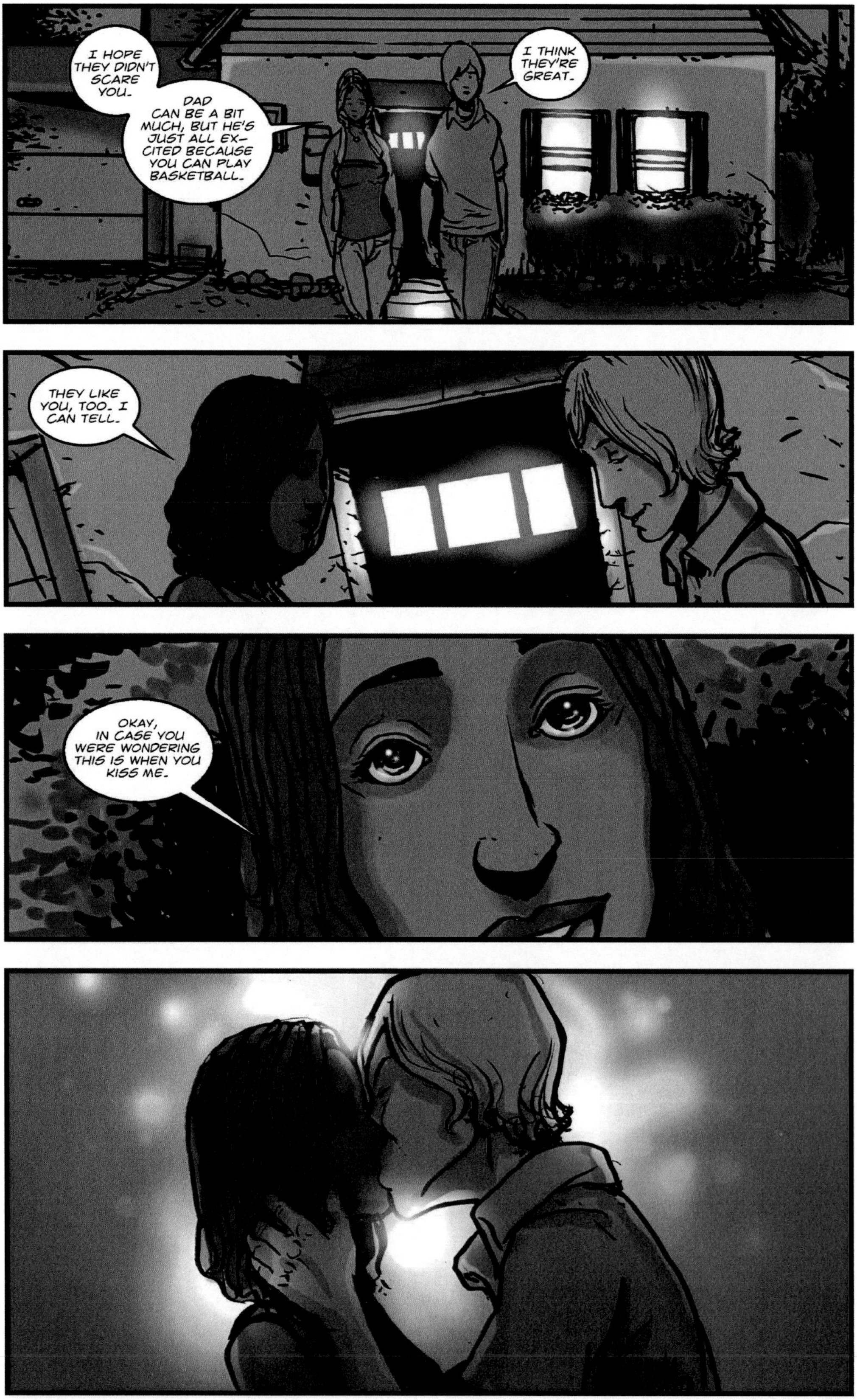
I HOPE THEY DIDN'T SCARE YOU.
DAD CAN BE A BIT MUCH, BUT HE'S JUST ALL EX-CITED BECAUSE YOU CAN PLAY BASKETBALL.
I THINK THEY'RE GREAT.
THEY LIKE YOU, TOO. I CAN TELL.
OKAY, IN CASE YOU WERE WONDERING THIS IS WHEN YOU KISS ME.

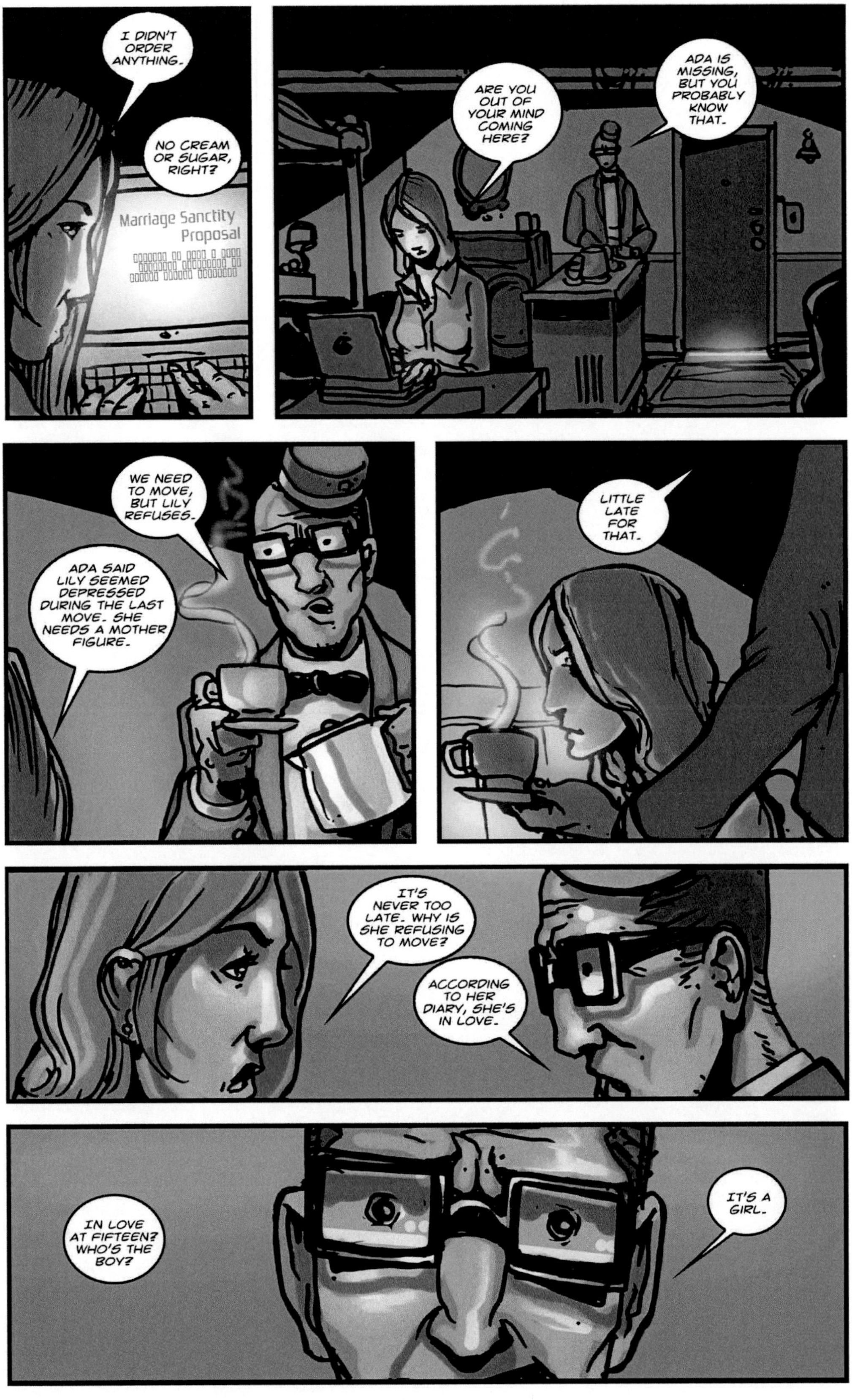
I DIDN'T ORDER ANYTHING.
NO CREAM OR SUGAR, RIGHT?
Marriage Sanctity Proposal
ARE YOU OUT OF YOUR MIND COMING HERE?
ADA IS MISSING, BUT YOU PROBABLY KNOW THAT.
WE NEED TO MOVE, BUT LILY REFUSES.
ADA SAID LILY SEEMED DEPRESSED DURING THE LAST MOVE. SHE NEEDS A MOTHER FIGURE.
LITTLE LATE FOR THAT.
IT'S NEVER TOO LATE. WHY IS SHE REFUSING TO MOVE?
ACCORDING TO HER DIARY, SHE'S IN LOVE.
IN LOVE AT FIFTEEN? WHO'S THE BOY?
IT'S A GIRL.

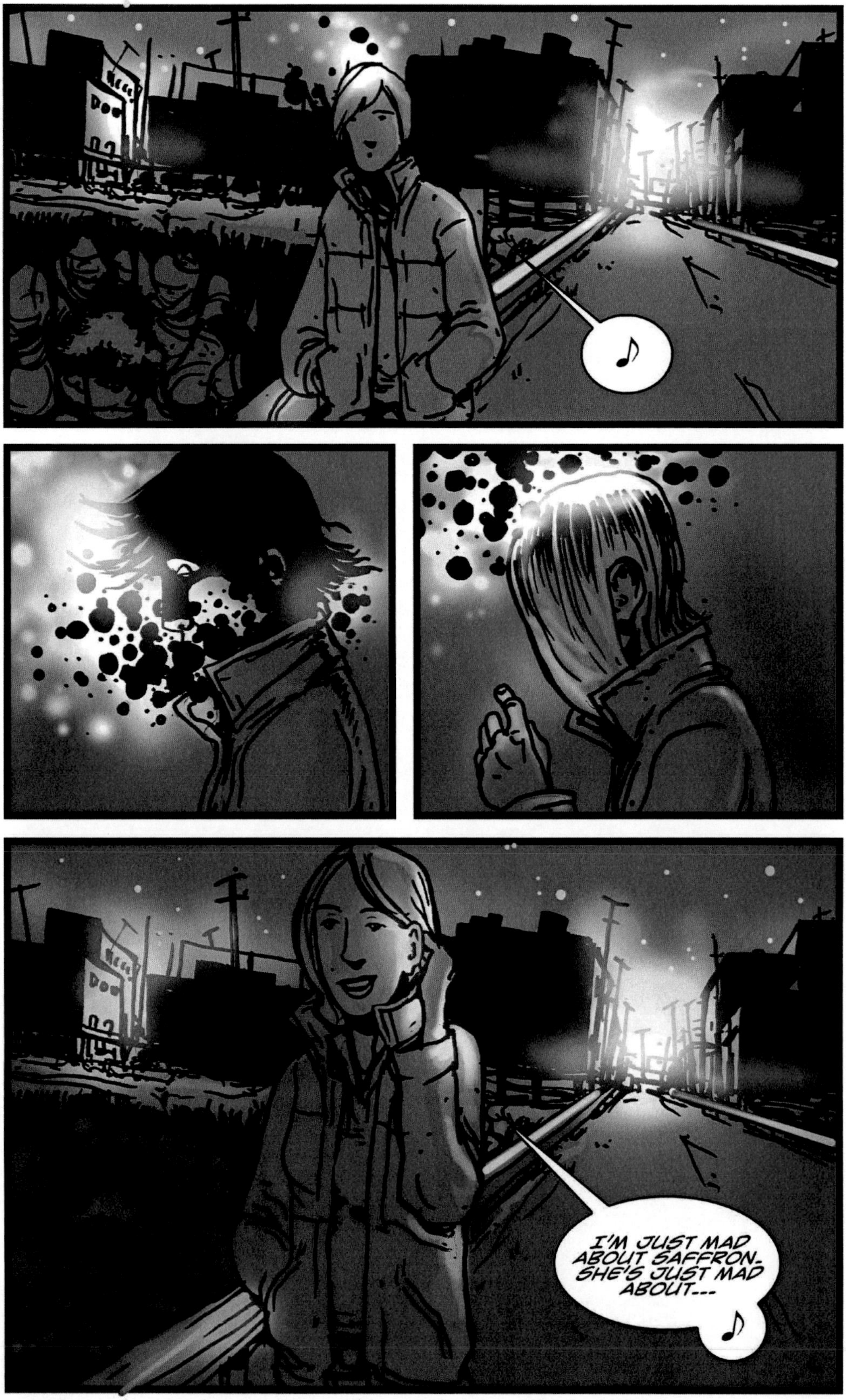
♪
I'M JUST MAD ABOUT SAFFRON- SHE'S JUST MAD ABOUT---
♪

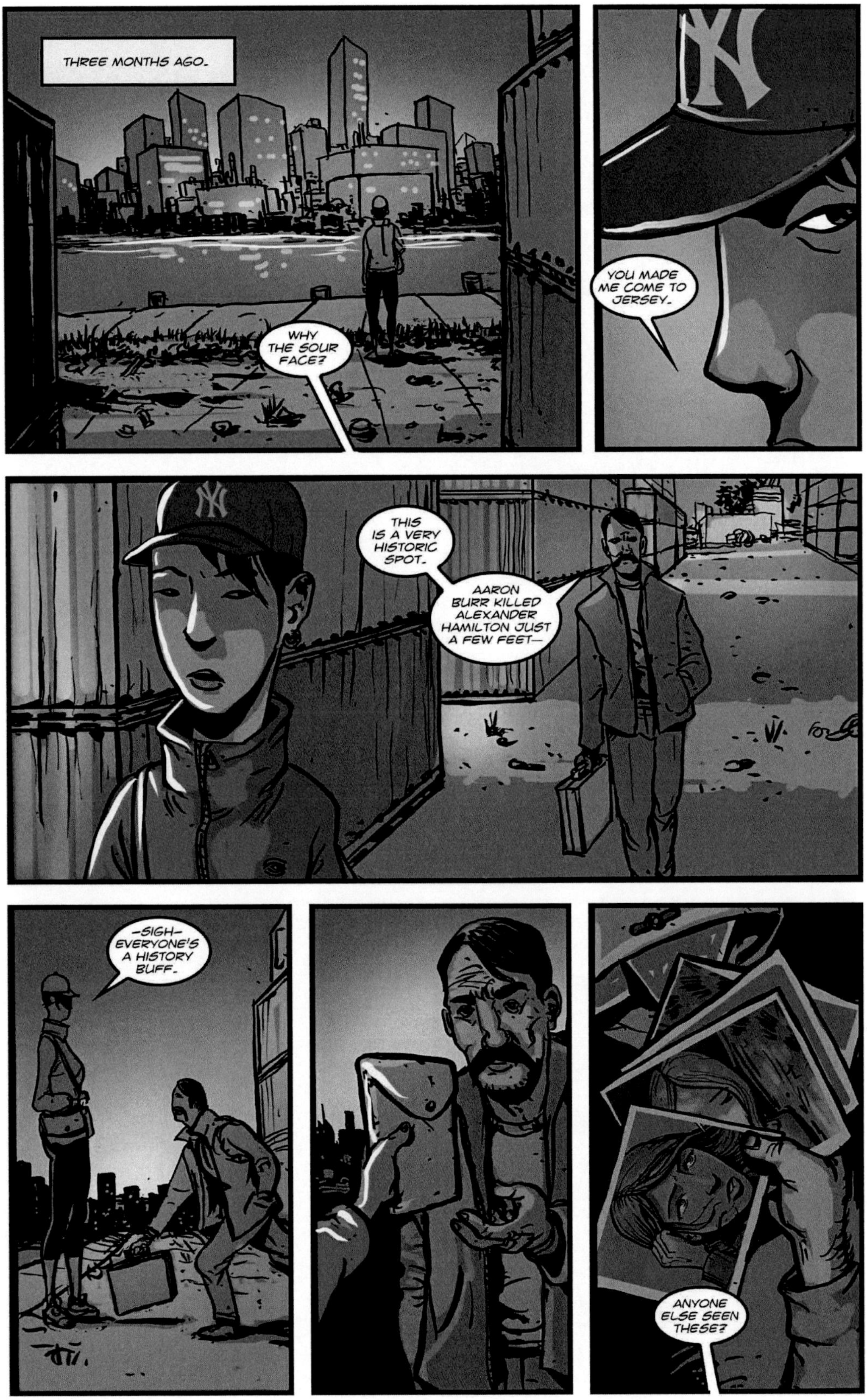

THREE MONTHS AGO...
WHY THE SOUR FACE?
YOU MADE ME COME TO JERSEY...
THIS IS A VERY HISTORIC SPOT...
AARON BURR KILLED ALEXANDER HAMILTON JUST A FEW FEET—
—SIGH— EVERYONE'S A HISTORY BUFF...
ANYONE ELSE SEEN THESE?

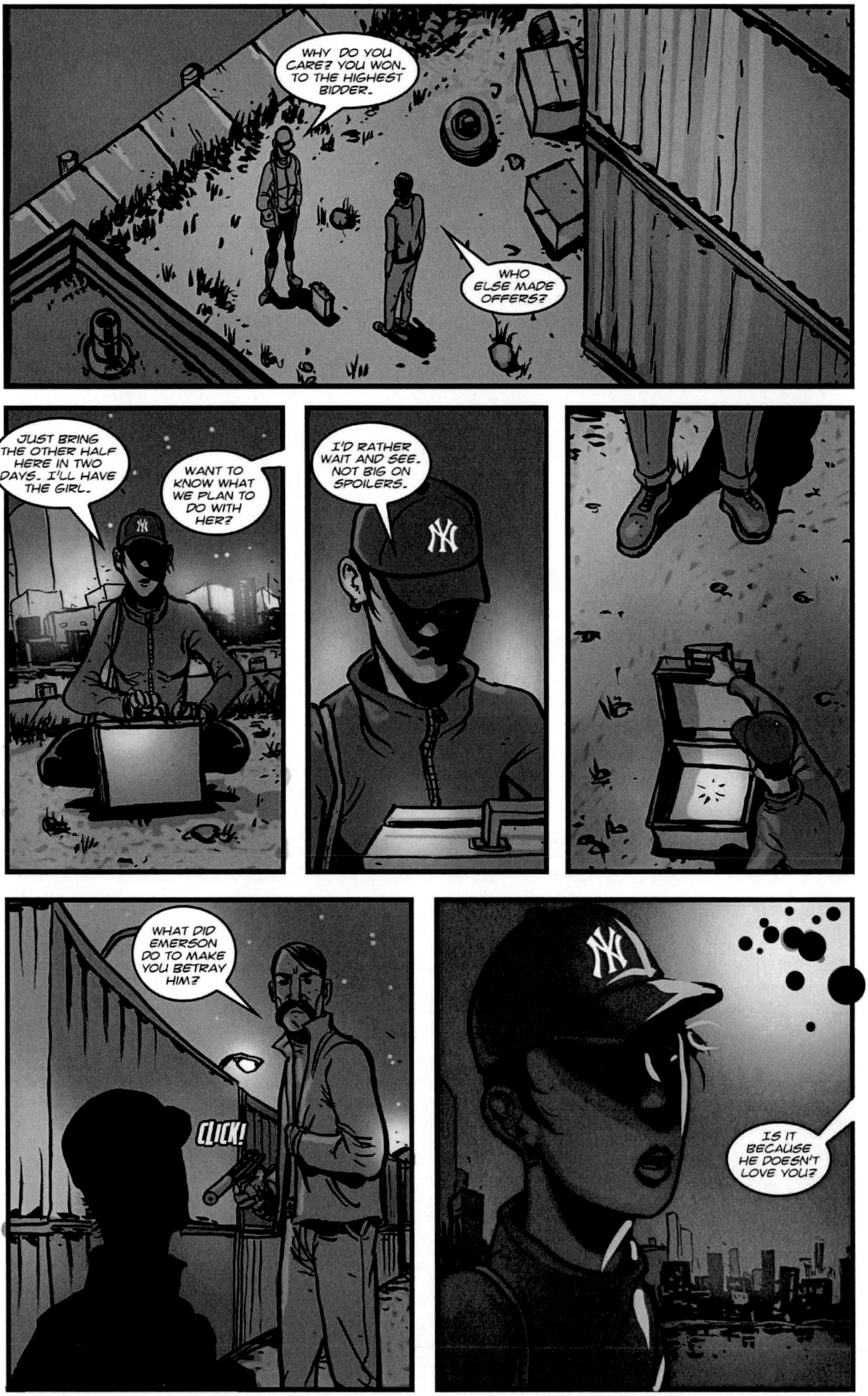
WHY DO YOU CARE? YOU WON. TO THE HIGHEST BIDDER.
WHO ELSE MADE OFFERS?
JUST BRING THE OTHER HALF HERE IN TWO DAYS. I'LL HAVE THE GIRL.
WANT TO KNOW WHAT WE PLAN TO DO WITH HER?
I'D RATHER WAIT AND SEE. NOT BIG ON SPOILERS.
WHAT DID EMERSON DO TO MAKE YOU BETRAY HIM?
CLICK!
IS IT BECAUSE HE DOESN'T LOVE YOU?

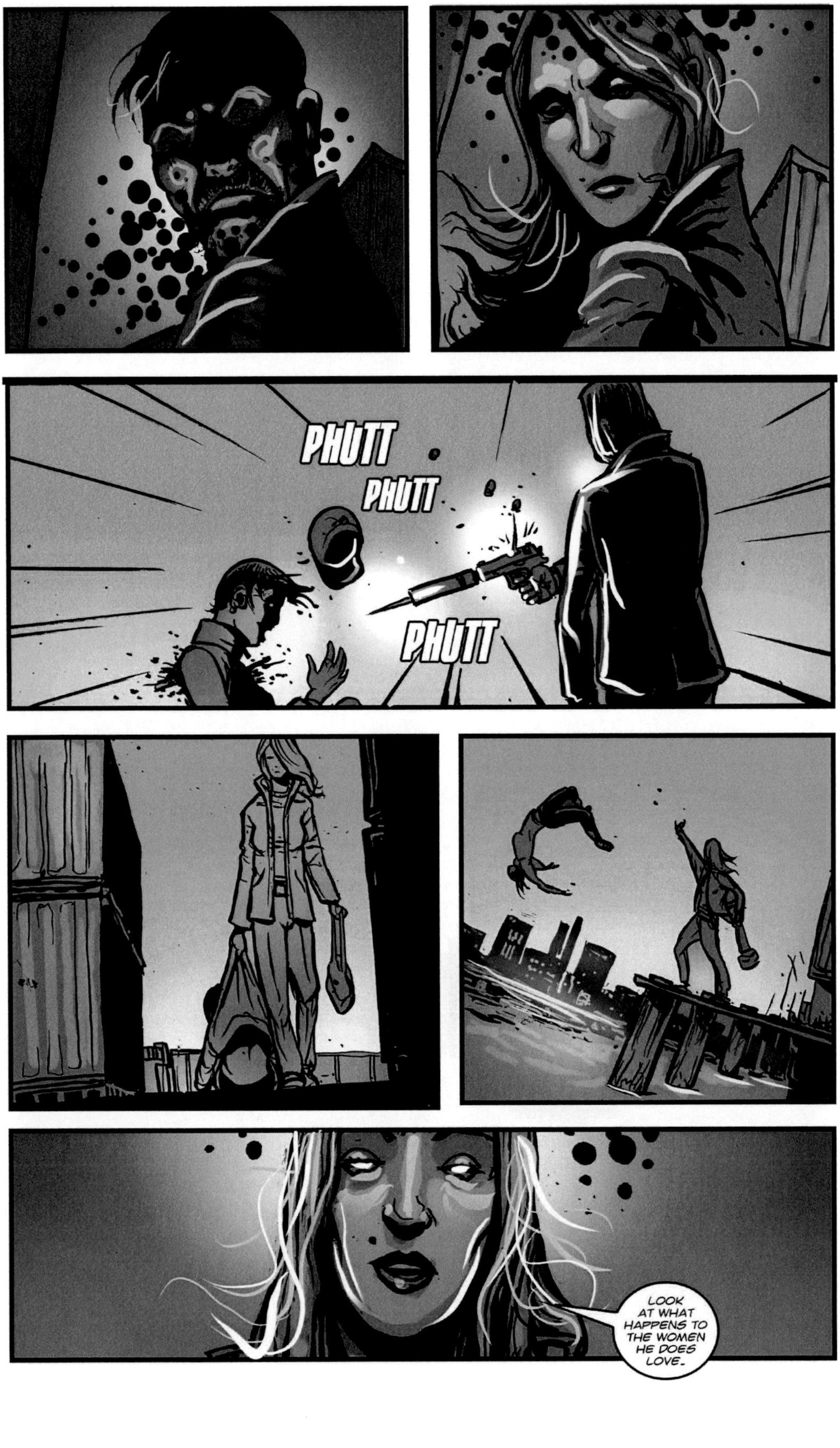
PHUTT
PHUTT
PHUTT
LOOK AT WHAT HAPPENS TO THE WOMEN HE DOES LOVE.

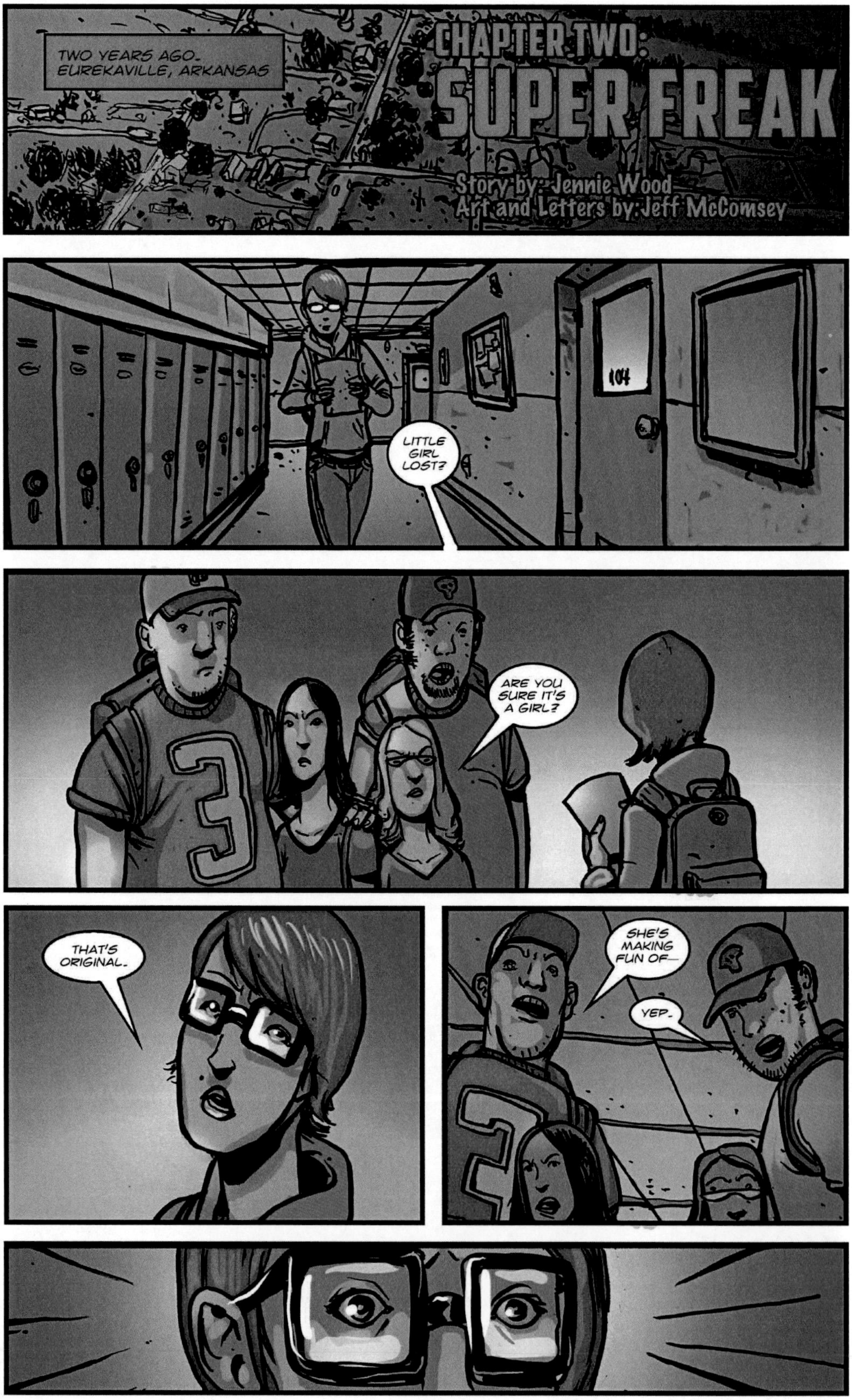
TWO YEARS AGO.
EUREKAVILLE, ARKANSAS
CHAPTER TWO:
SUPER FREAK
Story by: Jennie Wood
Art and Letters by: Jeff McComsey
104
LITTLE GIRL LOST?
ARE YOU SURE IT'S A GIRL?
THAT'S ORIGINAL.
SHE'S MAKING FUN OF—
YEP.

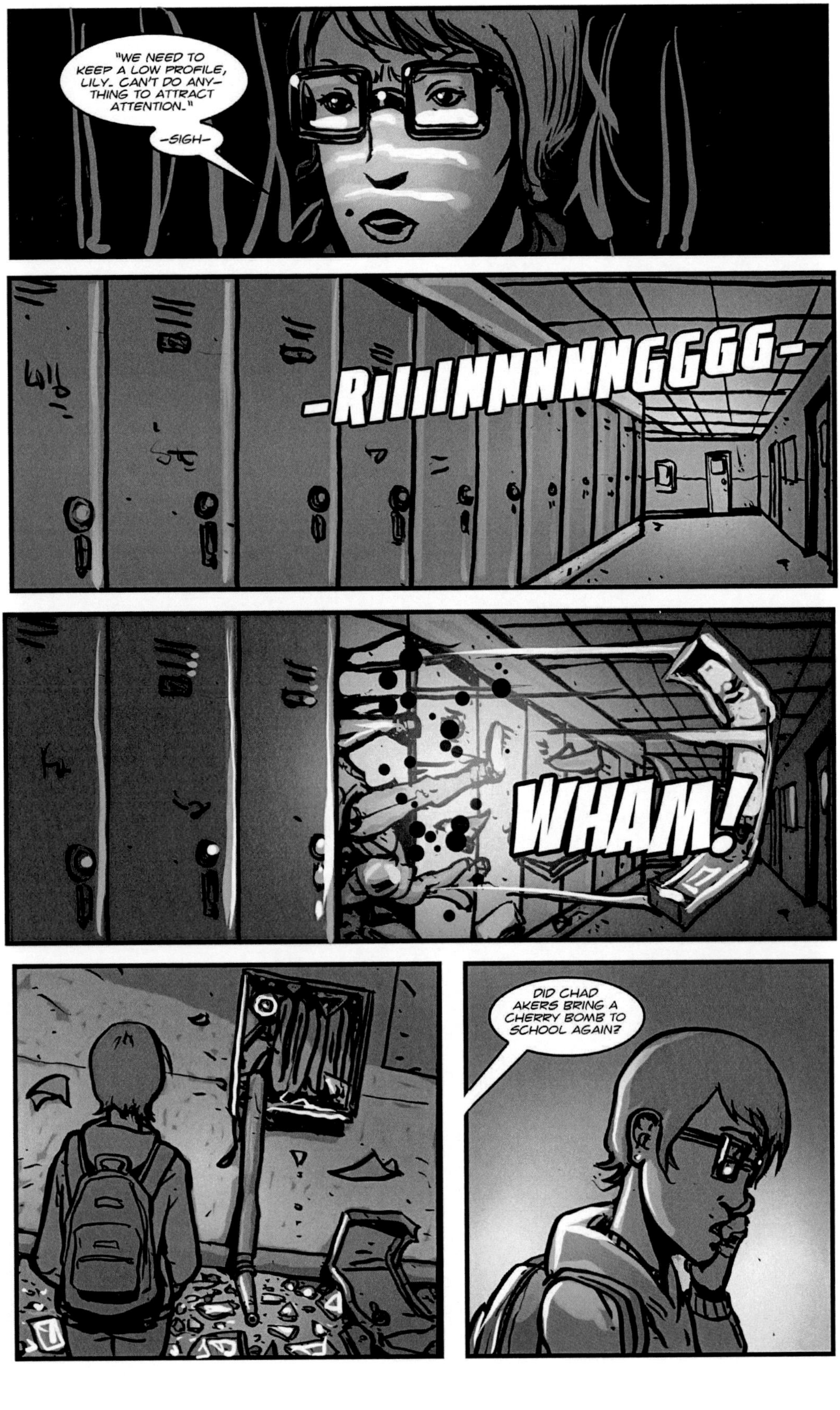
"WE NEED TO KEEP A LOW PROFILE, LILY. CAN'T DO ANY-THING TO ATTRACT ATTENTION."
-SIGH-
-RIIIINNNNNGGGG-
WHAM!
DID CHAD AKERS BRING A CHERRY BOMB TO SCHOOL AGAIN?

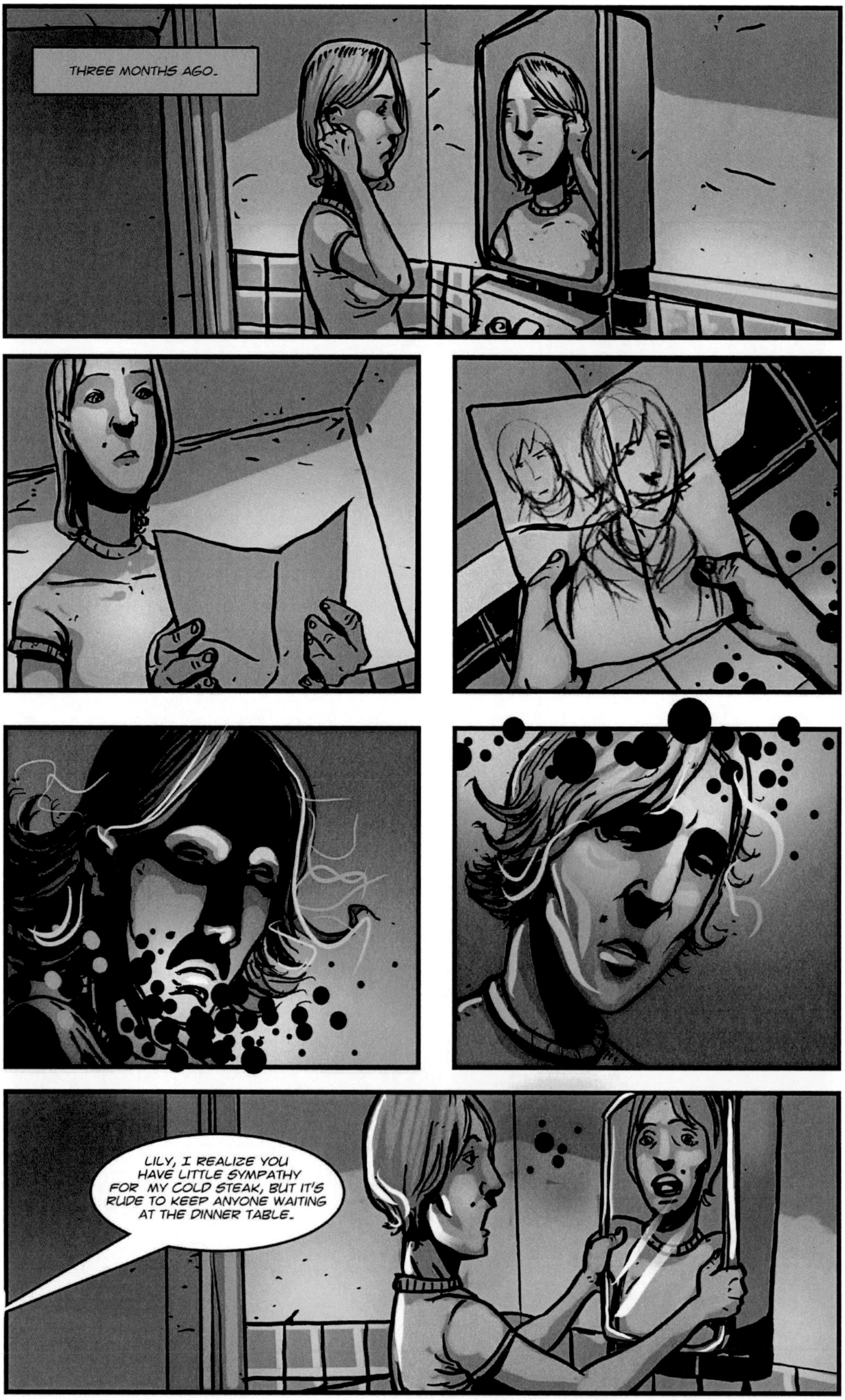
THREE MONTHS AGO...
LILY, I REALIZE YOU HAVE LITTLE SYMPATHY FOR MY COLD STEAK, BUT IT'S RUDE TO KEEP ANYONE WAITING AT THE DINNER TABLE.

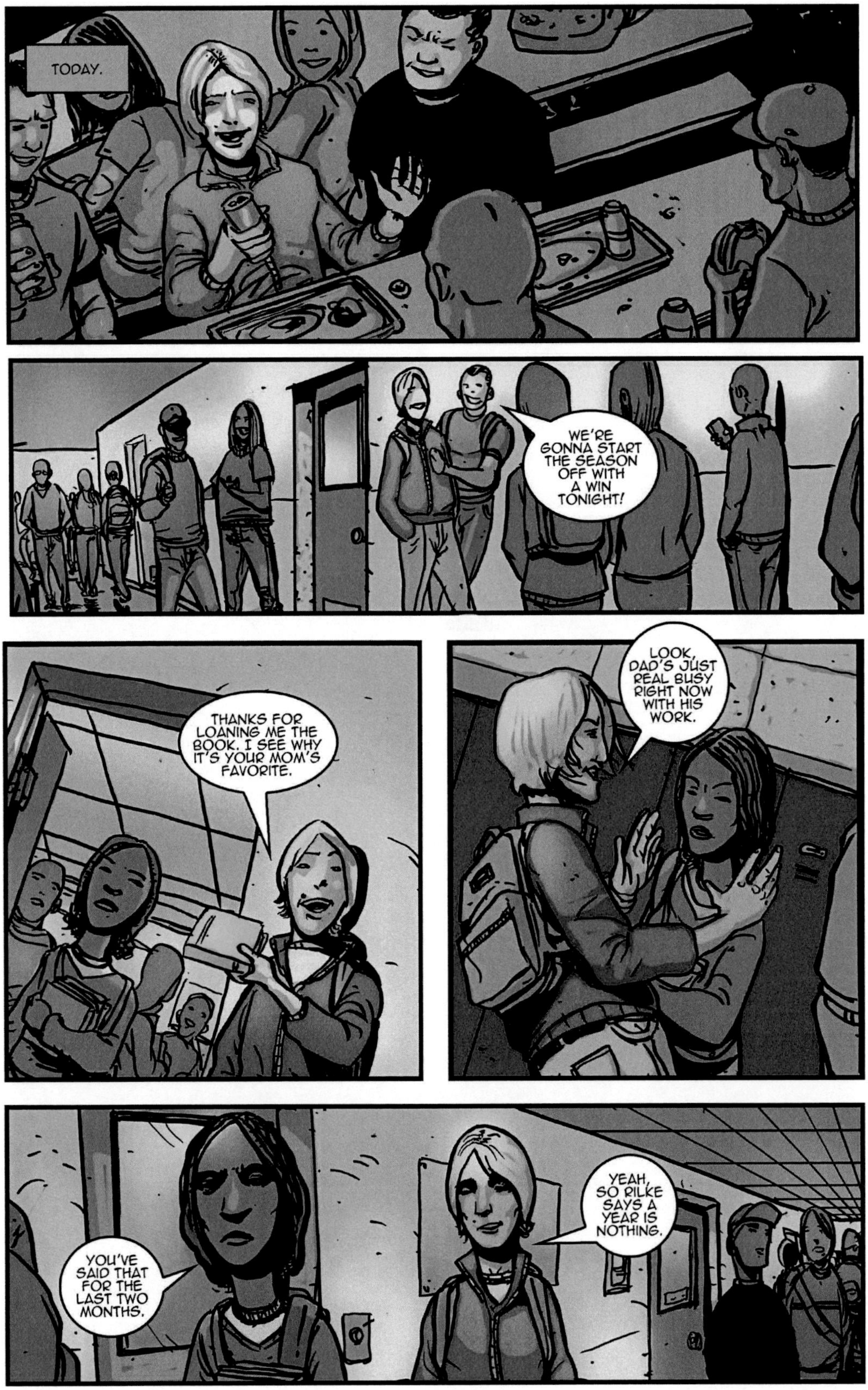
TODAY.
WE'RE GONNA START THE SEASON OFF WITH A WIN TONIGHT!
THANKS FOR LOANING ME THE BOOK. I SEE WHY IT'S YOUR MOM'S FAVORITE.
LOOK, DAD'S JUST REAL BUSY RIGHT NOW WITH HIS WORK.
YOU'VE SAID THAT FOR THE LAST TWO MONTHS.
YEAH, SO RILKE SAYS A YEAR IS NOTHING.

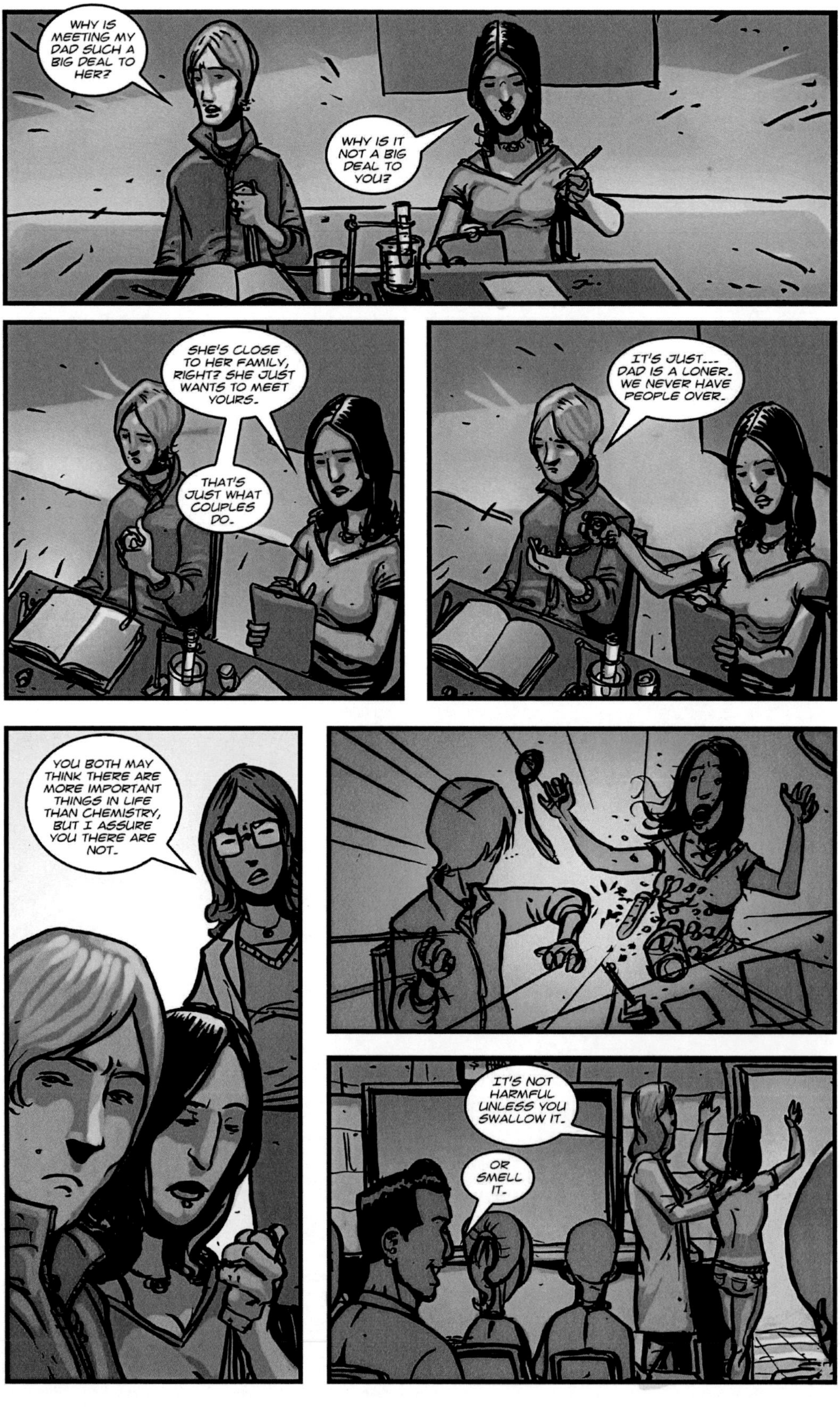
WHY IS MEETING MY DAD SUCH A BIG DEAL TO HER?
WHY IS IT NOT A BIG DEAL TO YOU?
SHE'S CLOSE TO HER FAMILY, RIGHT? SHE JUST WANTS TO MEET YOURS.
THAT'S JUST WHAT COUPLES DO.
IT'S JUST... DAD IS A LONER. WE NEVER HAVE PEOPLE OVER.
YOU BOTH MAY THINK THERE ARE MORE IMPORTANT THINGS IN LIFE THAN CHEMISTRY, BUT I ASSURE YOU THERE ARE NOT.
IT'S NOT HARMFUL UNLESS YOU SWALLOW IT.
OR SMELL IT.

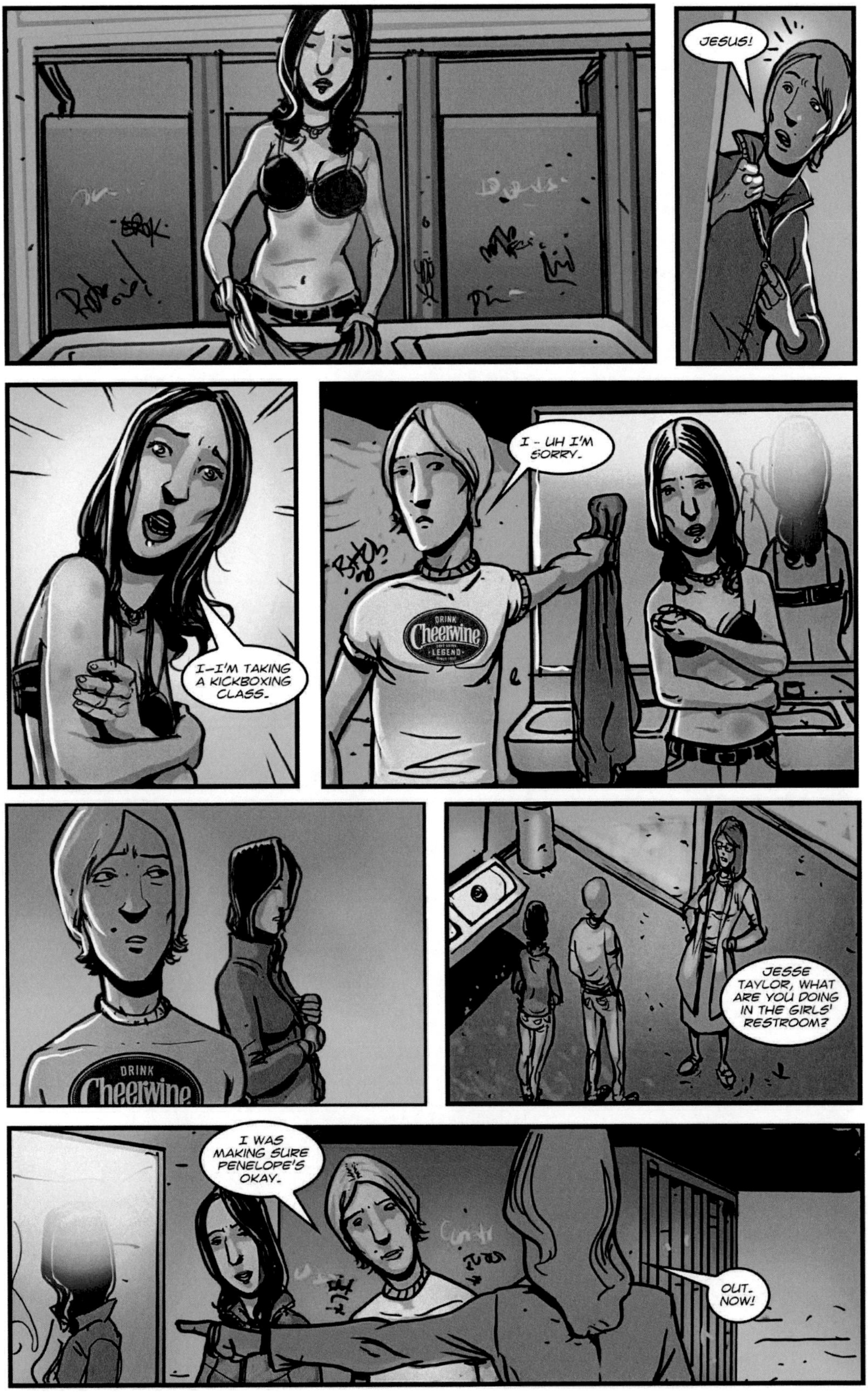
JESUS!
I–I'M TAKING A KICKBOXING CLASS.
I – UH I'M SORRY.
DRINK
Cheerwine
LEGEND
DRINK
Cheerwine
JESSE TAYLOR, WHAT ARE YOU DOING IN THE GIRLS' RESTROOM?
I WAS MAKING SURE PENELOPE'S OKAY.
OUT. NOW!

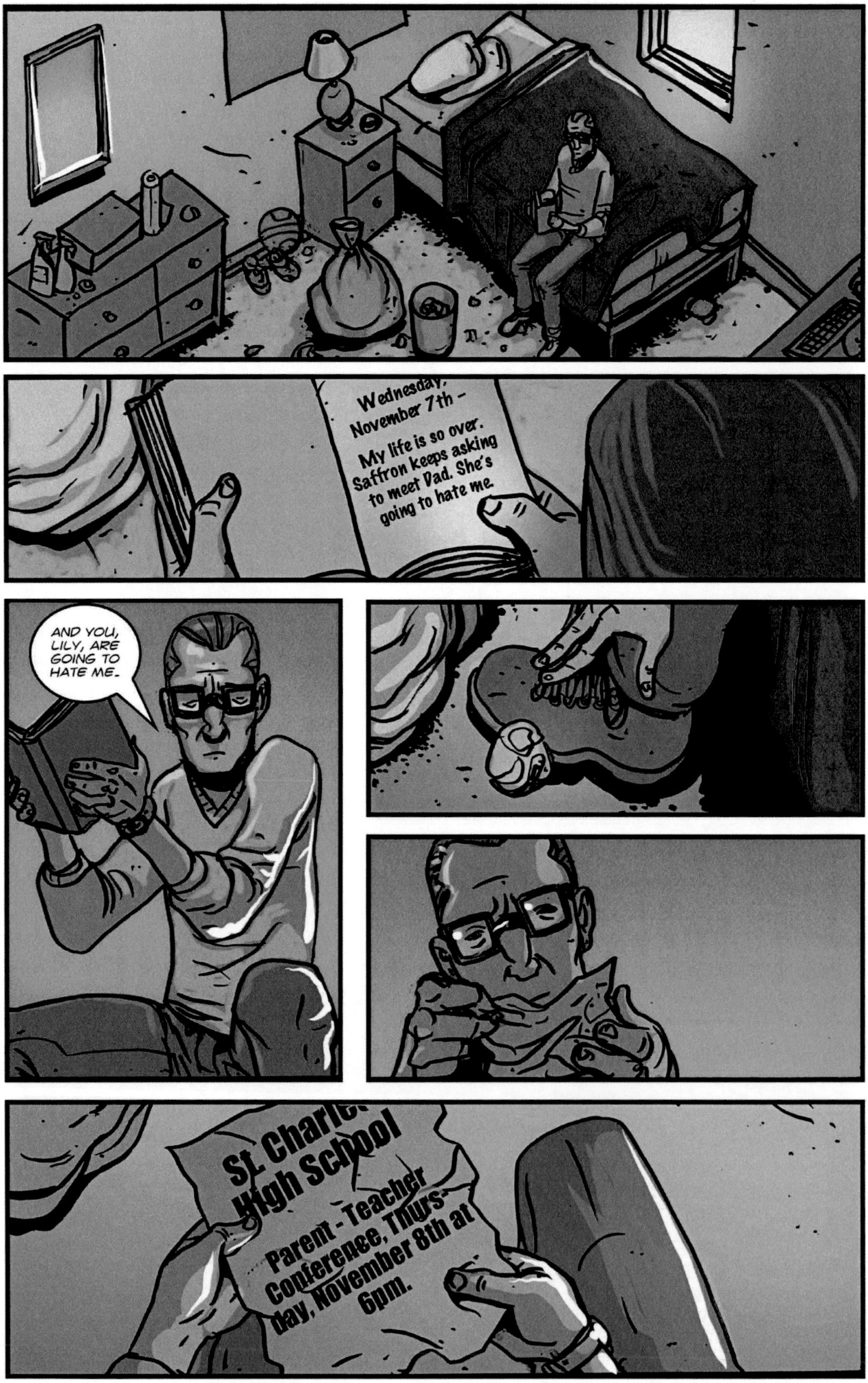
Wednesday, November 7th –
My life is so over. Saffron keeps asking to meet Dad. She's going to hate me.
AND YOU, LILY, ARE GOING TO HATE ME.
High School
Parent - Teacher Conference, Thurs-day, November 8th at 6pm.

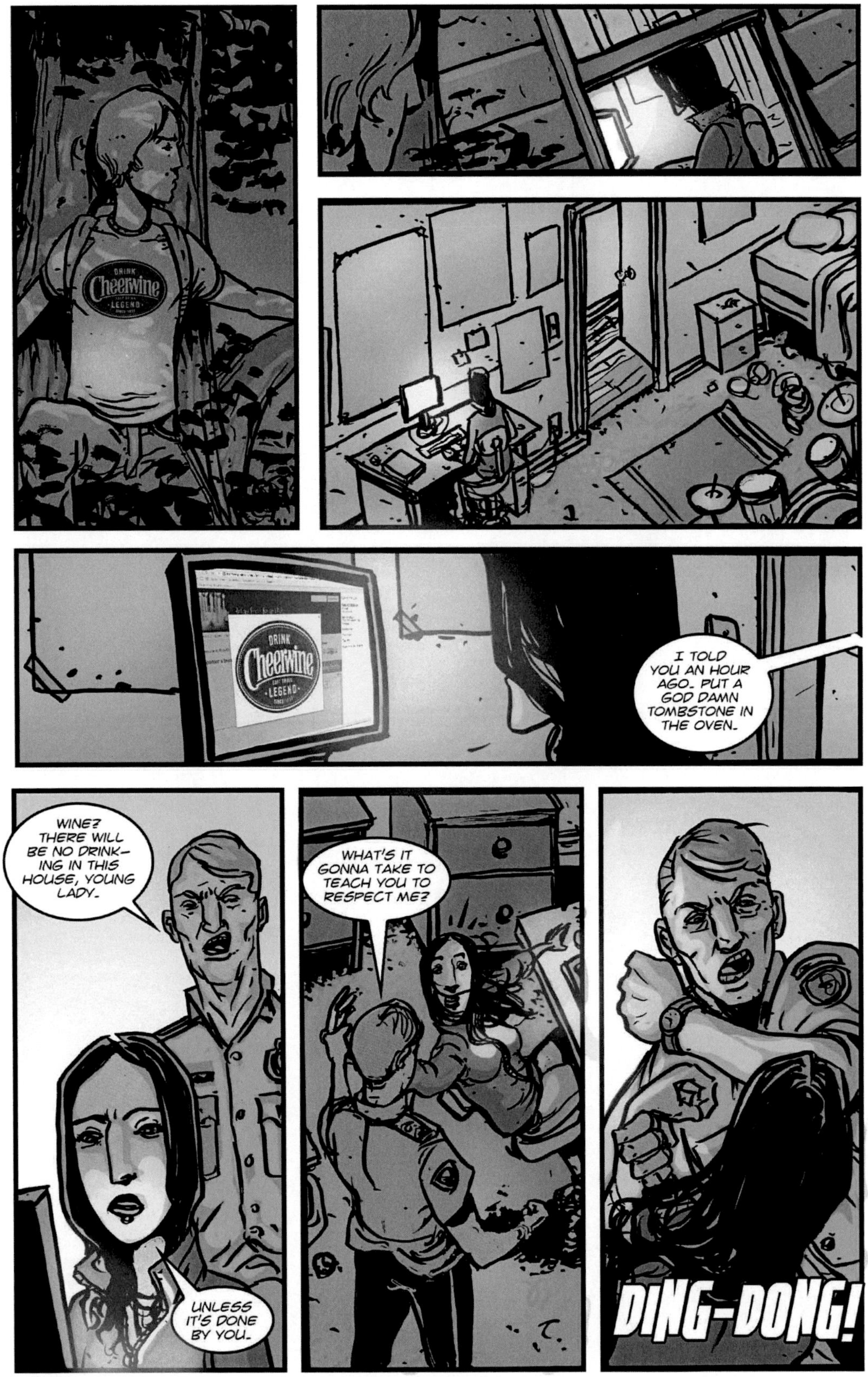
DRINK Cheerwine LEGEND
DRINK Cheerwine LEGEND
I TOLD YOU AN HOUR AGO. PUT A GOD DAMN TOMBSTONE IN THE OVEN.
WINE? THERE WILL BE NO DRINKING IN THIS HOUSE, YOUNG LADY.
UNLESS IT'S DONE BY YOU.
WHAT'S IT GONNA TAKE TO TEACH YOU TO RESPECT ME?
DING-DONG!

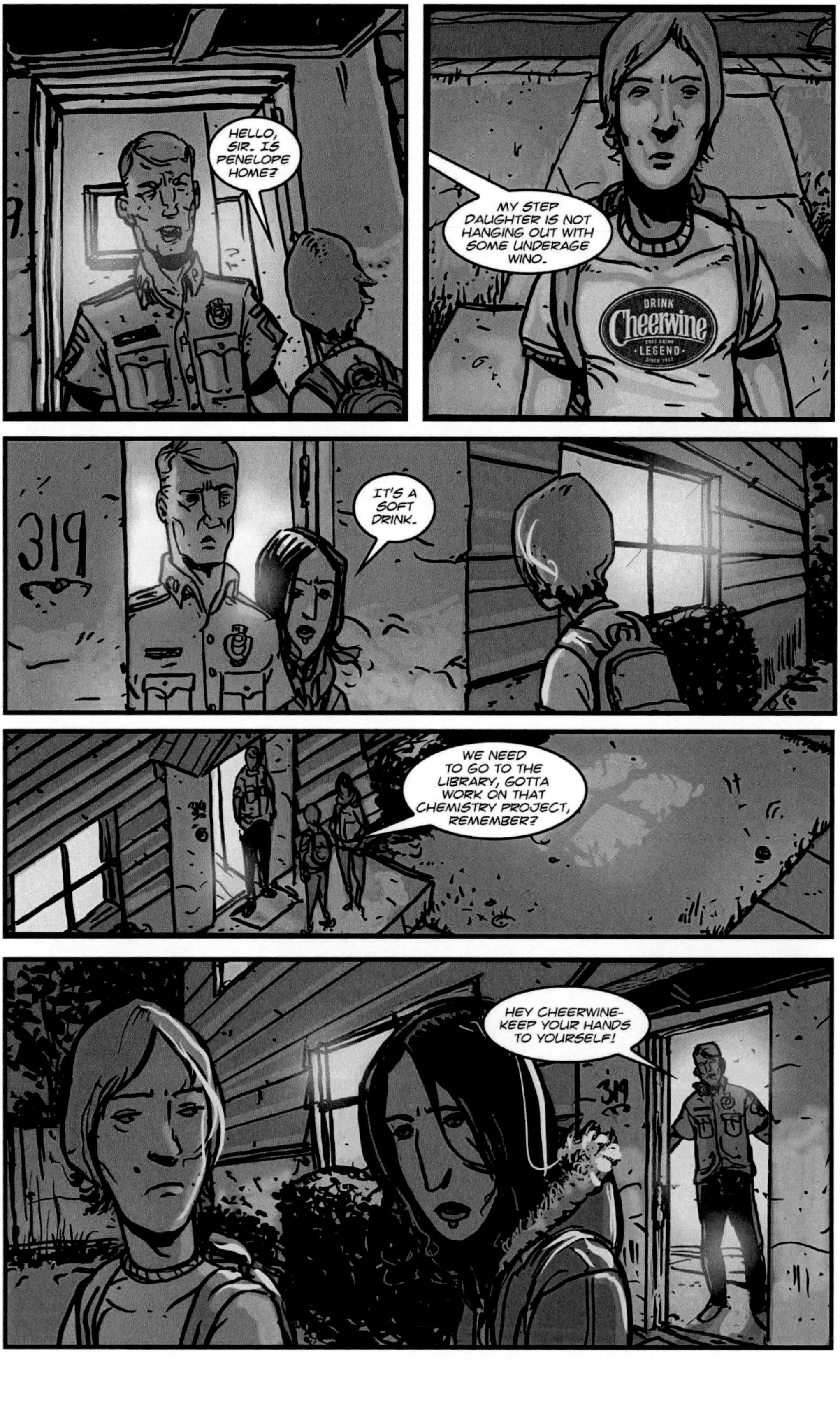
HELLO, SIR. IS PENELOPE HOME?
MY STEP DAUGHTER IS NOT HANGING OUT WITH SOME UNDERAGE WINO.
DRINK Cheerwine LEGEND
IT'S A SOFT DRINK.
319
WE NEED TO GO TO THE LIBRARY, GOTTA WORK ON THAT CHEMISTRY PROJECT, REMEMBER?
HEY CHEERWINE-KEEP YOUR HANDS TO YOURSELF!
319

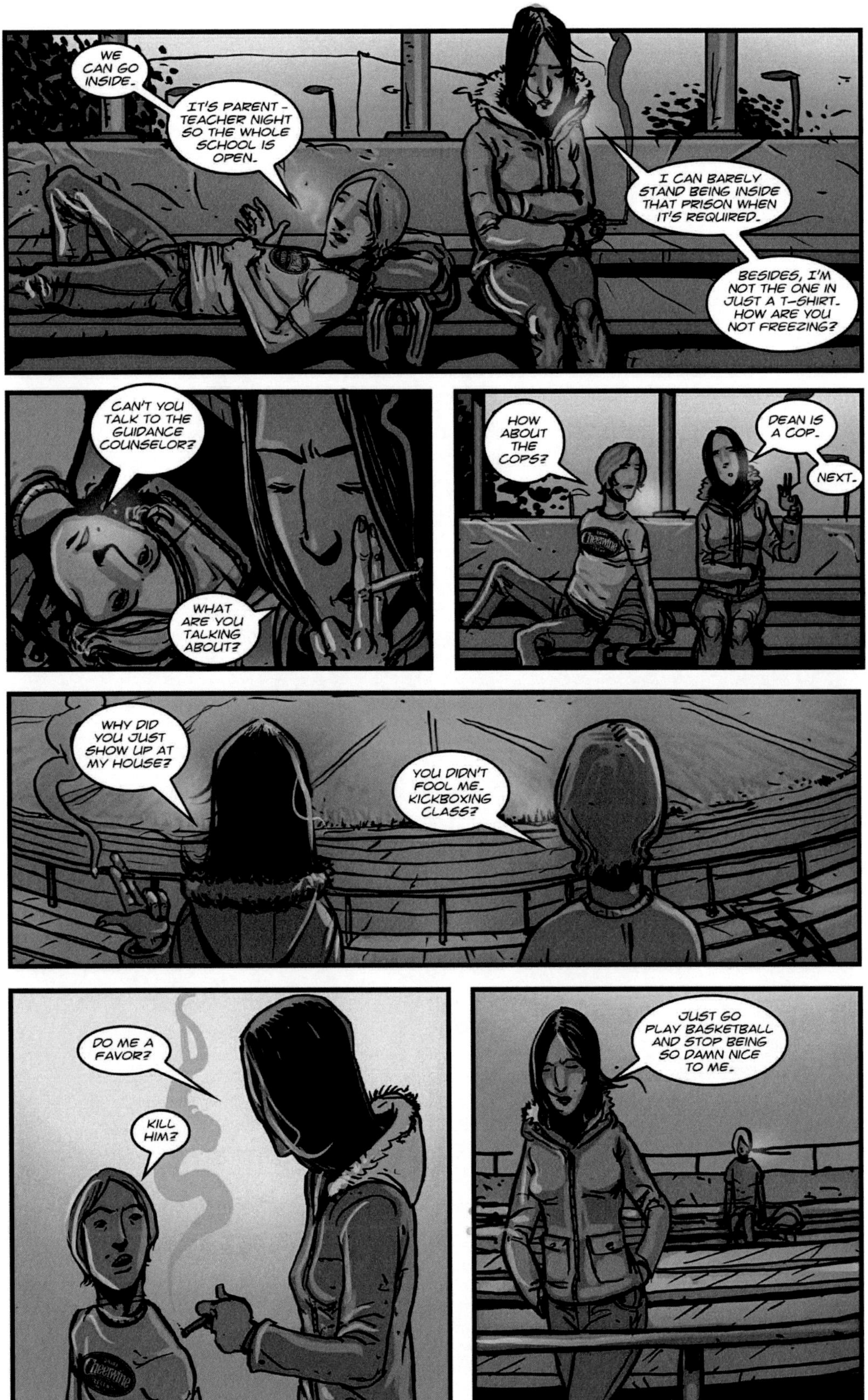
WE CAN GO INSIDE.
IT'S PARENT-TEACHER NIGHT SO THE WHOLE SCHOOL IS OPEN.
I CAN BARELY STAND BEING INSIDE THAT PRISON WHEN IT'S REQUIRED.
BESIDES, I'M NOT THE ONE IN JUST A T-SHIRT. HOW ARE YOU NOT FREEZING?
CAN'T YOU TALK TO THE GUIDANCE COUNSELOR?
WHAT ARE YOU TALKING ABOUT?
HOW ABOUT THE COPS?
DEAN IS A COP.
NEXT.
WHY DID YOU JUST SHOW UP AT MY HOUSE?
YOU DIDN'T FOOL ME. KICKBOXING CLASS?
DO ME A FAVOR?
KILL HIM?
JUST GO PLAY BASKETBALL AND STOP BEING SO DAMN NICE TO ME.

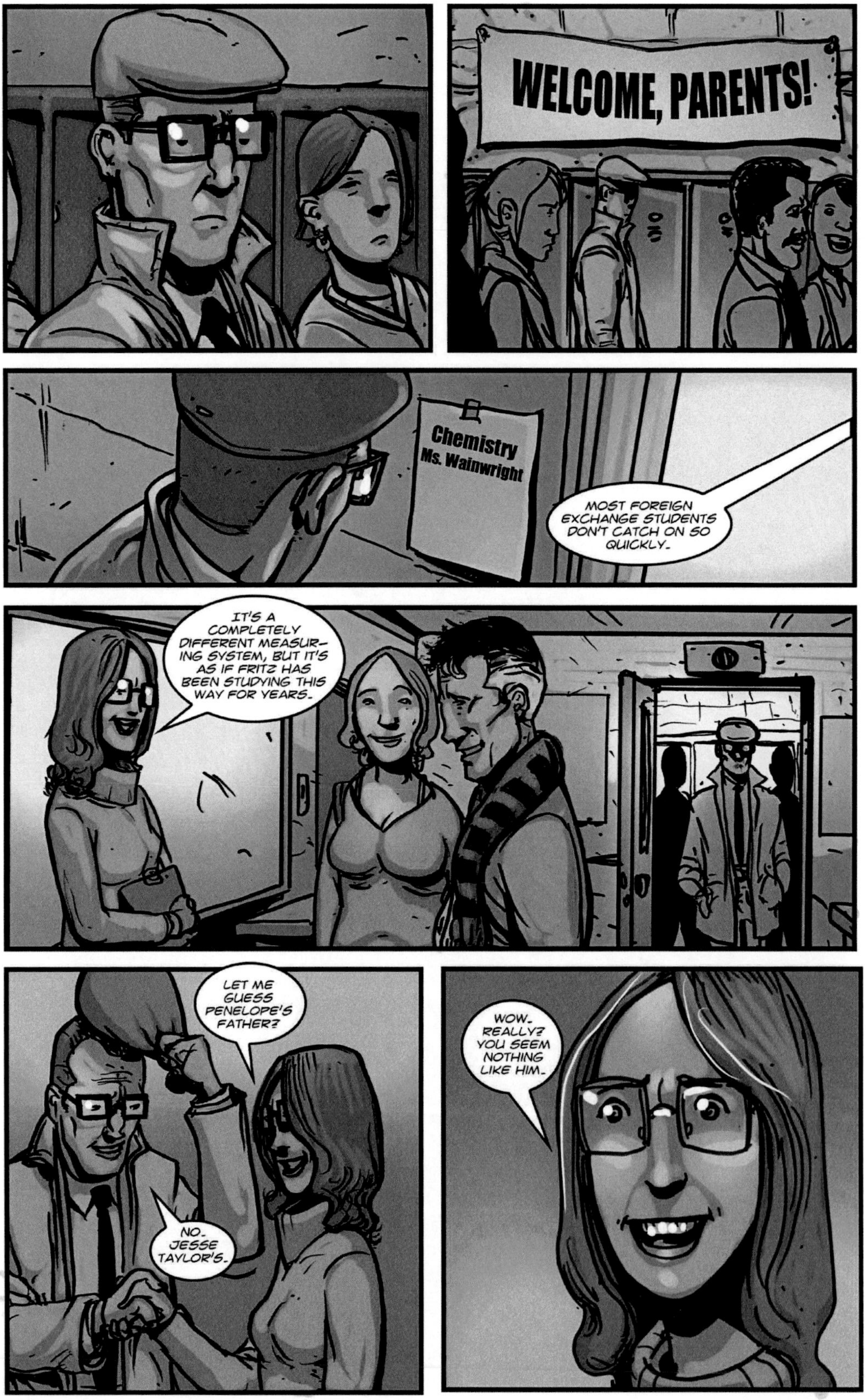
WELCOME, PARENTS!
Chemistry
Ms. Wainwright
MOST FOREIGN EXCHANGE STUDENTS DON'T CATCH ON SO QUICKLY.
IT'S A COMPLETELY DIFFERENT MEASURING SYSTEM, BUT IT'S AS IF FRITZ HAS BEEN STUDYING THIS WAY FOR YEARS.
LET ME GUESS PENELOPE'S FATHER?
NO. JESSE TAYLOR'S.
WOW. REALLY? YOU SEEM NOTHING LIKE HIM.

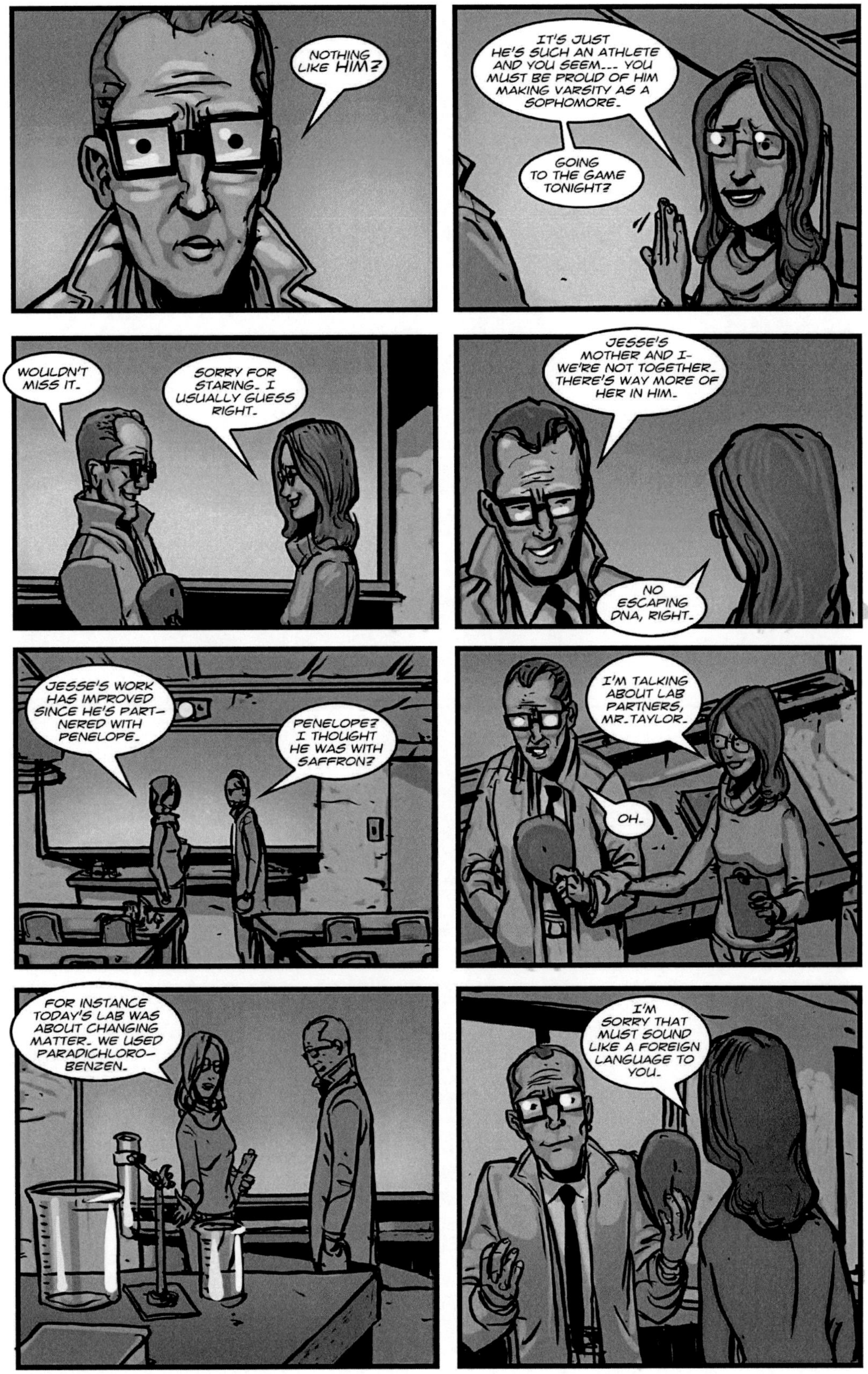
NOTHING LIKE HIM?
IT'S JUST HE'S SUCH AN ATHLETE AND YOU SEEM... YOU MUST BE PROUD OF HIM MAKING VARSITY AS A SOPHOMORE.
GOING TO THE GAME TONIGHT?
WOULDN'T MISS IT.
SORRY FOR STARING. I USUALLY GUESS RIGHT.
JESSE'S MOTHER AND I- WE'RE NOT TOGETHER. THERE'S WAY MORE OF HER IN HIM.
NO ESCAPING DNA, RIGHT.
JESSE'S WORK HAS IMPROVED SINCE HE'S PART-NERED WITH PENELOPE.
PENELOPE? I THOUGHT HE WAS WITH SAFFRON?
I'M TALKING ABOUT LAB PARTNERS, MR. TAYLOR.
OH.
FOR INSTANCE TODAY'S LAB WAS ABOUT CHANGING MATTER. WE USED PARADICHLORO-BENZEN.
I'M SORRY THAT MUST SOUND LIKE A FOREIGN LANGUAGE TO YOU.

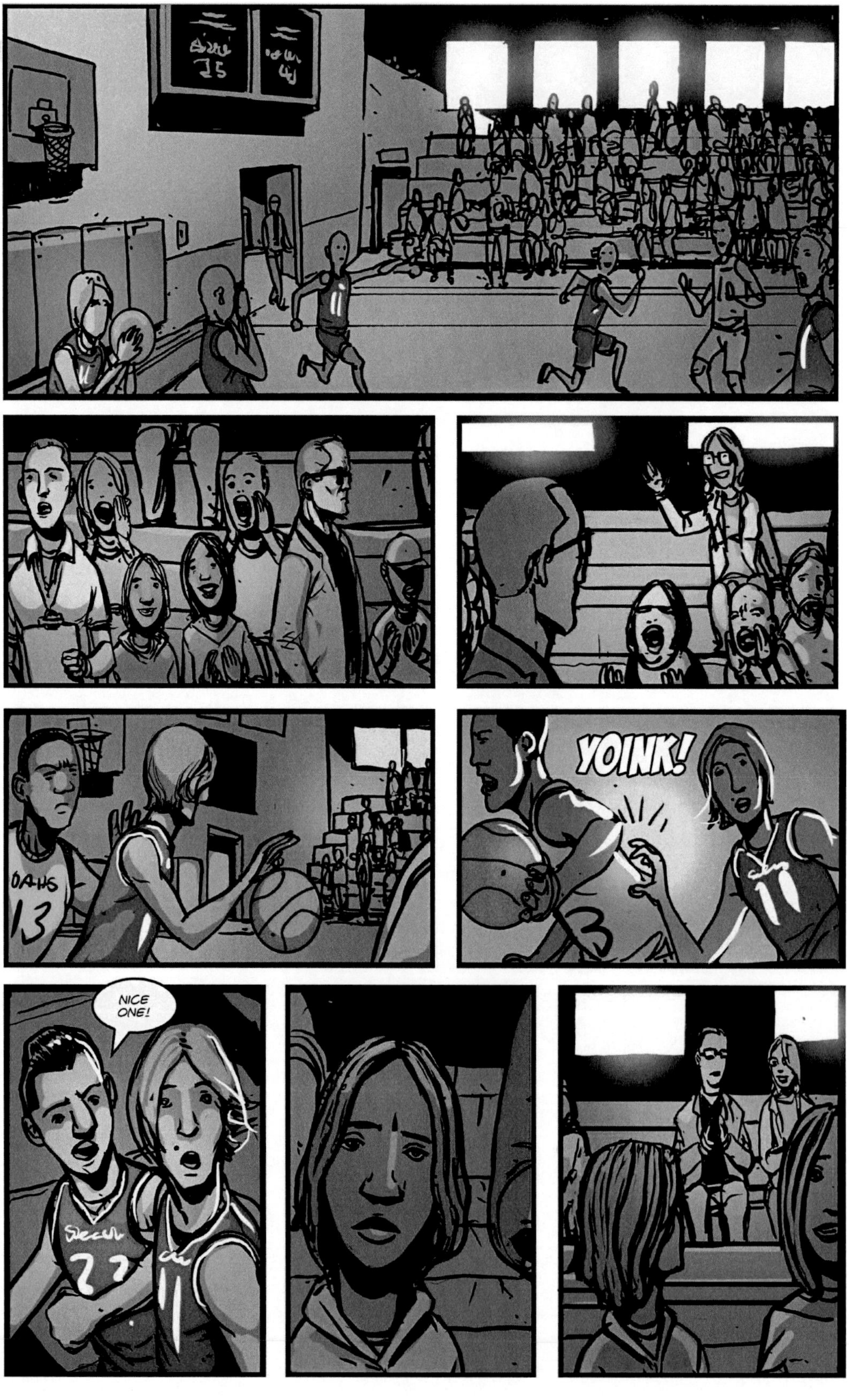
YOINK!
NICE ONE!

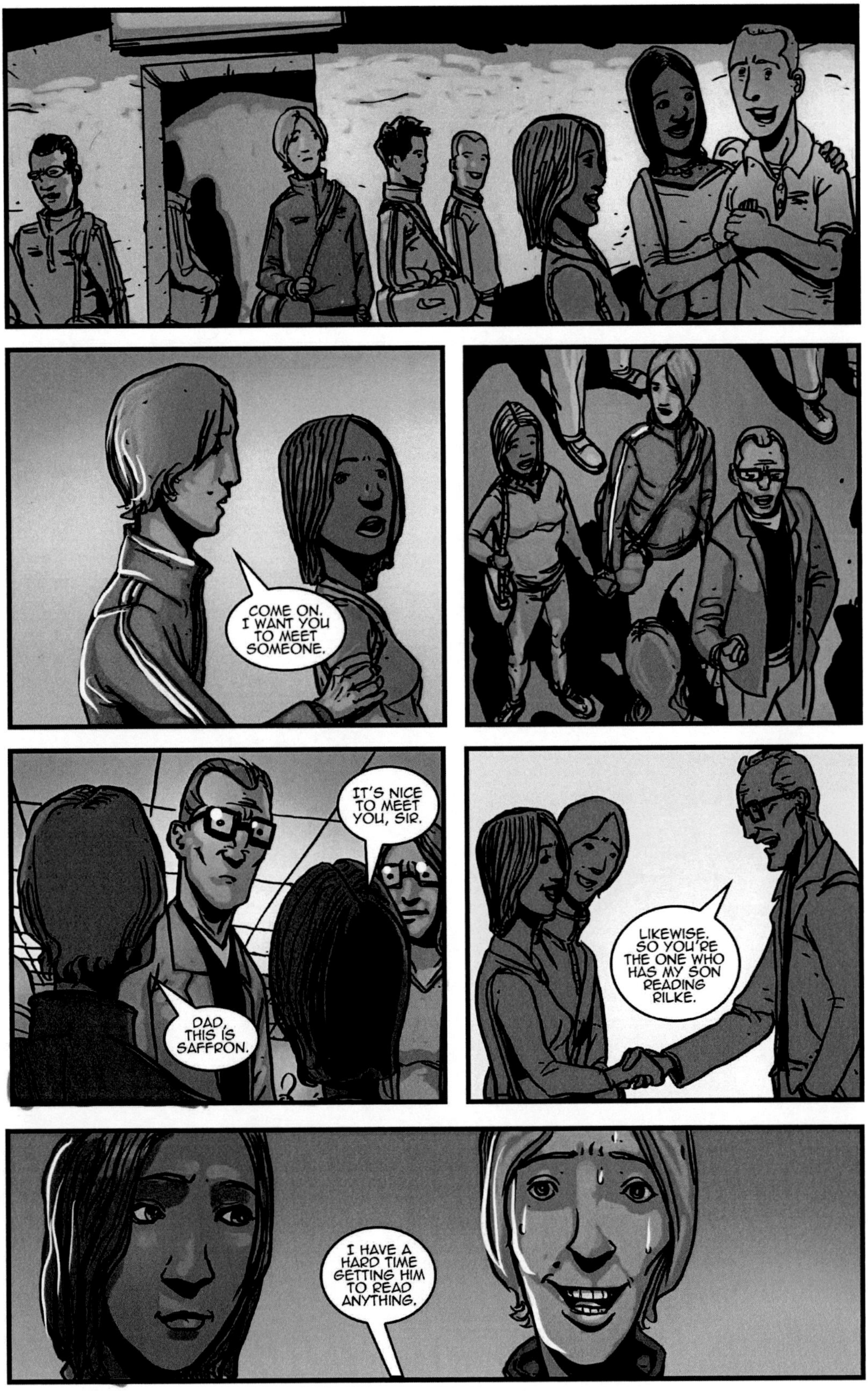
COME ON. I WANT YOU TO MEET SOMEONE.
IT'S NICE TO MEET YOU, SIR.
DAD, THIS IS SAFFRON.
LIKEWISE. SO YOU'RE THE ONE WHO HAS MY SON READING RILKE.
I HAVE A HARD TIME GETTING HIM TO READ ANYTHING.

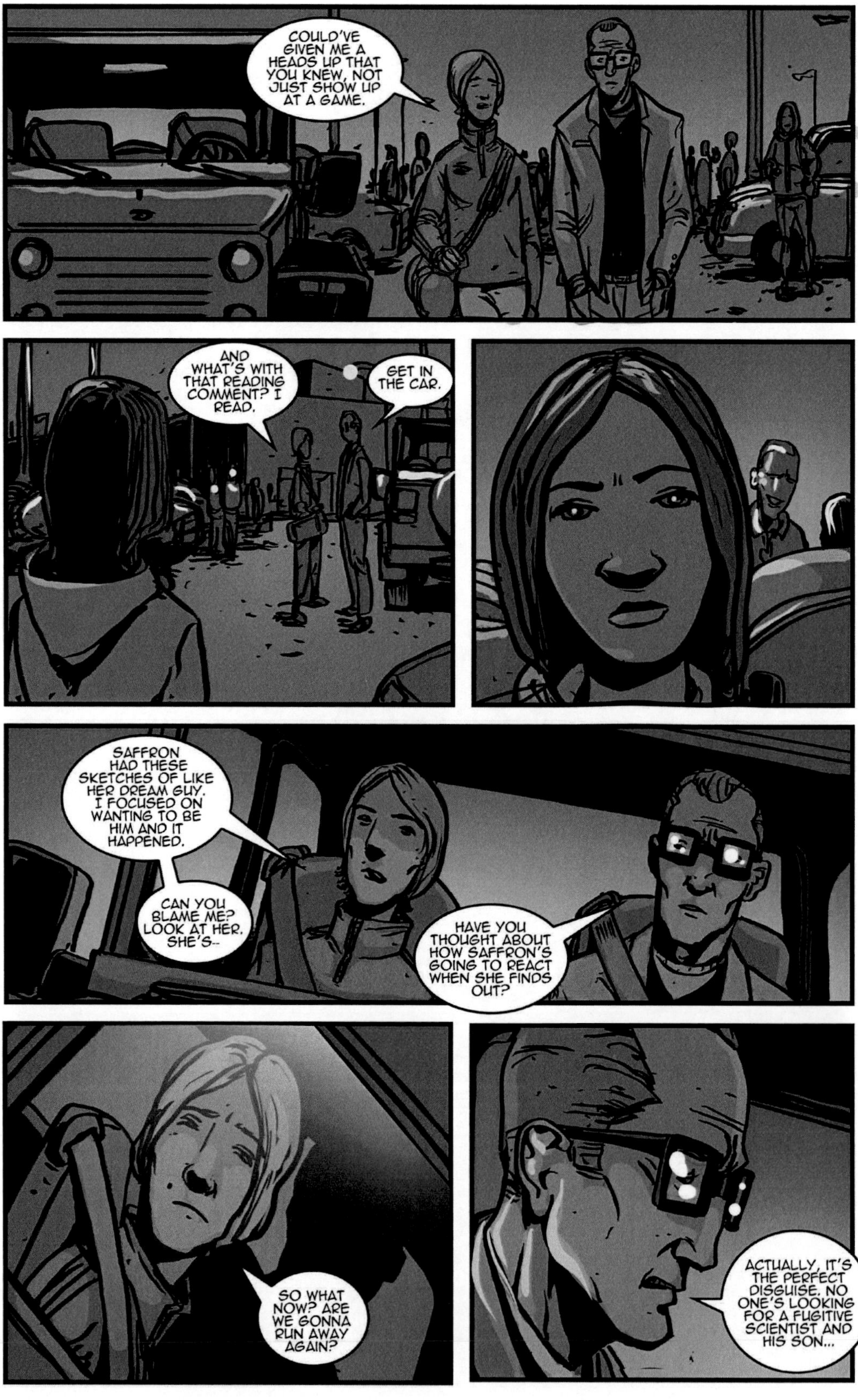
COULD'VE GIVEN ME A HEADS UP THAT YOU KNEW, NOT JUST SHOW UP AT A GAME.
AND WHAT'S WITH THAT READING COMMENT? I READ.
GET IN THE CAR.
SAFFRON HAD THESE SKETCHES OF LIKE HER DREAM GUY. I FOCUSED ON WANTING TO BE HIM AND IT HAPPENED.
CAN YOU BLAME ME? LOOK AT HER. SHE'S--
HAVE YOU THOUGHT ABOUT HOW SAFFRON'S GOING TO REACT WHEN SHE FINDS OUT?
SO WHAT NOW? ARE WE GONNA RUN AWAY AGAIN?
ACTUALLY, IT'S THE PERFECT DISGUISE. NO ONE'S LOOKING FOR A FUGITIVE SCIENTIST AND HIS SON...

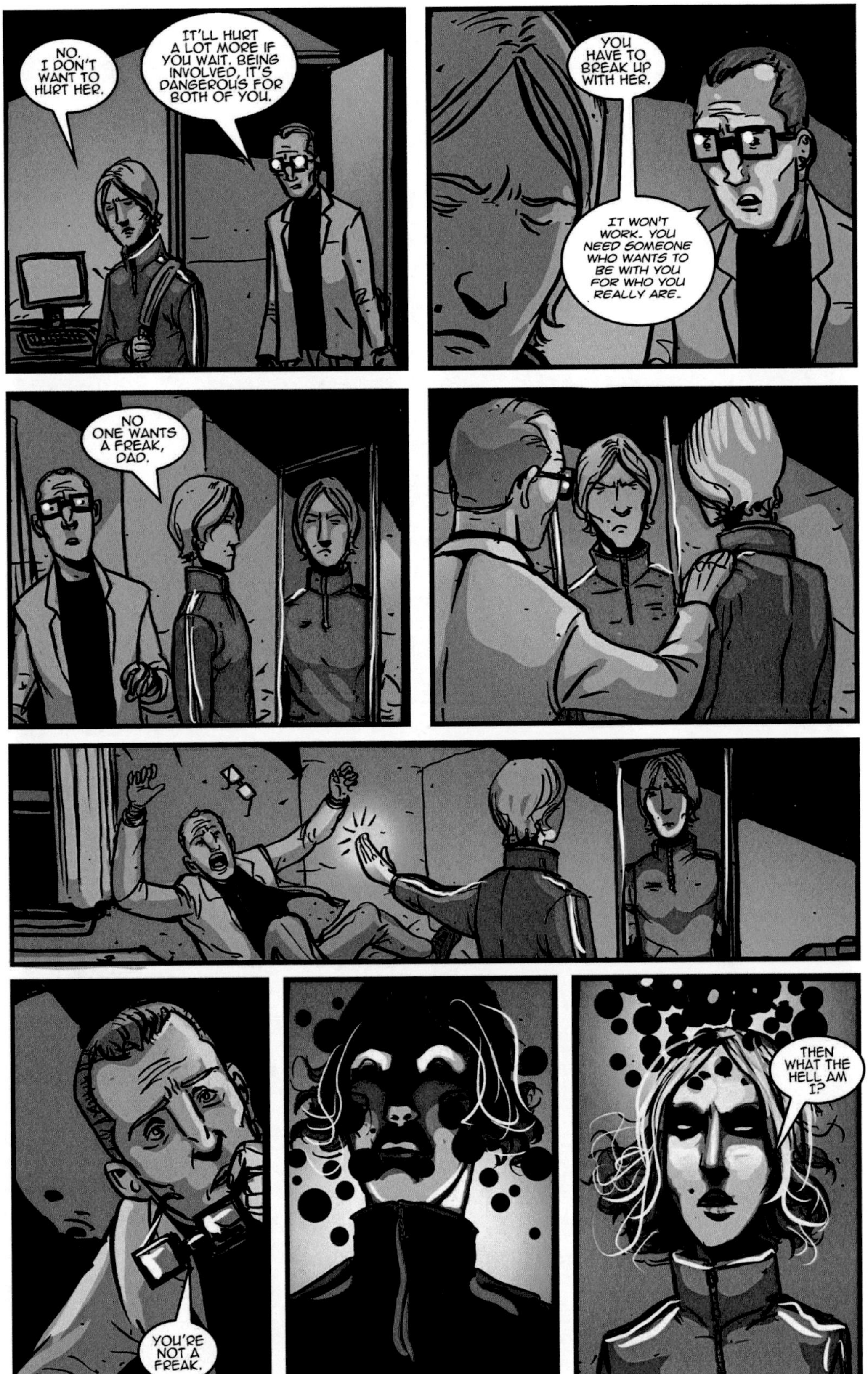
NO, I DON'T WANT TO HURT HER.
IT'LL HURT A LOT MORE IF YOU WAIT. BEING INVOLVED, IT'S DANGEROUS FOR BOTH OF YOU.
YOU HAVE TO BREAK UP WITH HER.
IT WON'T WORK. YOU NEED SOMEONE WHO WANTS TO BE WITH YOU FOR WHO YOU REALLY ARE.
NO ONE WANTS A FREAK, DAD.
YOU'RE NOT A FREAK.
THEN WHAT THE HELL AM I?

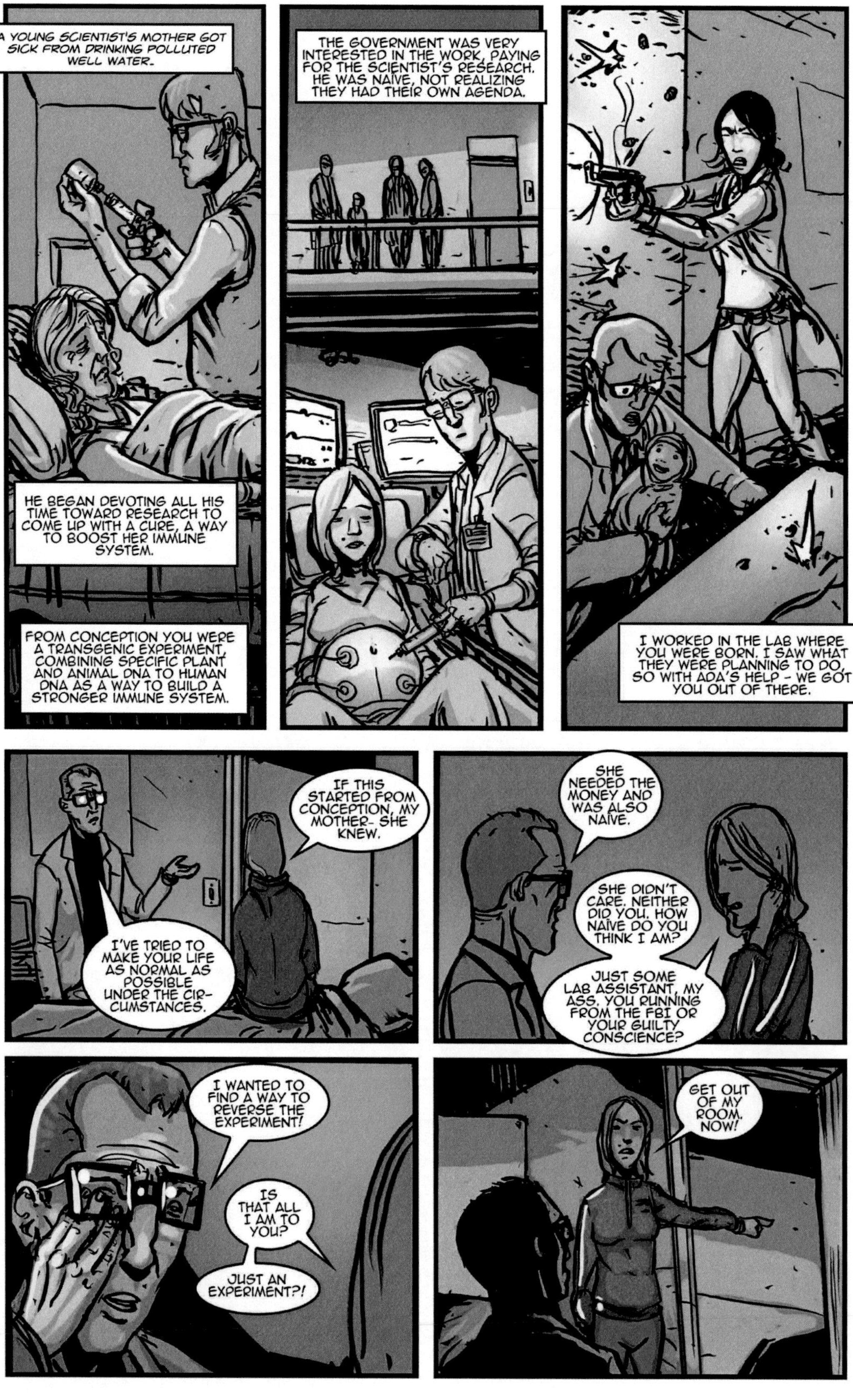
A YOUNG SCIENTIST'S MOTHER GOT SICK FROM DRINKING POLLUTED WELL WATER.
HE BEGAN DEVOTING ALL HIS TIME TOWARD RESEARCH TO COME UP WITH A CURE, A WAY TO BOOST HER IMMUNE SYSTEM.
FROM CONCEPTION YOU WERE A TRANSGENIC EXPERIMENT, COMBINING SPECIFIC PLANT AND ANIMAL DNA TO HUMAN DNA AS A WAY TO BUILD A STRONGER IMMUNE SYSTEM.
THE GOVERNMENT WAS VERY INTERESTED IN THE WORK, PAYING FOR THE SCIENTIST'S RESEARCH. HE WAS NAIVE, NOT REALIZING THEY HAD THEIR OWN AGENDA.
I WORKED IN THE LAB WHERE YOU WERE BORN. I SAW WHAT THEY WERE PLANNING TO DO, SO WITH ADA'S HELP - WE GOT YOU OUT OF THERE.
IF THIS STARTED FROM CONCEPTION, MY MOTHER- SHE KNEW.
I'VE TRIED TO MAKE YOUR LIFE AS NORMAL AS POSSIBLE UNDER THE CIR-CUMSTANCES.
SHE NEEDED THE MONEY AND WAS ALSO NAIVE.
SHE DIDN'T CARE. NEITHER DID YOU. HOW NAIVE DO YOU THINK I AM?
JUST SOME LAB ASSISTANT, MY ASS. YOU RUNNING FROM THE FBI OR YOUR GUILTY CONSCIENCE?
I WANTED TO FIND A WAY TO REVERSE THE EXPERIMENT!
IS THAT ALL I AM TO YOU?
JUST AN EXPERIMENT?!
GET OUT OF MY ROOM. NOW!

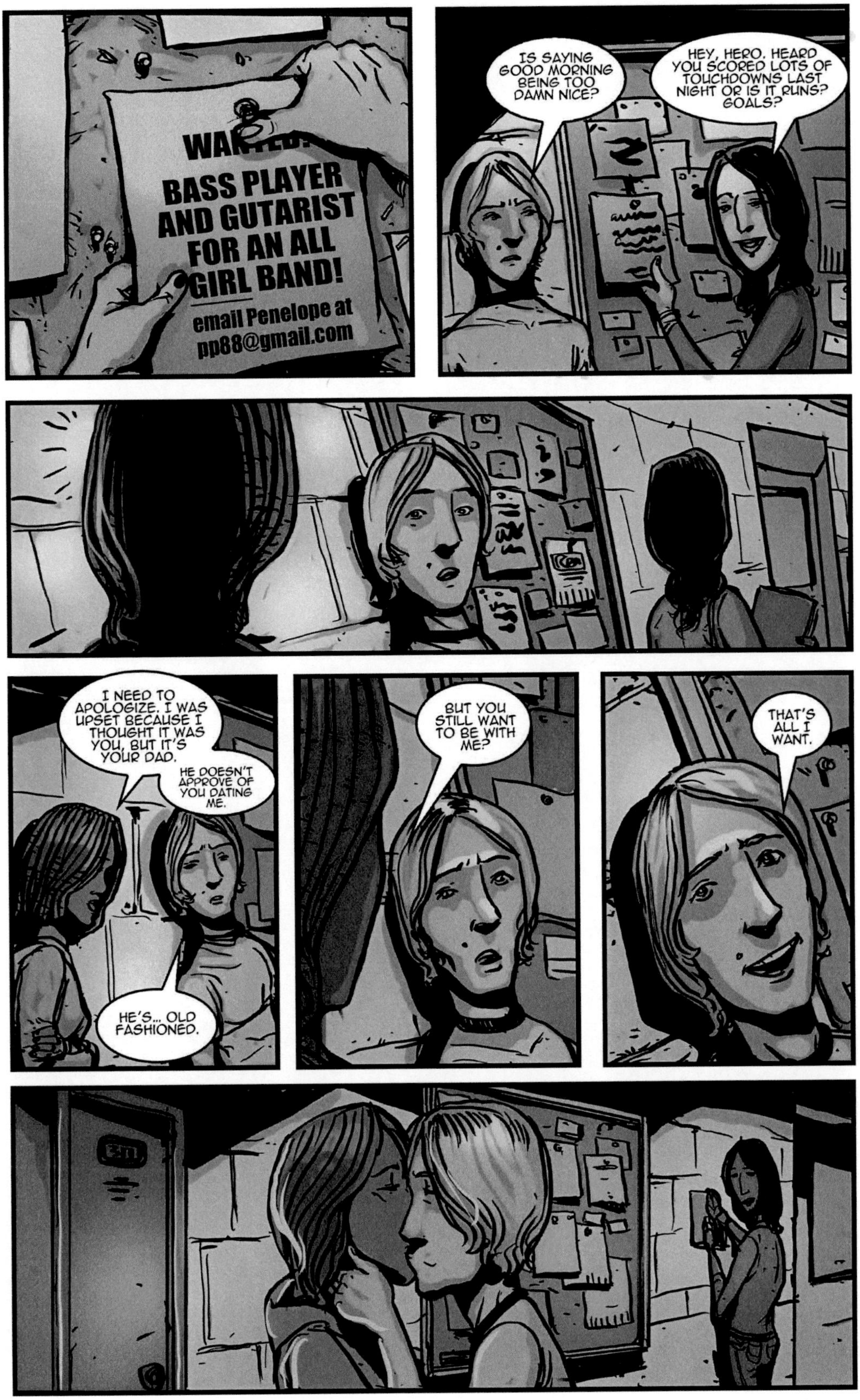

BASS PLAYER AND GUTARIST FOR AN ALL GIRL BAND!
email Penelope at pp88@gmail.com
IS SAYING GOOD MORNING BEING TOO DAMN NICE?
HEY, HERO. HEARD YOU SCORED LOTS OF TOUCHDOWNS LAST NIGHT OR IS IT RUNS? GOALS?
I NEED TO APOLOGIZE. I WAS UPSET BECAUSE I THOUGHT IT WAS YOU, BUT IT'S YOUR DAD.
HE DOESN'T APPROVE OF YOU DATING ME.
HE'S... OLD FASHIONED.
BUT YOU STILL WANT TO BE WITH ME?
THAT'S ALL I WANT.

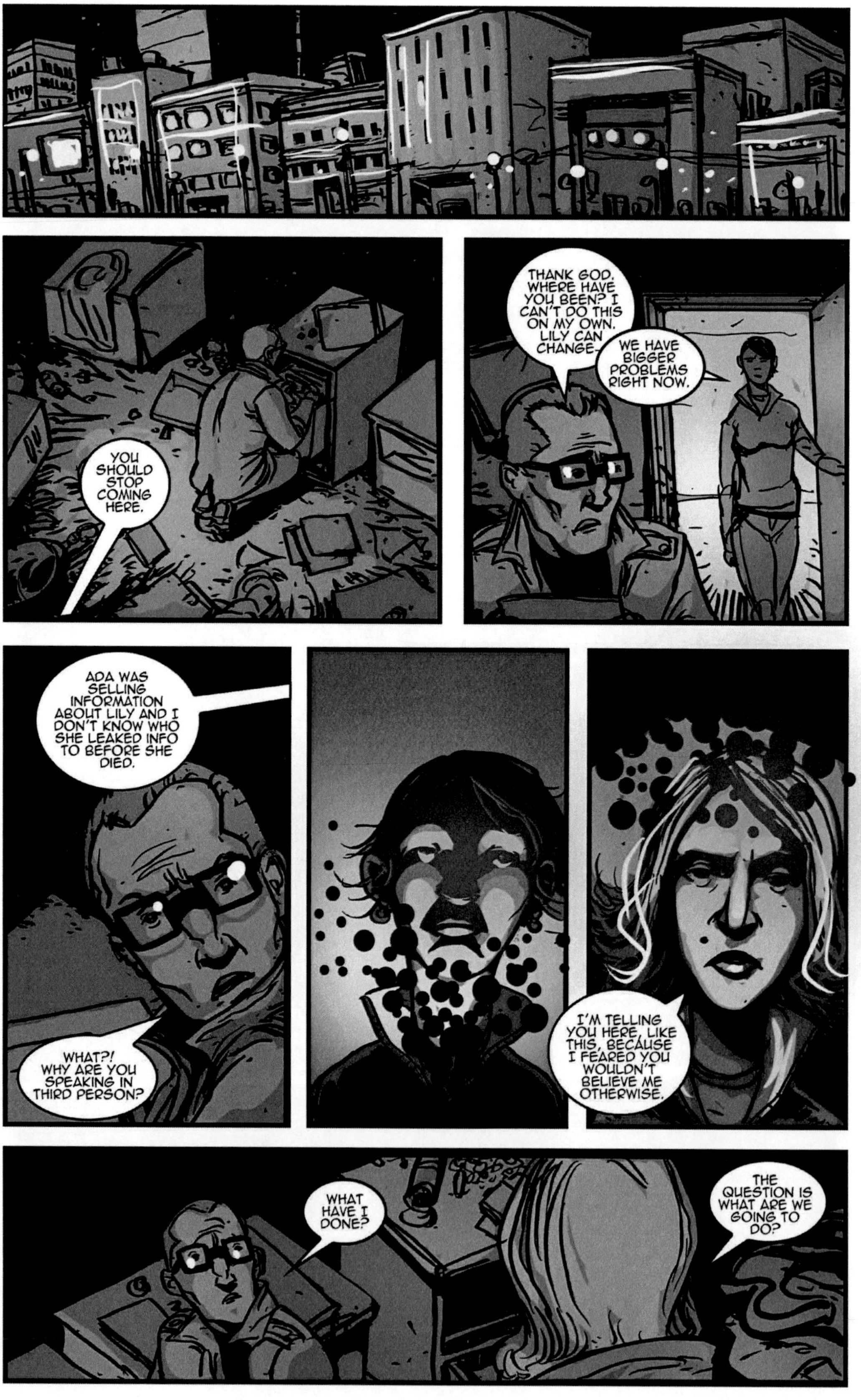
YOU SHOULD STOP COMING HERE.
THANK GOD. WHERE HAVE YOU BEEN? I CAN'T DO THIS ON MY OWN. LILY CAN CHANGE-
WE HAVE BIGGER PROBLEMS RIGHT NOW.
ADA WAS SELLING INFORMATION ABOUT LILY AND I DON'T KNOW WHO SHE LEAKED INFO TO BEFORE SHE DIED.
WHAT?! WHY ARE YOU SPEAKING IN THIRD PERSON?
I'M TELLING YOU HERE, LIKE THIS, BECAUSE I FEARED YOU WOULDN'T BELIEVE ME OTHERWISE.
WHAT HAVE I DONE?
THE QUESTION IS WHAT ARE WE GOING TO DO?

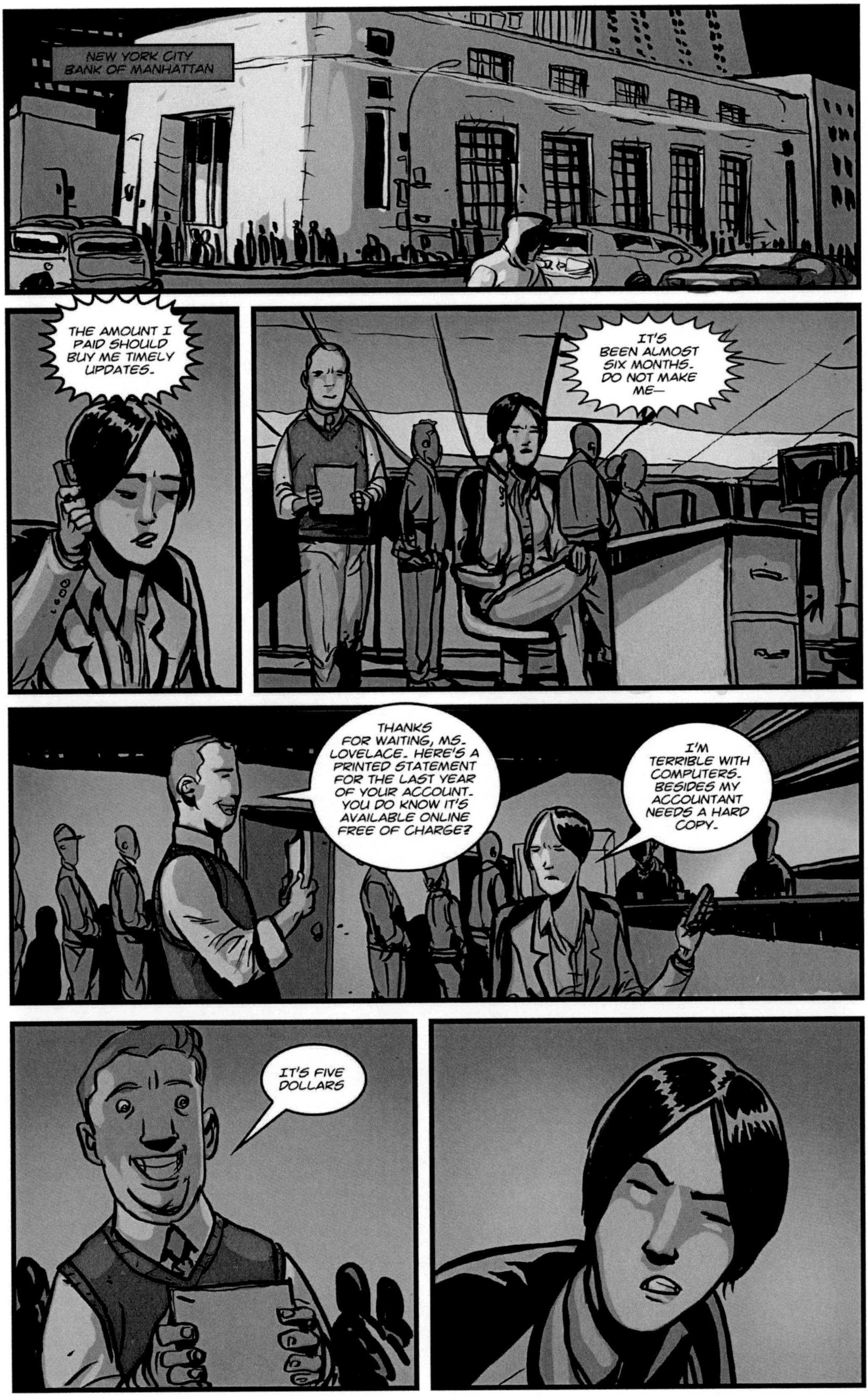
NEW YORK CITY
BANK OF MANHATTAN
THE AMOUNT I PAID SHOULD BUY ME TIMELY UPDATES.
IT'S BEEN ALMOST SIX MONTHS. DO NOT MAKE ME—
THANKS FOR WAITING, MS. LOVELACE. HERE'S A PRINTED STATEMENT FOR THE LAST YEAR OF YOUR ACCOUNT. YOU DO KNOW IT'S AVAILABLE ONLINE FREE OF CHARGE?
I'M TERRIBLE WITH COMPUTERS. BESIDES MY ACCOUNTANT NEEDS A HARD COPY.
IT'S FIVE DOLLARS

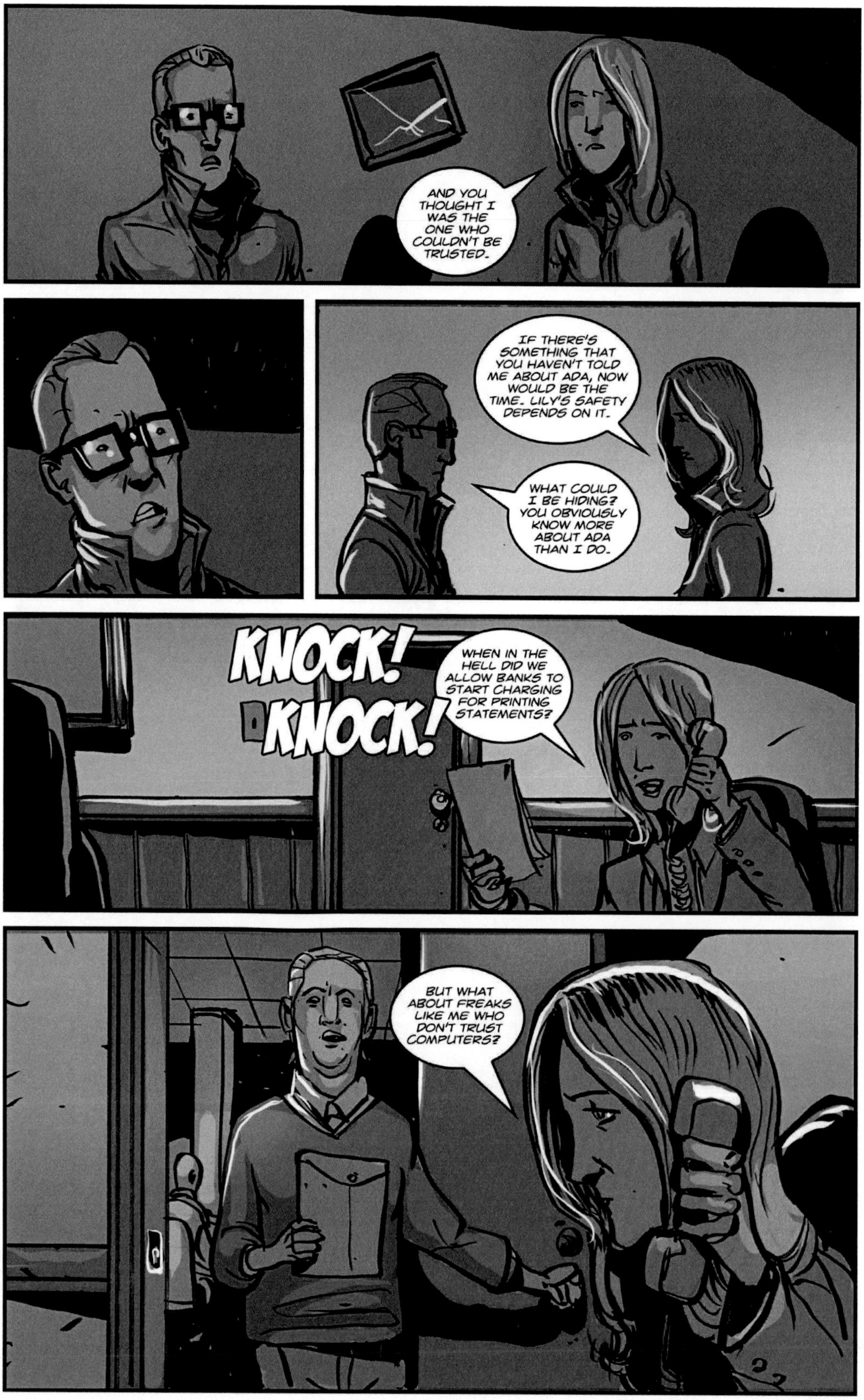
AND YOU THOUGHT I WAS THE ONE WHO COULDN'T BE TRUSTED.
IF THERE'S SOMETHING THAT YOU HAVEN'T TOLD ME ABOUT ADA, NOW WOULD BE THE TIME. LILY'S SAFETY DEPENDS ON IT.
WHAT COULD I BE HIDING? YOU OBVIOUSLY KNOW MORE ABOUT ADA THAN I DO.
KNOCK! KNOCK!
WHEN IN THE HELL DID WE ALLOW BANKS TO START CHARGING FOR PRINTING STATEMENTS?
BUT WHAT ABOUT FREAKS LIKE ME WHO DON'T TRUST COMPUTERS?

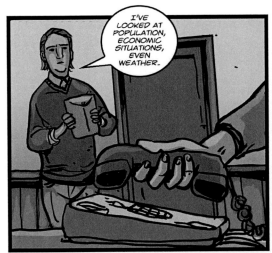

I'VE LOOKED AT POPULATION, ECONOMIC SITUATIONS, EVEN WEATHER.

THERE IS NOT ONE THING THAT ALL THESE TOWNS HAVE IN COMMON, EXCEPT THEY'RE ALL SMALL AND ONLY A REDNECK WOULD BE CONTENT LIV—

THERE HAS TO BE SOMETHING.

MAYBE IF YOU TELL ME WHAT I'M LOOKING FOR.

WHY THESE TOWNS? WHAT'S THE COMMON DENOMINATOR FOR YOU? ONLY ONE IS IN NEW YORK.

JUST KEEP DIGGING. LOOK AT SCIENTIFIC, GEOLOGICAL, ENVIRONMENTAL DATA, SIMILAR NEWS EVENTS.

MARK, I NEED YOU TO DO THIS. I CAN'T TRUST ANYONE ELSE.

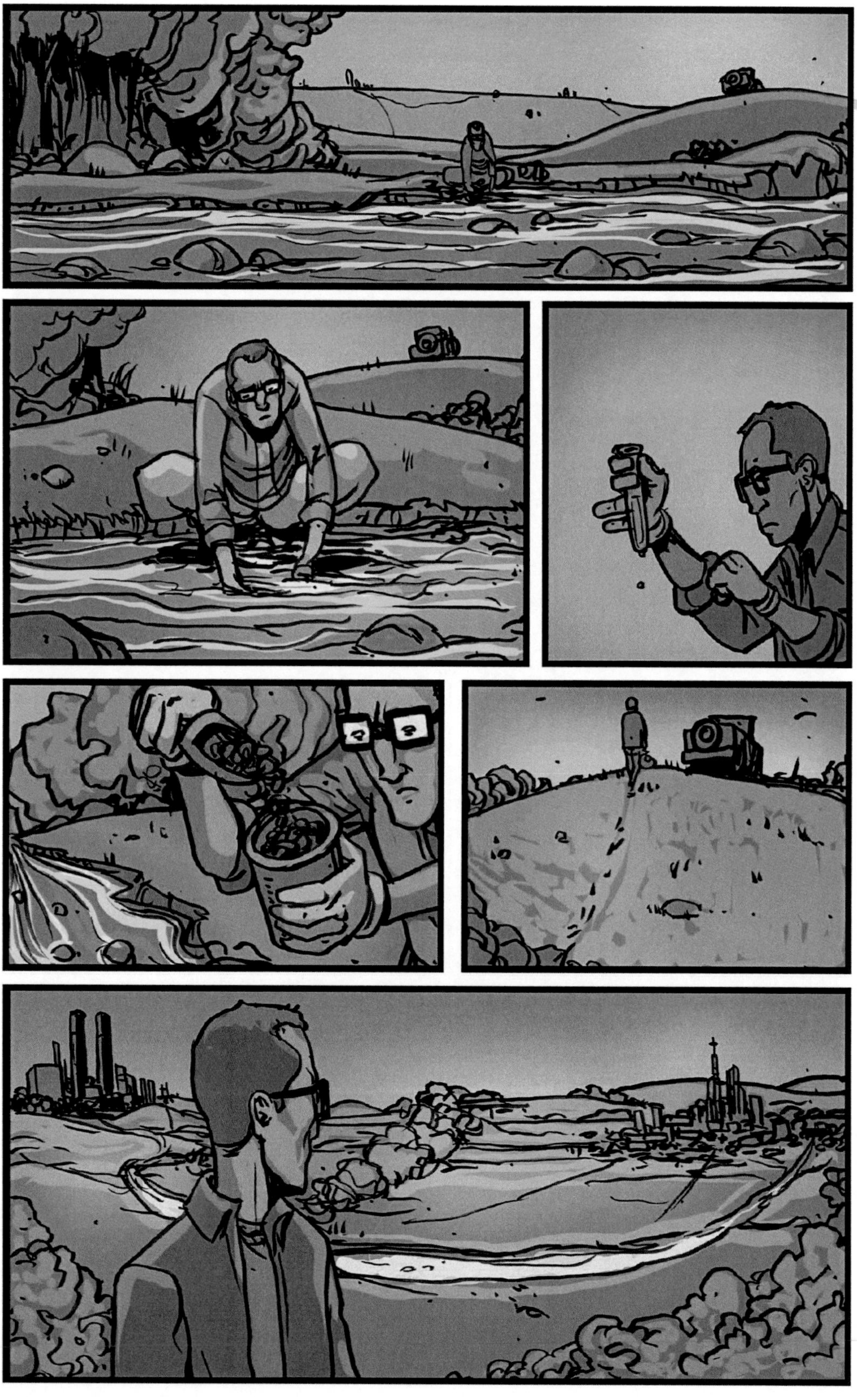

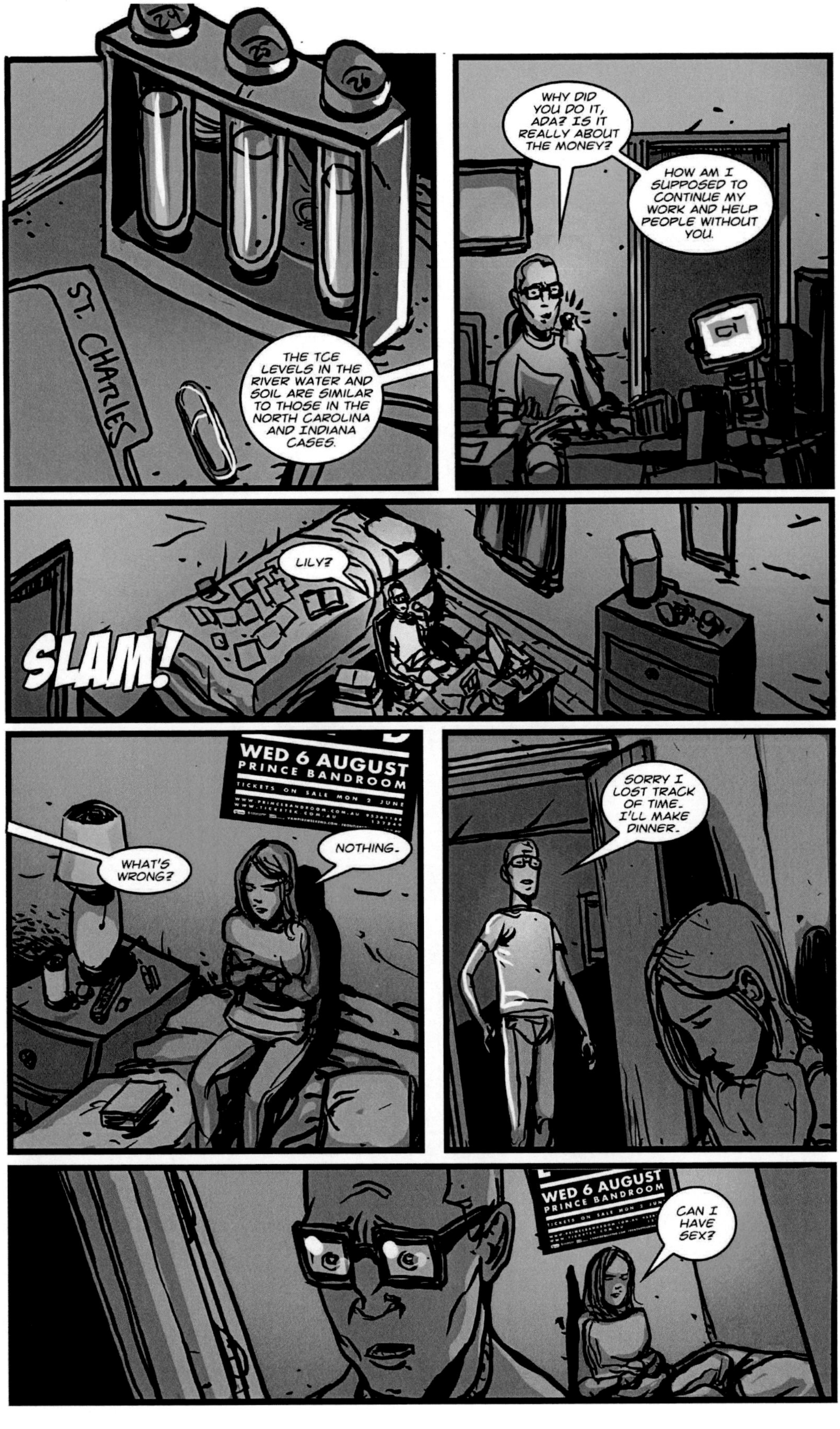
ST. CHARLES
THE TCE LEVELS IN THE RIVER WATER AND SOIL ARE SIMILAR TO THOSE IN THE NORTH CAROLINA AND INDIANA CASES.
WHY DID YOU DO IT, ADA? IS IT REALLY ABOUT THE MONEY?
HOW AM I SUPPOSED TO CONTINUE MY WORK AND HELP PEOPLE WITHOUT YOU.
LILY?
SLAM!
WED 6 AUGUST
PRINCE BANDROOM
TICKETS ON SALE MON 2 JUNE
WHAT'S WRONG?
NOTHING.
SORRY I LOST TRACK OF TIME. I'LL MAKE DINNER.
WED 6 AUGUST
PRINCE BANDROOM
CAN I HAVE SEX?

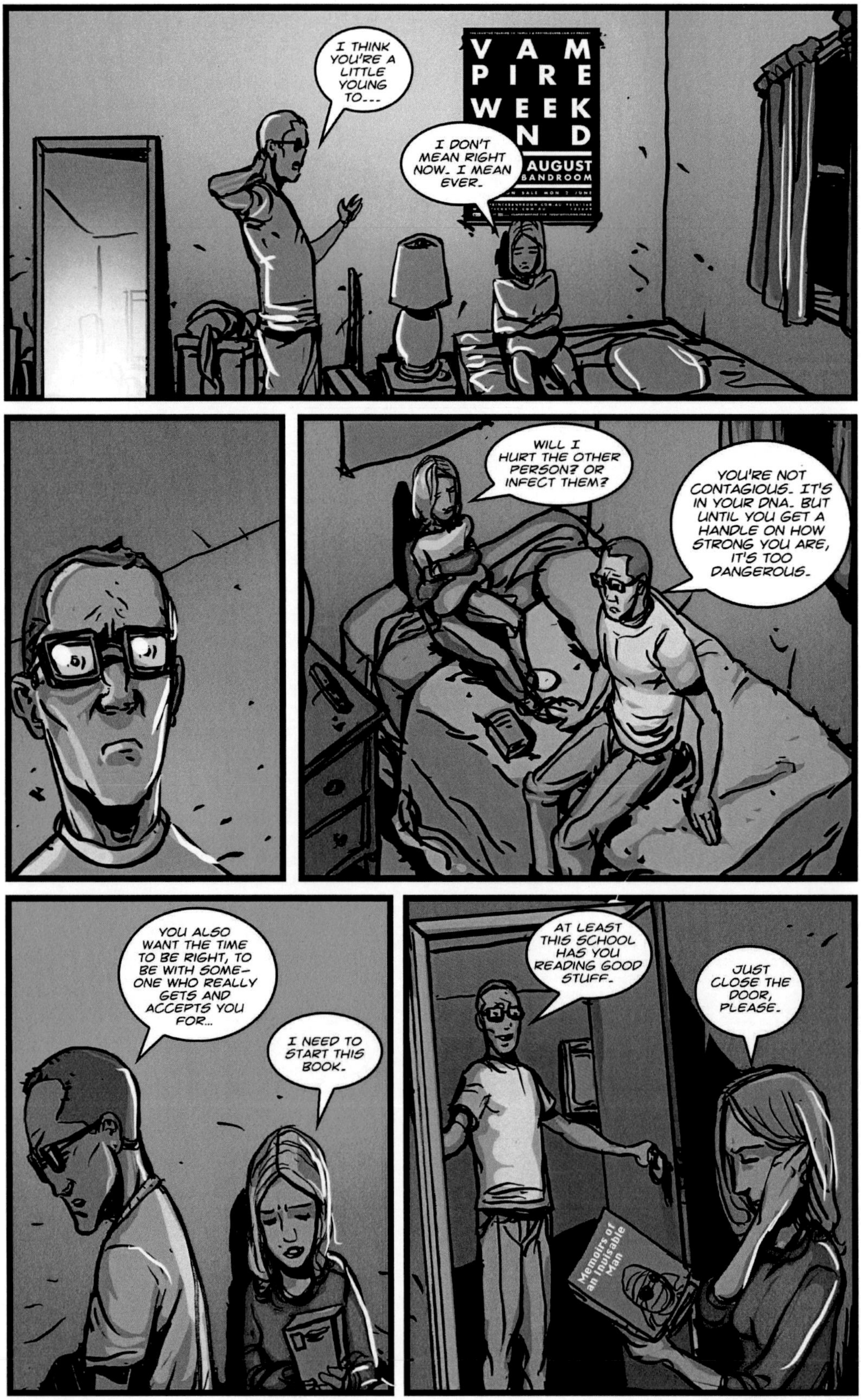
I THINK YOU'RE A LITTLE YOUNG TO...
VAM
PIRE
WEEK
ND
AUGUST
BANDROOM
I DON'T MEAN RIGHT NOW. I MEAN EVER.
WILL I HURT THE OTHER PERSON? OR INFECT THEM?
YOU'RE NOT CONTAGIOUS. IT'S IN YOUR DNA. BUT UNTIL YOU GET A HANDLE ON HOW STRONG YOU ARE, IT'S TOO DANGEROUS.
YOU ALSO WANT THE TIME TO BE RIGHT, TO BE WITH SOME-ONE WHO REALLY GETS AND ACCEPTS YOU FOR...
I NEED TO START THIS BOOK.
AT LEAST THIS SCHOOL HAS YOU READING GOOD STUFF.
JUST CLOSE THE DOOR, PLEASE.
Memoirs of an Invisible Man

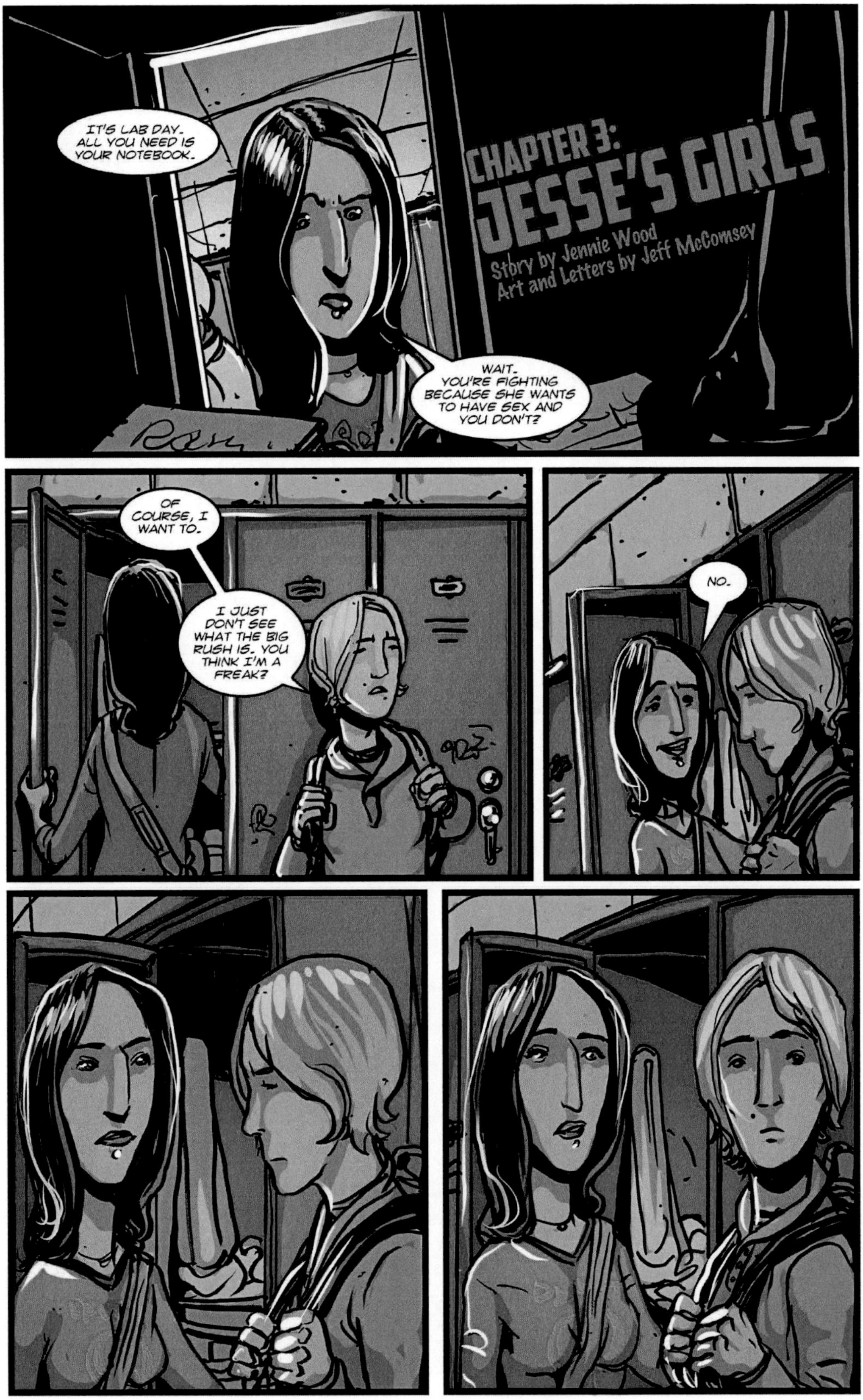
IT'S LAB DAY. ALL YOU NEED IS YOUR NOTEBOOK.
CHAPTER 3: JESSE'S GIRLS
Story by Jennie Wood
Art and Letters by Jeff McComsey
WAIT. YOU'RE FIGHTING BECAUSE SHE WANTS TO HAVE SEX AND YOU DON'T?
OF COURSE, I WANT TO.
I JUST DON'T SEE WHAT THE BIG RUSH IS. YOU THINK I'M A FREAK?
NO.

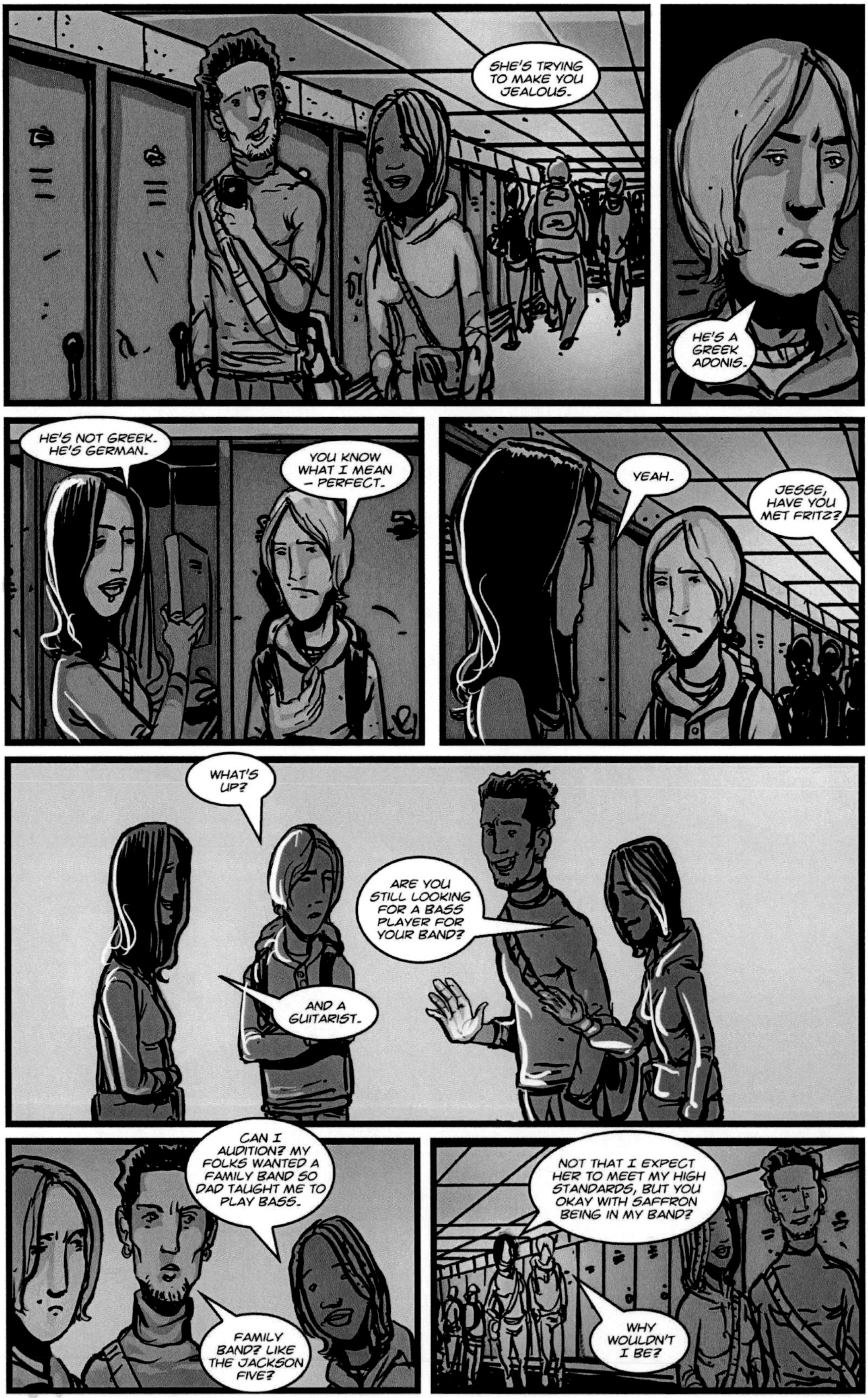
SHE'S TRYING TO MAKE YOU JEALOUS.
HE'S A GREEK ADONIS.
HE'S NOT GREEK. HE'S GERMAN.
YOU KNOW WHAT I MEAN – PERFECT.
YEAH.
JESSE, HAVE YOU MET FRITZ?
WHAT'S UP?
ARE YOU STILL LOOKING FOR A BASS PLAYER FOR YOUR BAND?
AND A GUITARIST.
CAN I AUDITION? MY FOLKS WANTED A FAMILY BAND SO DAD TAUGHT ME TO PLAY BASS.
FAMILY BAND? LIKE THE JACKSON FIVE?
NOT THAT I EXPECT HER TO MEET MY HIGH STANDARDS, BUT YOU OKAY WITH SAFFRON BEING IN MY BAND?
WHY WOULDN'T I BE?

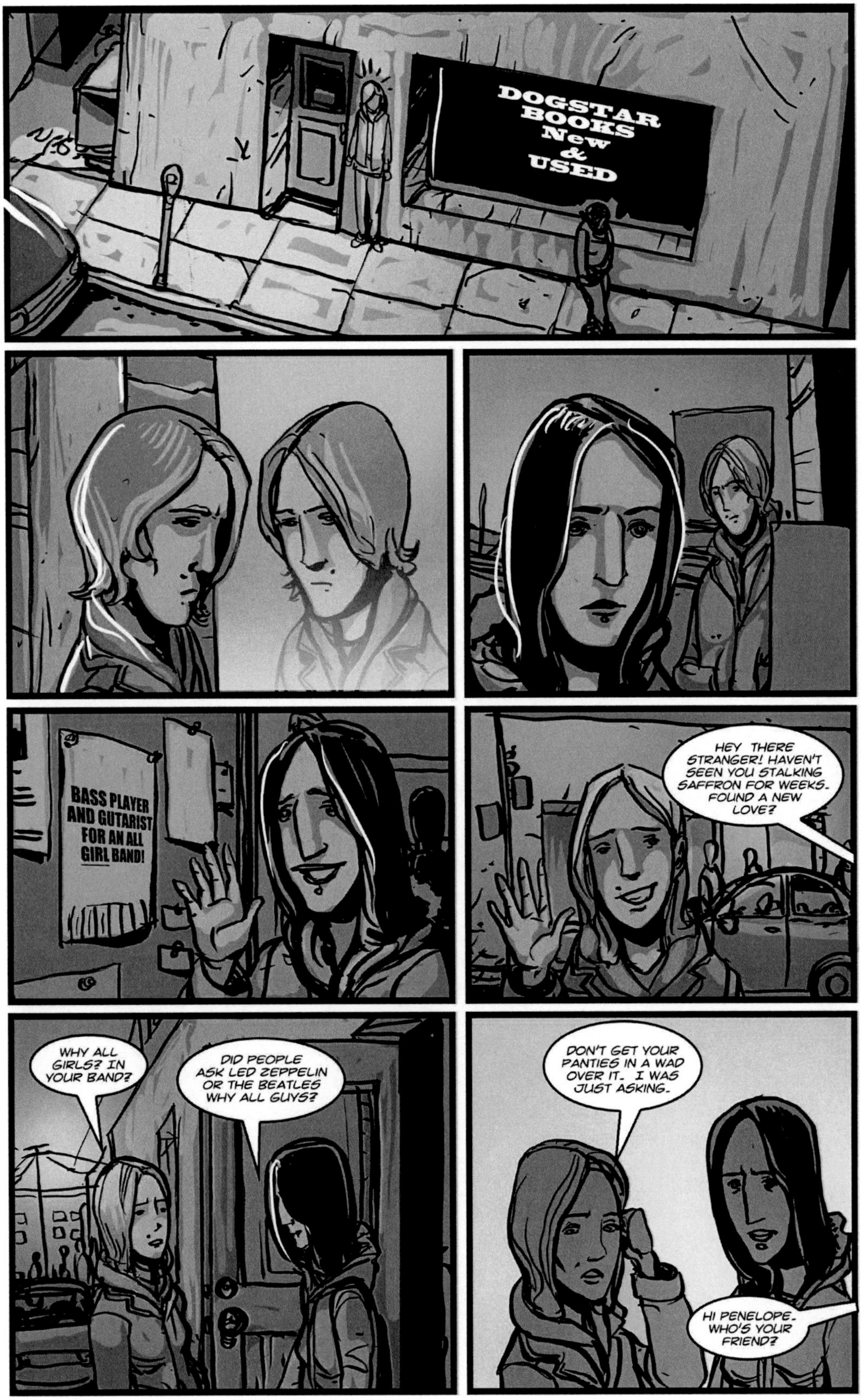
DOGSTAR BOOKS New & USED
BASS PLAYER AND GUTARIST FOR AN ALL GIRL BAND!
HEY THERE STRANGER! HAVEN'T SEEN YOU STALKING SAFFRON FOR WEEKS. FOUND A NEW LOVE?
WHY ALL GIRLS? IN YOUR BAND?
DID PEOPLE ASK LED ZEPPELIN OR THE BEATLES WHY ALL GUYS?
DON'T GET YOUR PANTIES IN A WAD OVER IT. I WAS JUST ASKING.
HI PENELOPE. WHO'S YOUR FRIEND?

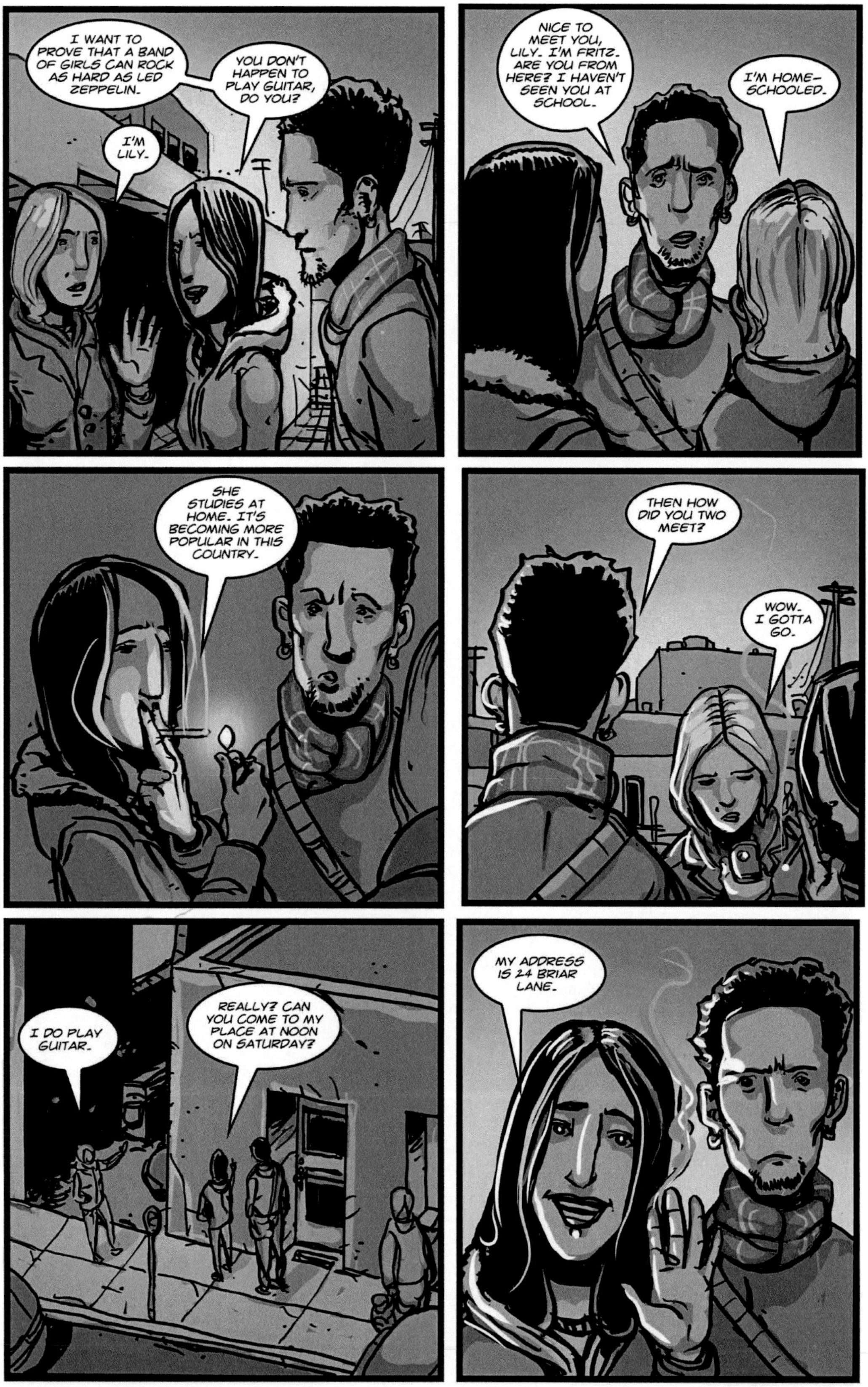
I WANT TO PROVE THAT A BAND OF GIRLS CAN ROCK AS HARD AS LED ZEPPELIN.
YOU DON'T HAPPEN TO PLAY GUITAR, DO YOU?
I'M LILY.
NICE TO MEET YOU, LILY. I'M FRITZ. ARE YOU FROM HERE? I HAVEN'T SEEN YOU AT SCHOOL.
I'M HOME-SCHOOLED.
SHE STUDIES AT HOME. IT'S BECOMING MORE POPULAR IN THIS COUNTRY.
THEN HOW DID YOU TWO MEET?
WOW. I GOTTA GO.
I DO PLAY GUITAR.
REALLY? CAN YOU COME TO MY PLACE AT NOON ON SATURDAY?
MY ADDRESS IS 24 BRIAR LANE.

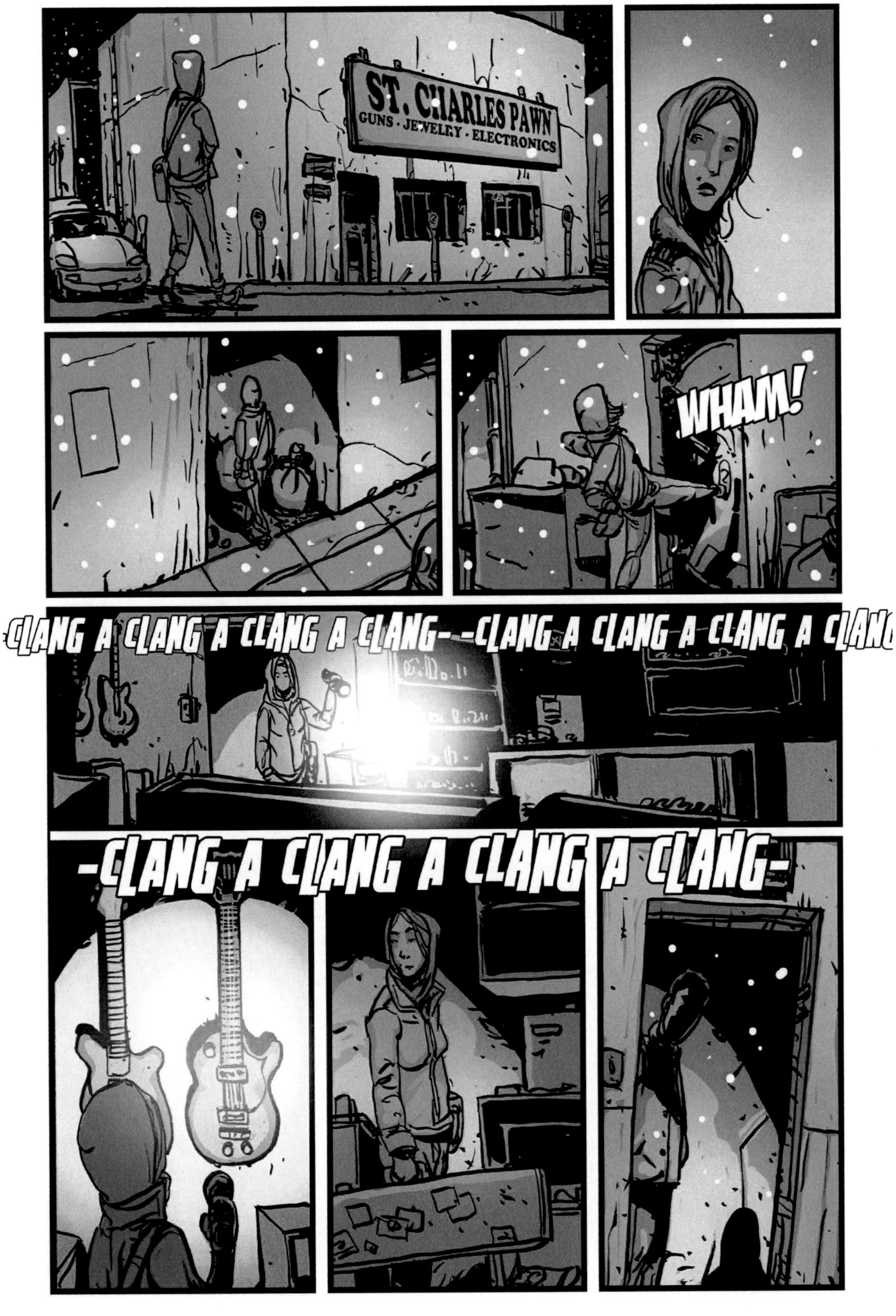
ST. CHARLES PAWN
GUNS · JEWELRY · ELECTRONICS
WHAM!
-CLANG A CLANG A CLANG A CLANG- -CLANG A CLANG A CLANG A CLANG
-CLANG A CLANG A CLANG A CLANG-

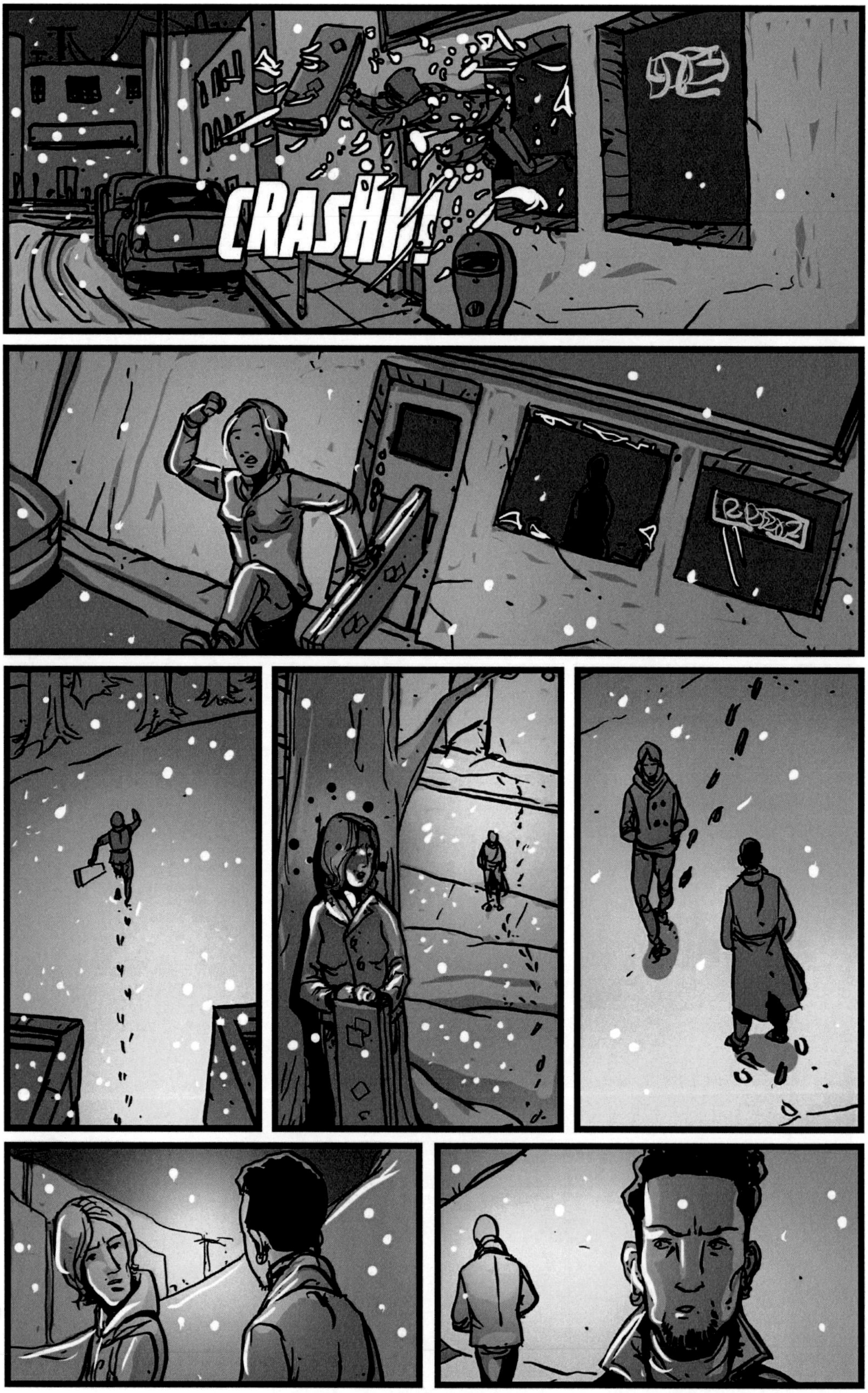
CRASH!!

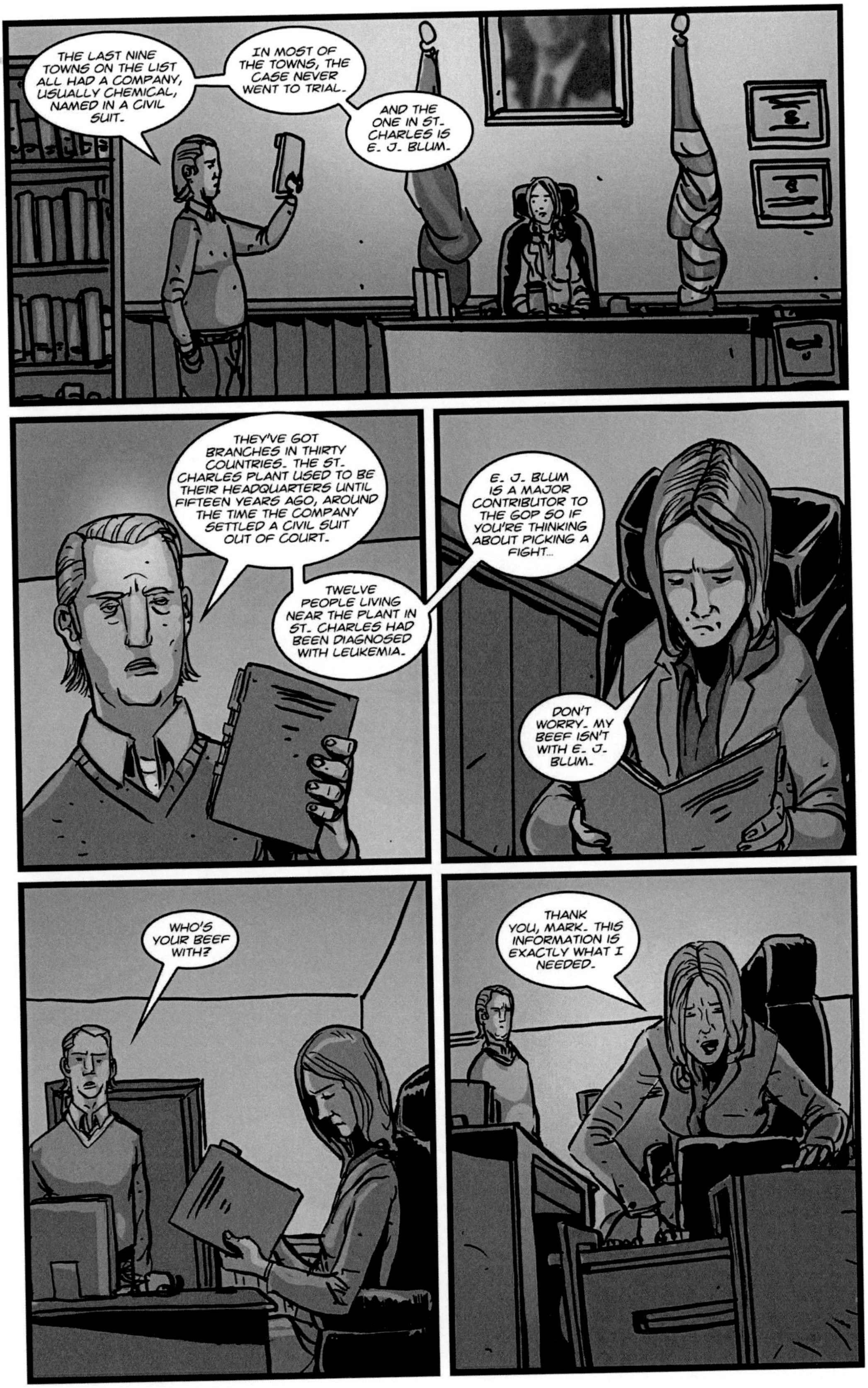
THE LAST NINE TOWNS ON THE LIST ALL HAD A COMPANY, USUALLY CHEMICAL, NAMED IN A CIVIL SUIT.
IN MOST OF THE TOWNS, THE CASE NEVER WENT TO TRIAL.
AND THE ONE IN ST. CHARLES IS E. J. BLUM.
THEY'VE GOT BRANCHES IN THIRTY COUNTRIES. THE ST. CHARLES PLANT USED TO BE THEIR HEADQUARTERS UNTIL FIFTEEN YEARS AGO, AROUND THE TIME THE COMPANY SETTLED A CIVIL SUIT OUT OF COURT.
TWELVE PEOPLE LIVING NEAR THE PLANT IN ST. CHARLES HAD BEEN DIAGNOSED WITH LEUKEMIA.
E. J. BLUM IS A MAJOR CONTRIBUTOR TO THE GOP SO IF YOU'RE THINKING ABOUT PICKING A FIGHT...
DON'T WORRY. MY BEEF ISN'T WITH E. J. BLUM.
WHO'S YOUR BEEF WITH?
THANK YOU, MARK. THIS INFORMATION IS EXACTLY WHAT I NEEDED.

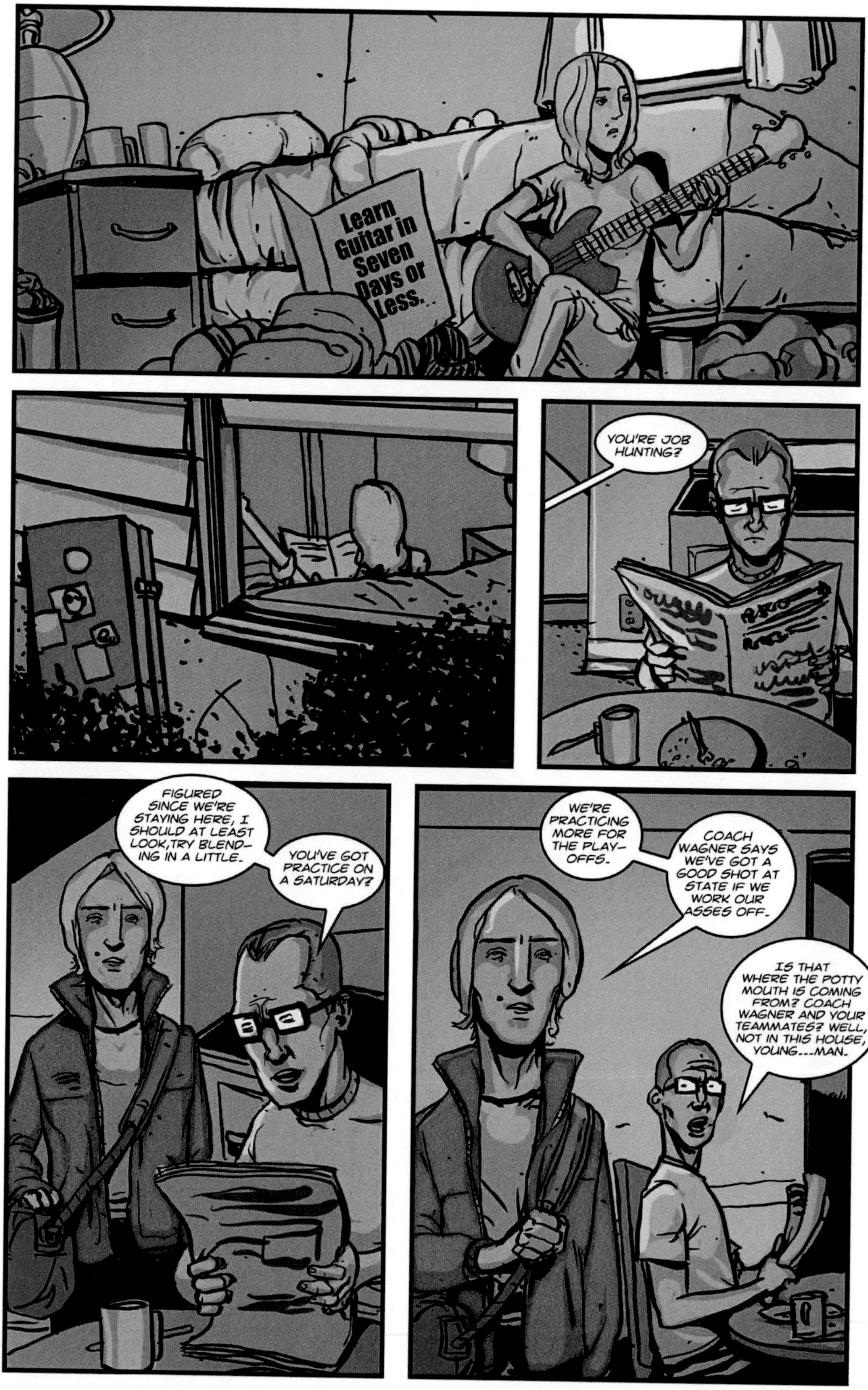
Learn Guitar in Seven Days or Less.
YOU'RE JOB HUNTING?
FIGURED SINCE WE'RE STAYING HERE, I SHOULD AT LEAST LOOK, TRY BLENDING IN A LITTLE.
YOU'VE GOT PRACTICE ON A SATURDAY?
WE'RE PRACTICING MORE FOR THE PLAY-OFFS.
COACH WAGNER SAYS WE'VE GOT A GOOD SHOT AT STATE IF WE WORK OUR ASSES OFF.
IS THAT WHERE THE POTTY MOUTH IS COMING FROM? COACH WAGNER AND YOUR TEAMMATES? WELL, NOT IN THIS HOUSE, YOUNG...MAN.

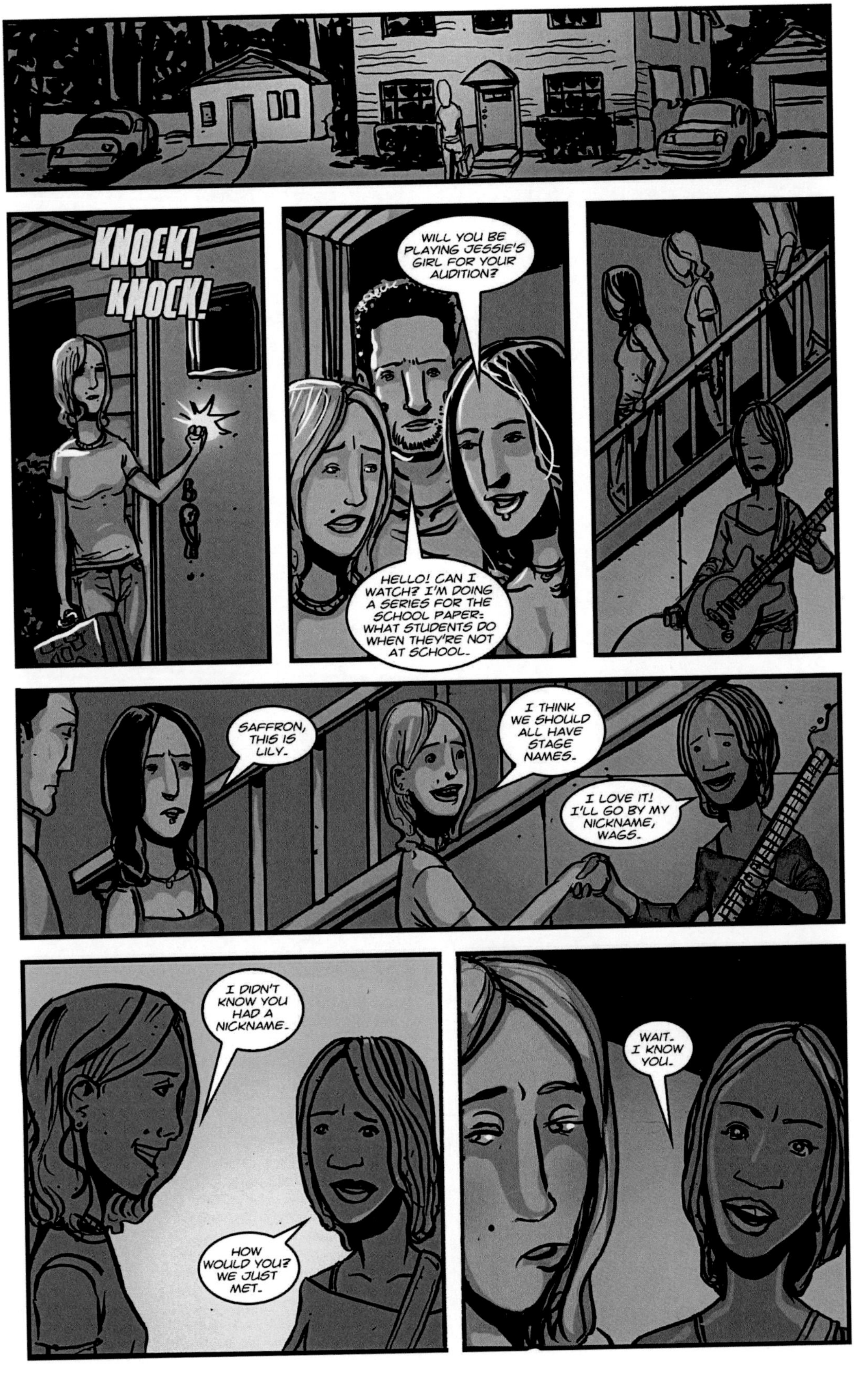
KNOCK! KNOCK!
WILL YOU BE PLAYING JESSIE'S GIRL FOR YOUR AUDITION?
HELLO! CAN I WATCH? I'M DOING A SERIES FOR THE SCHOOL PAPER: WHAT STUDENTS DO WHEN THEY'RE NOT AT SCHOOL.
SAFFRON, THIS IS LILY.
I THINK WE SHOULD ALL HAVE STAGE NAMES.
I LOVE IT! I'LL GO BY MY NICKNAME, WAGS.
I DIDN'T KNOW YOU HAD A NICKNAME.
HOW WOULD YOU? WE JUST MET.
WAIT. I KNOW YOU.

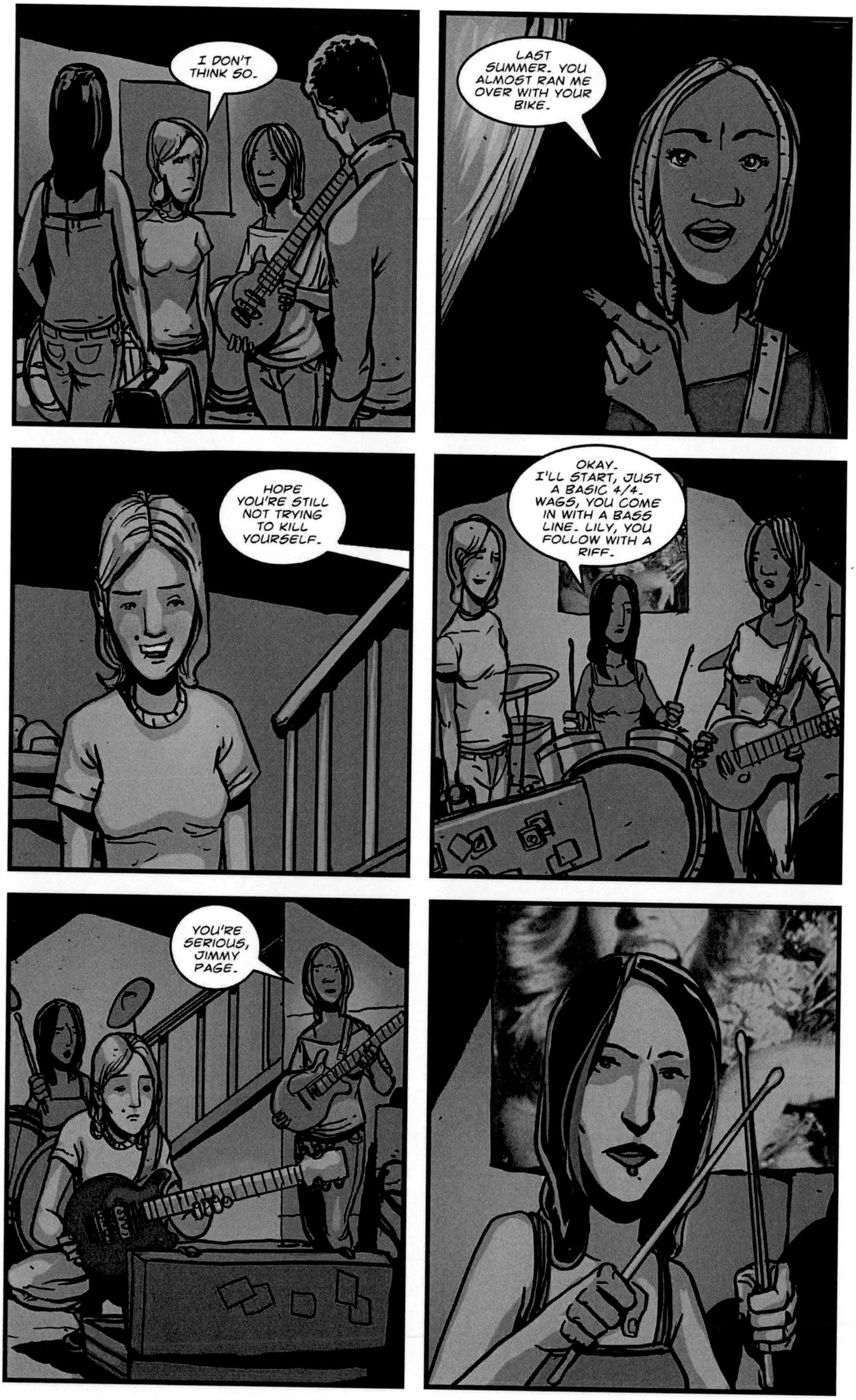
I DON'T THINK SO.
LAST SUMMER. YOU ALMOST RAN ME OVER WITH YOUR BIKE.
HOPE YOU'RE STILL NOT TRYING TO KILL YOURSELF.
OKAY. I'LL START, JUST A BASIC 4/4. WAGS, YOU COME IN WITH A BASS LINE. LILY, YOU FOLLOW WITH A RIFF.
YOU'RE SERIOUS, JIMMY PAGE.

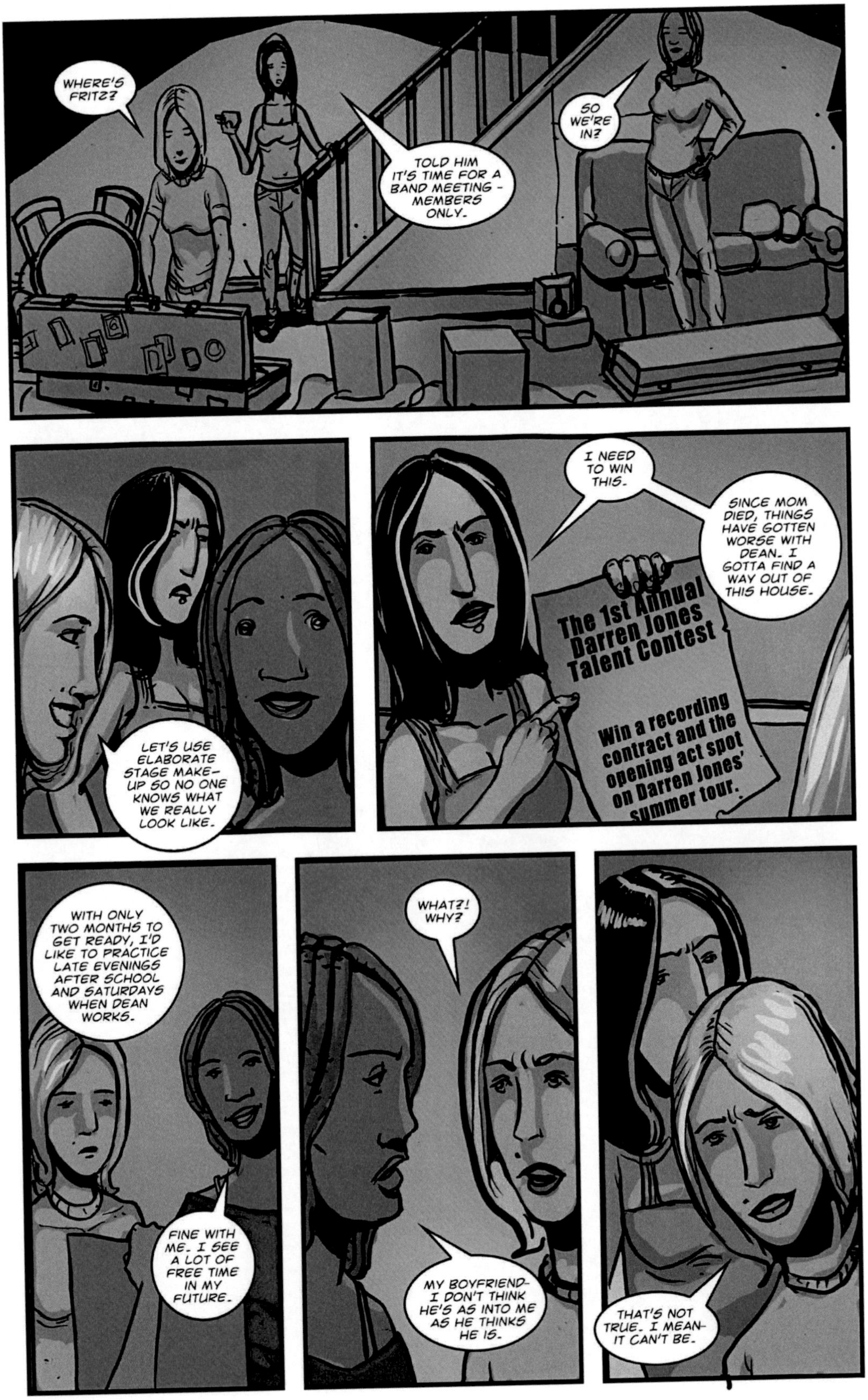
WHERE'S FRITZ?
TOLD HIM IT'S TIME FOR A BAND MEETING - MEMBERS ONLY.
SO WE'RE IN?
LET'S USE ELABORATE STAGE MAKE-UP SO NO ONE KNOWS WHAT WE REALLY LOOK LIKE.
I NEED TO WIN THIS.
SINCE MOM DIED, THINGS HAVE GOTTEN WORSE WITH DEAN. I GOTTA FIND A WAY OUT OF THIS HOUSE.
The 1st Annual Darren Jones Talent Contest
Win a recording contract and the opening act spot on Darren Jones' summer tour.
WITH ONLY TWO MONTHS TO GET READY, I'D LIKE TO PRACTICE LATE EVENINGS AFTER SCHOOL AND SATURDAYS WHEN DEAN WORKS.
FINE WITH ME. I SEE A LOT OF FREE TIME IN MY FUTURE.
WHAT?! WHY?
MY BOYFRIEND-I DON'T THINK HE'S AS INTO ME AS HE THINKS HE IS.
THAT'S NOT TRUE. I MEAN-IT CAN'T BE.

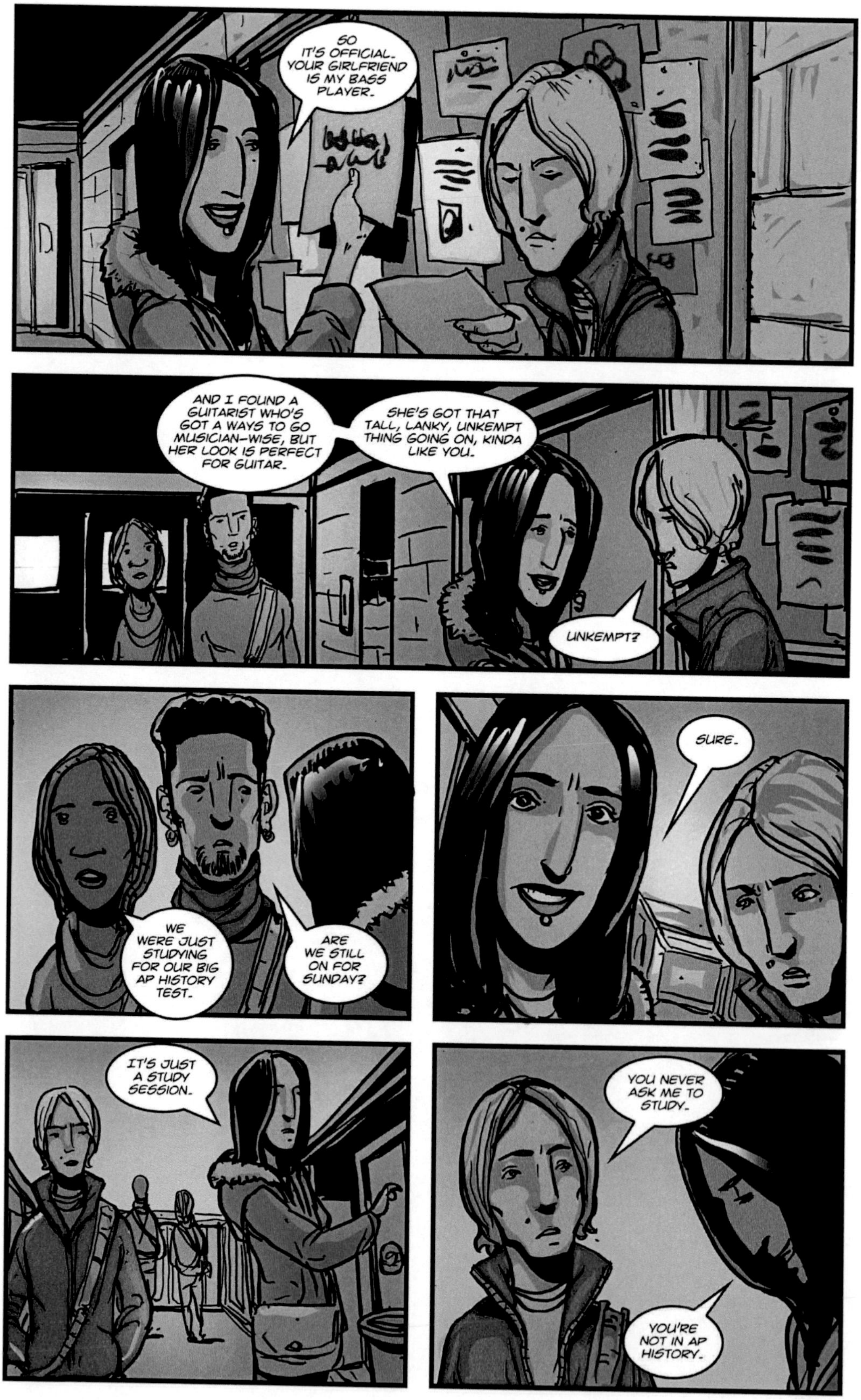
SO IT'S OFFICIAL. YOUR GIRLFRIEND IS MY BASS PLAYER.
AND I FOUND A GUITARIST WHO'S GOT A WAYS TO GO MUSICIAN-WISE, BUT HER LOOK IS PERFECT FOR GUITAR.
SHE'S GOT THAT TALL, LANKY, UNKEMPT THING GOING ON, KINDA LIKE YOU.
UNKEMPT?
WE WERE JUST STUDYING FOR OUR BIG AP HISTORY TEST.
ARE WE STILL ON FOR SUNDAY?
SURE.
IT'S JUST A STUDY SESSION.
YOU NEVER ASK ME TO STUDY.
YOU'RE NOT IN AP HISTORY.

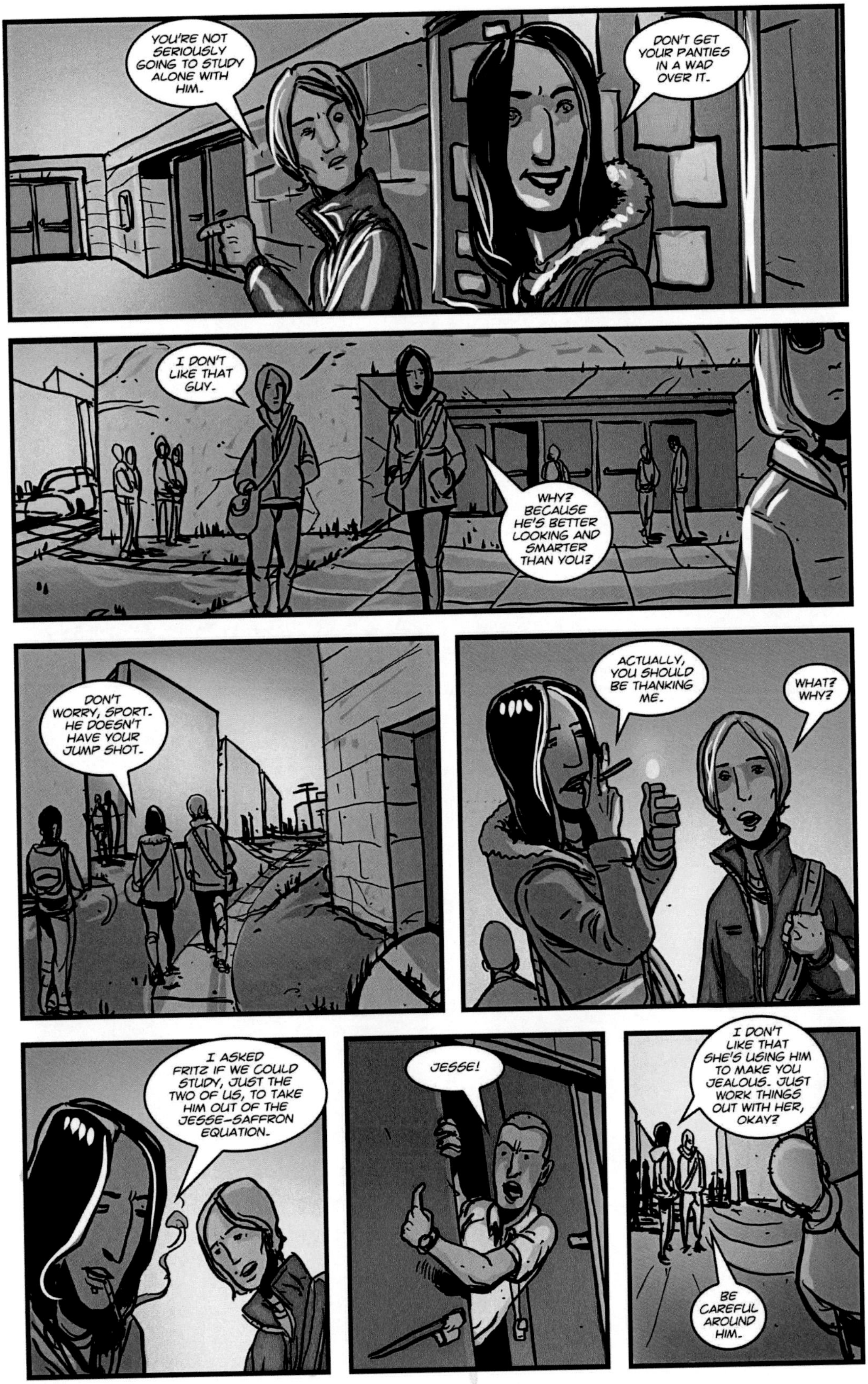
YOU'RE NOT SERIOUSLY GOING TO STUDY ALONE WITH HIM.
DON'T GET YOUR PANTIES IN A WAD OVER IT.
I DON'T LIKE THAT GUY.
WHY? BECAUSE HE'S BETTER LOOKING AND SMARTER THAN YOU?
DON'T WORRY, SPORT. HE DOESN'T HAVE YOUR JUMP SHOT.
ACTUALLY, YOU SHOULD BE THANKING ME.
WHAT? WHY?
I ASKED FRITZ IF WE COULD STUDY, JUST THE TWO OF US, TO TAKE HIM OUT OF THE JESSE-SAFFRON EQUATION.
JESSE!
I DON'T LIKE THAT SHE'S USING HIM TO MAKE YOU JEALOUS. JUST WORK THINGS OUT WITH HER, OKAY?
BE CAREFUL AROUND HIM.

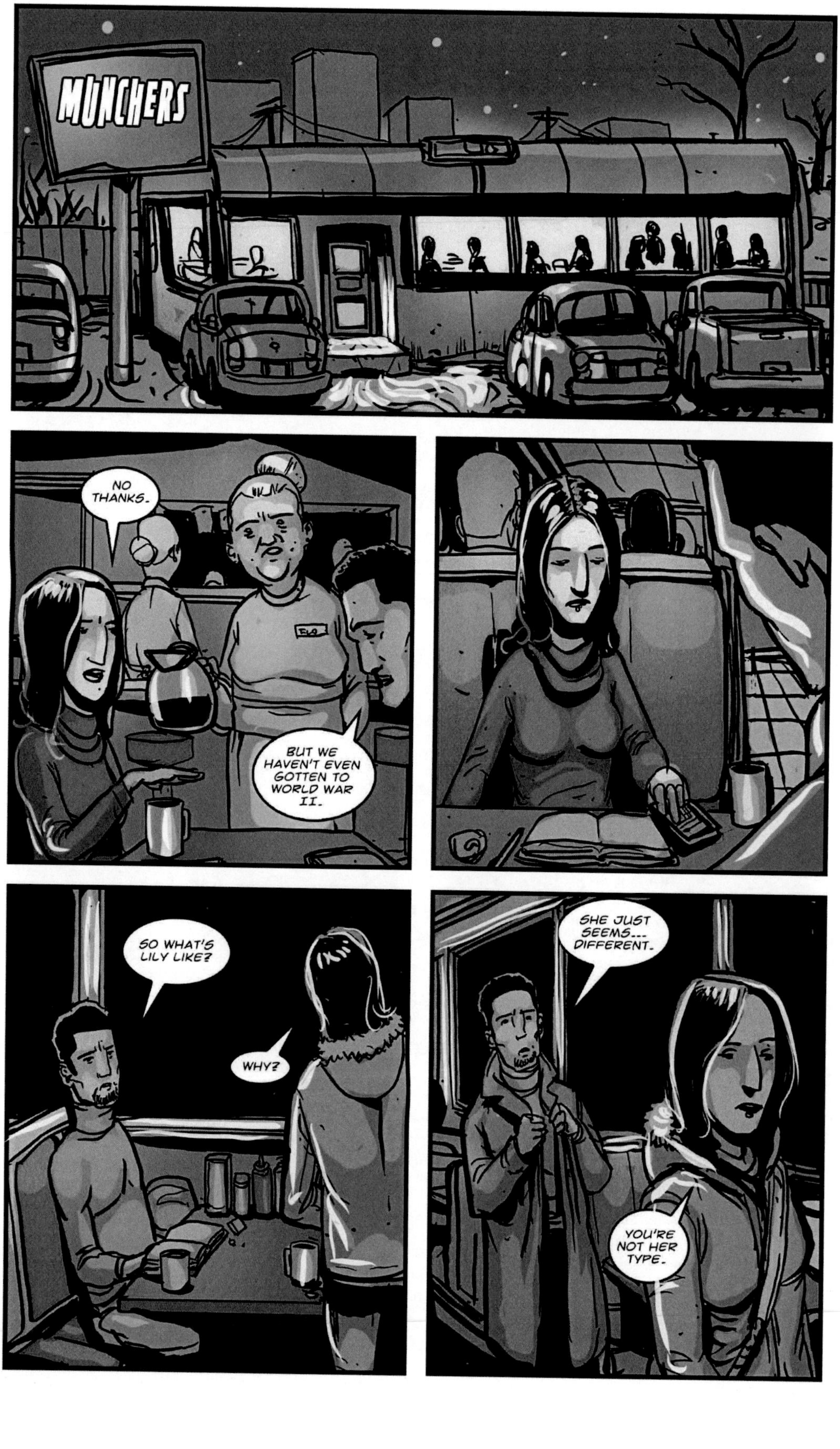
MUNCHERS
NO THANKS.
BUT WE HAVEN'T EVEN GOTTEN TO WORLD WAR II.
SO WHAT'S LILY LIKE?
WHY?
SHE JUST SEEMS... DIFFERENT.
YOU'RE NOT HER TYPE.

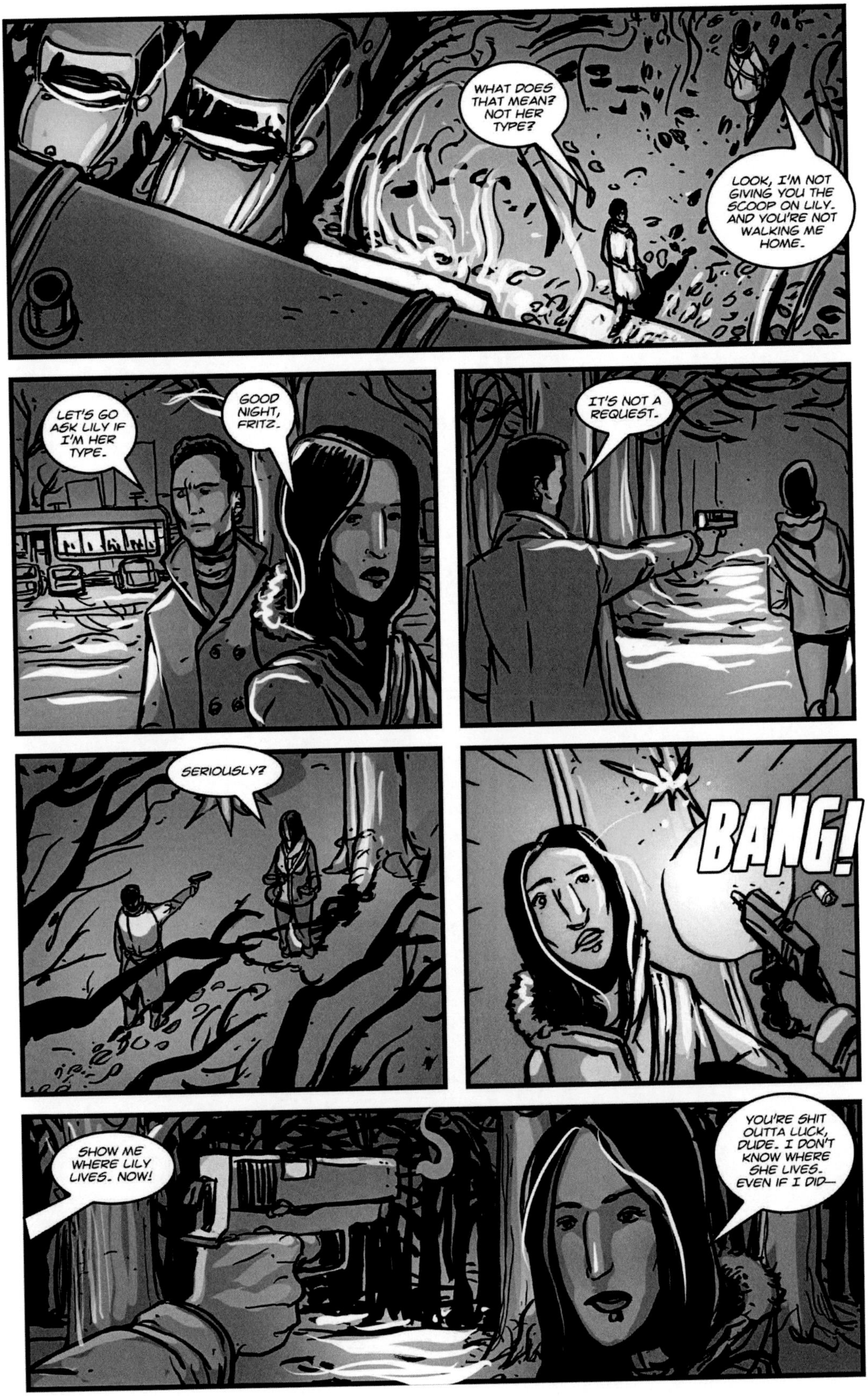
WHAT DOES THAT MEAN? NOT HER TYPE?
LOOK, I'M NOT GIVING YOU THE SCOOP ON LILY. AND YOU'RE NOT WALKING ME HOME.
LET'S GO ASK LILY IF I'M HER TYPE.
GOOD NIGHT, FRITZ.
IT'S NOT A REQUEST.
SERIOUSLY?
BANG!
SHOW ME WHERE LILY LIVES. NOW!
YOU'RE SHIT OUTTA LUCK, DUDE. I DON'T KNOW WHERE SHE LIVES. EVEN IF I DID—

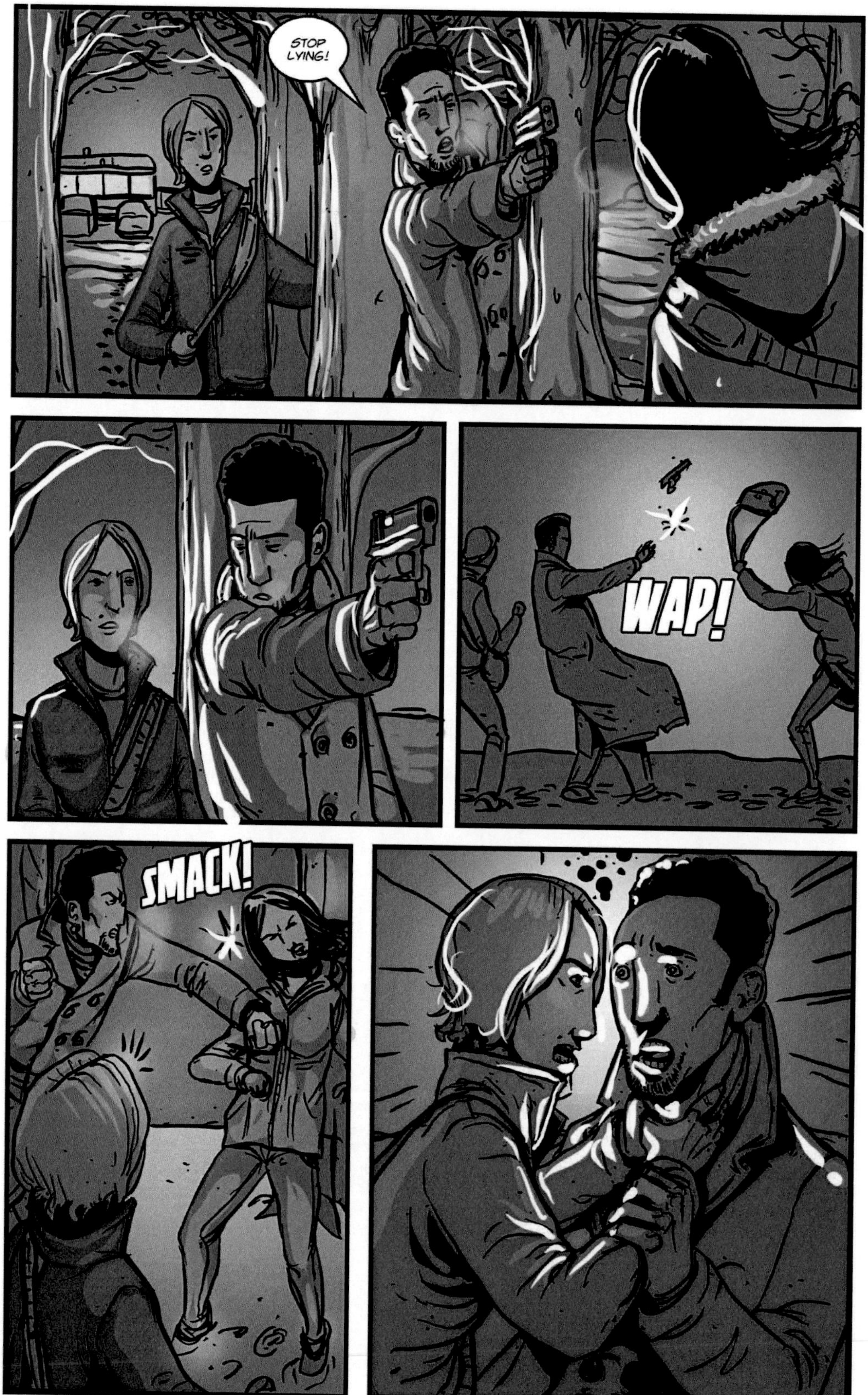
STOP LYING!
WAP!
SMACK!

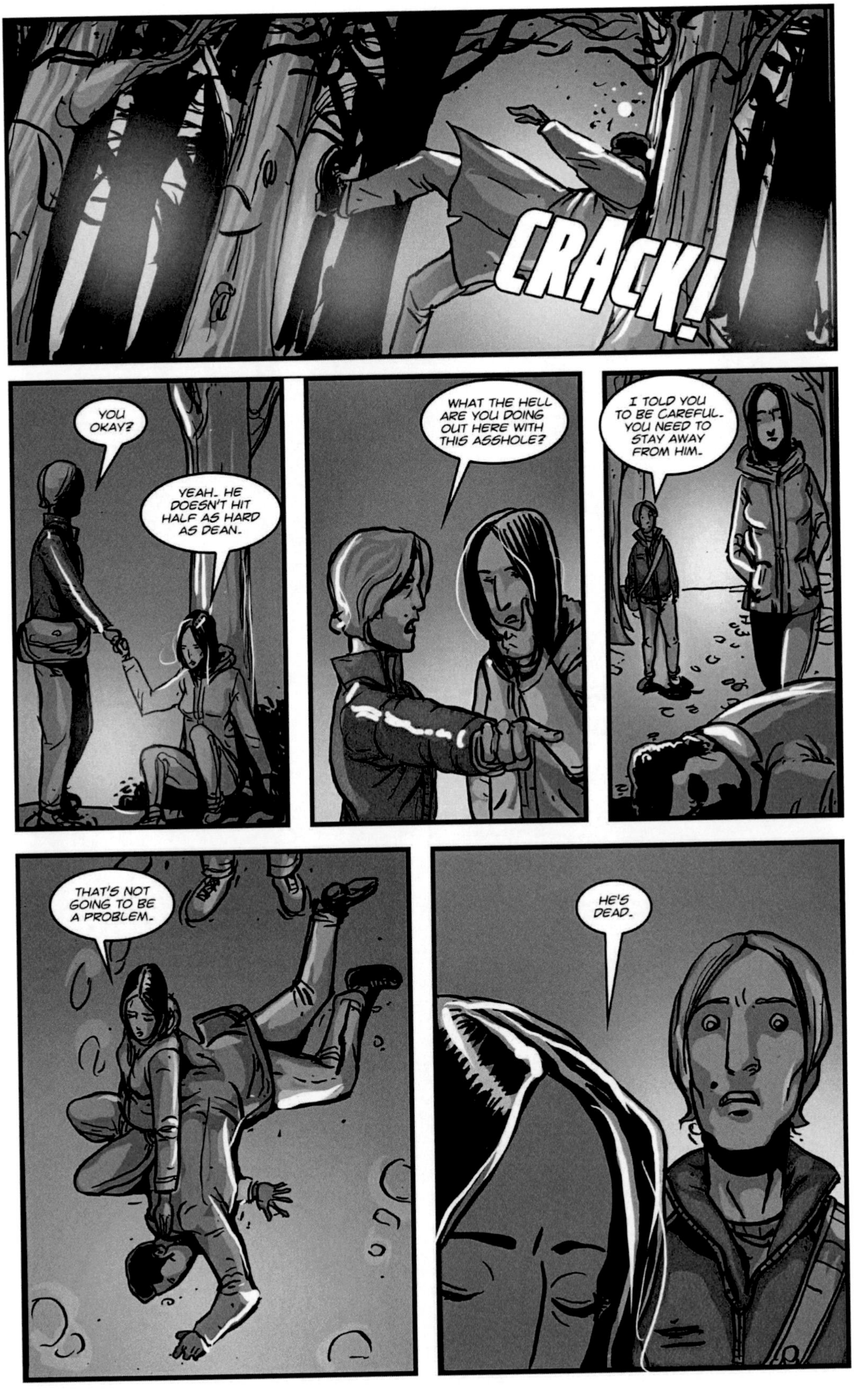
CRACK!
YOU OKAY?
YEAH. HE DOESN'T HIT HALF AS HARD AS DEAN.
WHAT THE HELL ARE YOU DOING OUT HERE WITH THIS ASSHOLE?
I TOLD YOU TO BE CAREFUL. YOU NEED TO STAY AWAY FROM HIM.
THAT'S NOT GOING TO BE A PROBLEM.
HE'S DEAD.

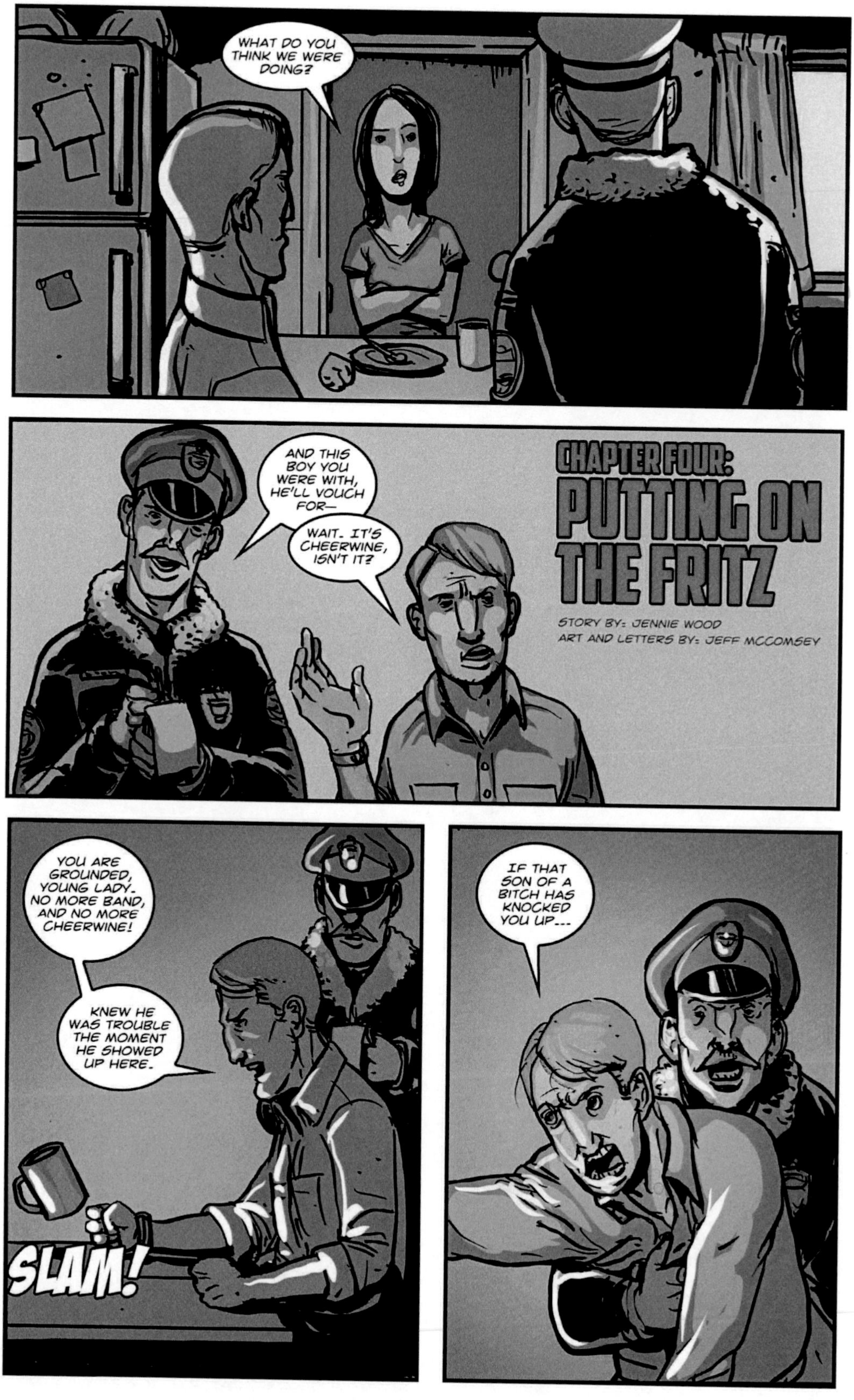
WHAT DO YOU THINK WE WERE DOING?
AND THIS BOY YOU WERE WITH, HE'LL VOUCH FOR—
WAIT. IT'S CHEERWINE, ISN'T IT?
CHAPTER FOUR:
PUTTING ON THE FRITZ
STORY BY: JENNIE WOOD
ART AND LETTERS BY: JEFF MCCOMSEY
YOU ARE GROUNDED, YOUNG LADY. NO MORE BAND, AND NO MORE CHEERWINE!
KNEW HE WAS TROUBLE THE MOMENT HE SHOWED UP HERE.
SLAM!
IF THAT SON OF A BITCH HAS KNOCKED YOU UP...

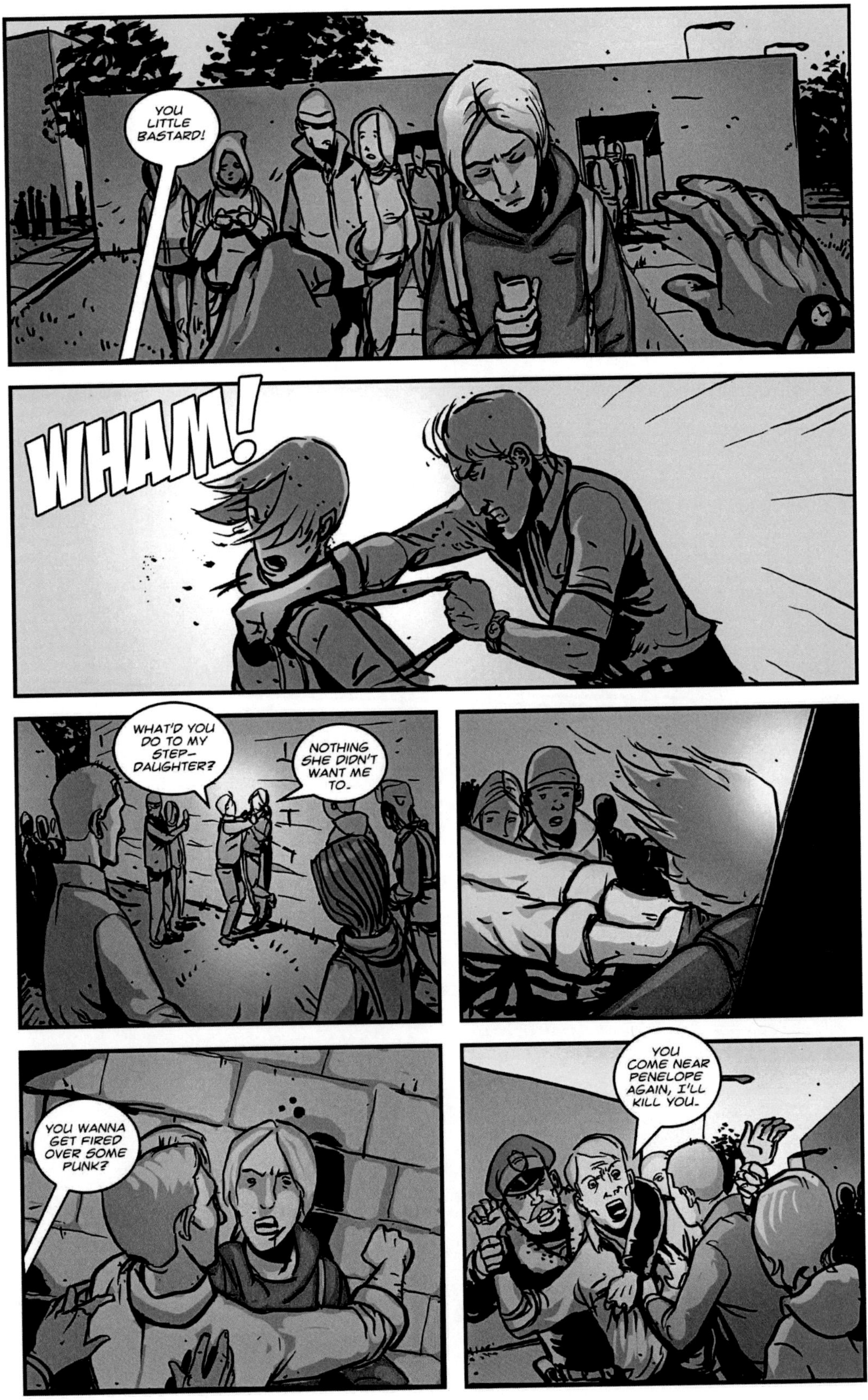
YOU LITTLE BASTARD!
WHAM!
WHAT'D YOU DO TO MY STEP-DAUGHTER?
NOTHING SHE DIDN'T WANT ME TO.
YOU WANNA GET FIRED OVER SOME PUNK?
YOU COME NEAR PENELOPE AGAIN, I'LL KILL YOU.

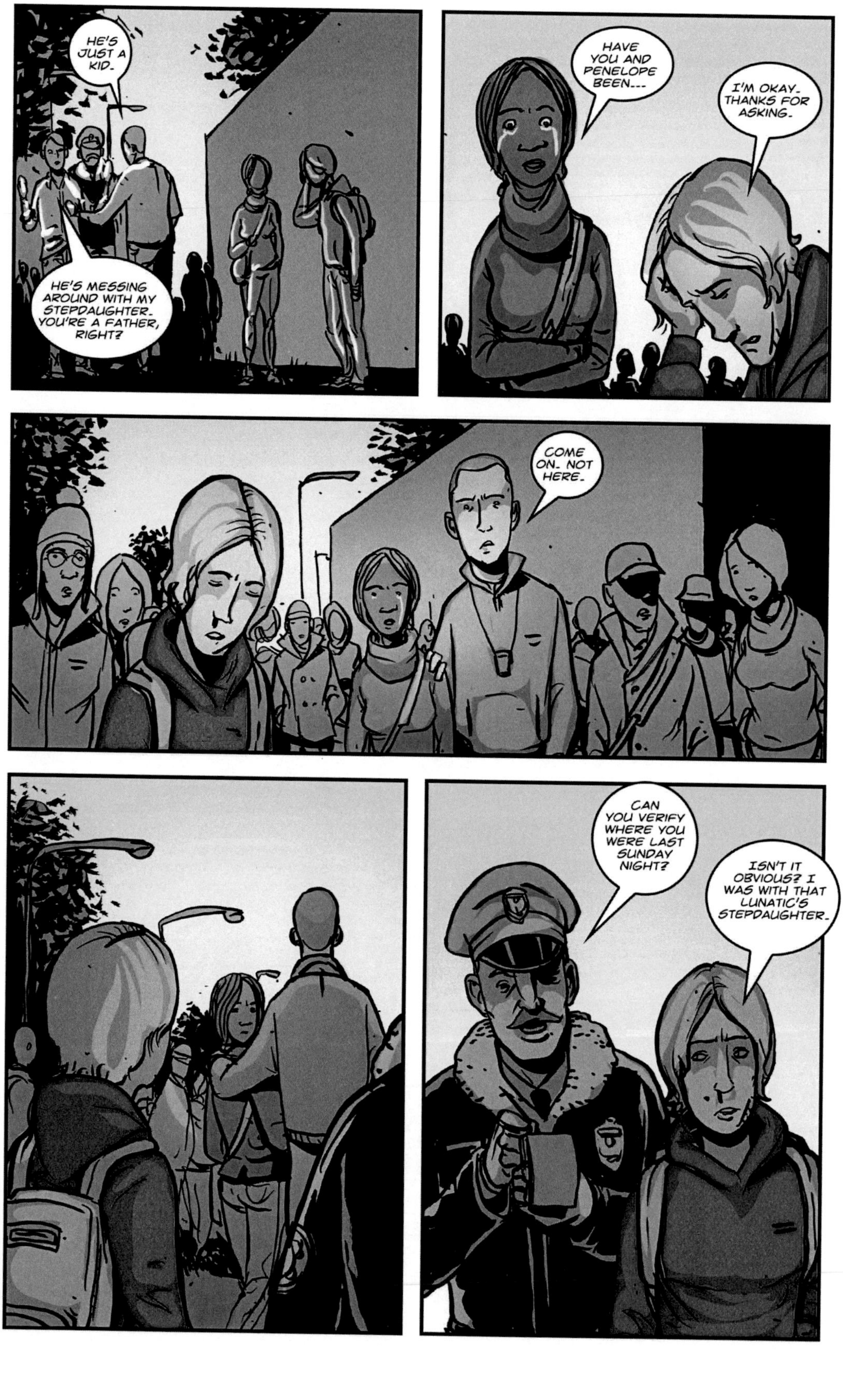
HE'S JUST A KID.
HE'S MESSING AROUND WITH MY STEPDAUGHTER. YOU'RE A FATHER, RIGHT?
HAVE YOU AND PENELOPE BEEN...
I'M OKAY. THANKS FOR ASKING.
COME ON. NOT HERE.
CAN YOU VERIFY WHERE YOU WERE LAST SUNDAY NIGHT?
ISN'T IT OBVIOUS? I WAS WITH THAT LUNATIC'S STEPDAUGHTER.

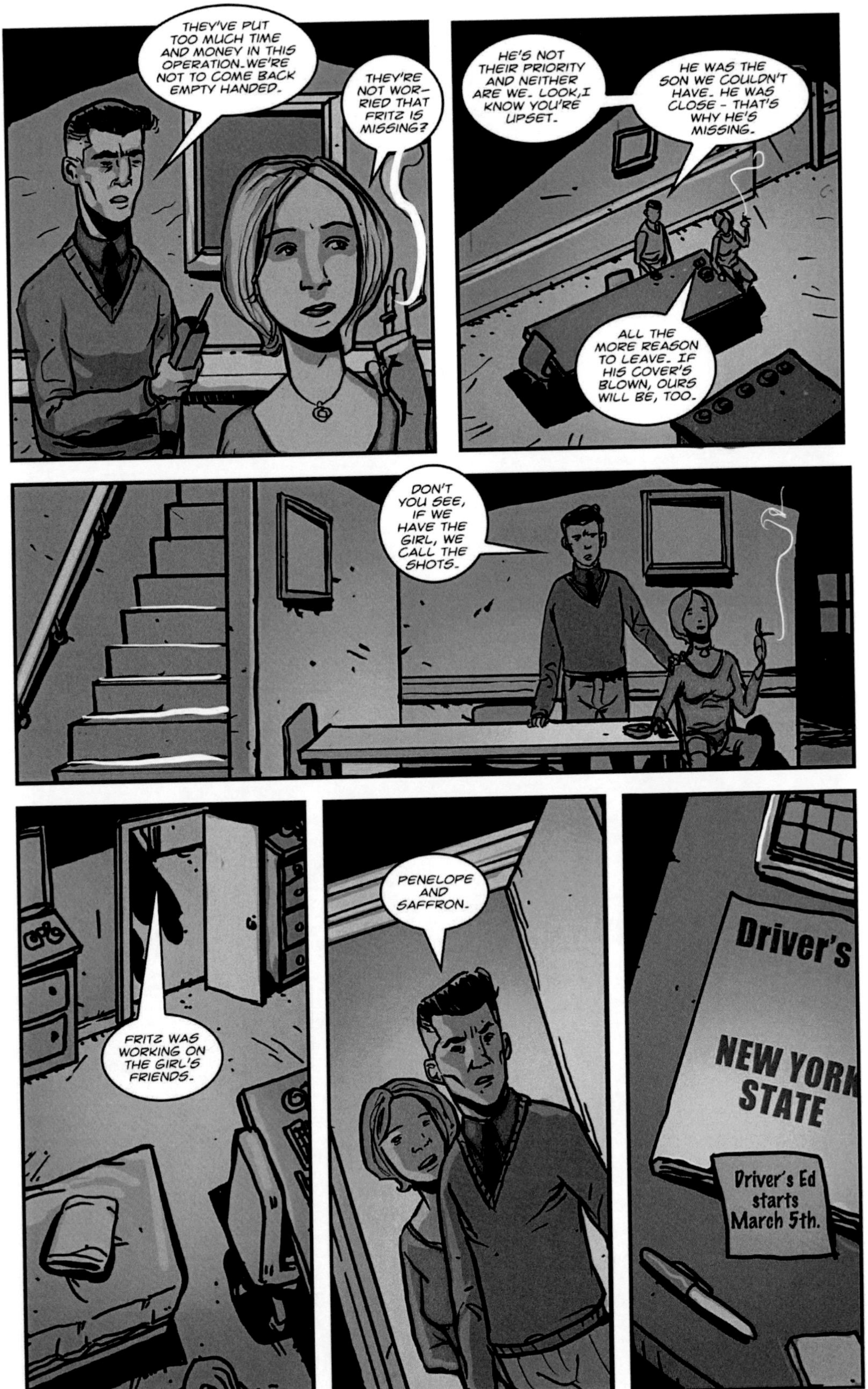
THEY'VE PUT TOO MUCH TIME AND MONEY IN THIS OPERATION. WE'RE NOT TO COME BACK EMPTY HANDED.
THEY'RE NOT WORRIED THAT FRITZ IS MISSING?
HE'S NOT THEIR PRIORITY AND NEITHER ARE WE. LOOK, I KNOW YOU'RE UPSET.
HE WAS THE SON WE COULDN'T HAVE. HE WAS CLOSE - THAT'S WHY HE'S MISSING.
ALL THE MORE REASON TO LEAVE. IF HIS COVER'S BLOWN, OURS WILL BE, TOO.
DON'T YOU SEE, IF WE HAVE THE GIRL, WE CALL THE SHOTS.
FRITZ WAS WORKING ON THE GIRL'S FRIENDS.
PENELOPE AND SAFFRON.
Driver's
NEW YORK
STATE
Driver's Ed starts March 5th.

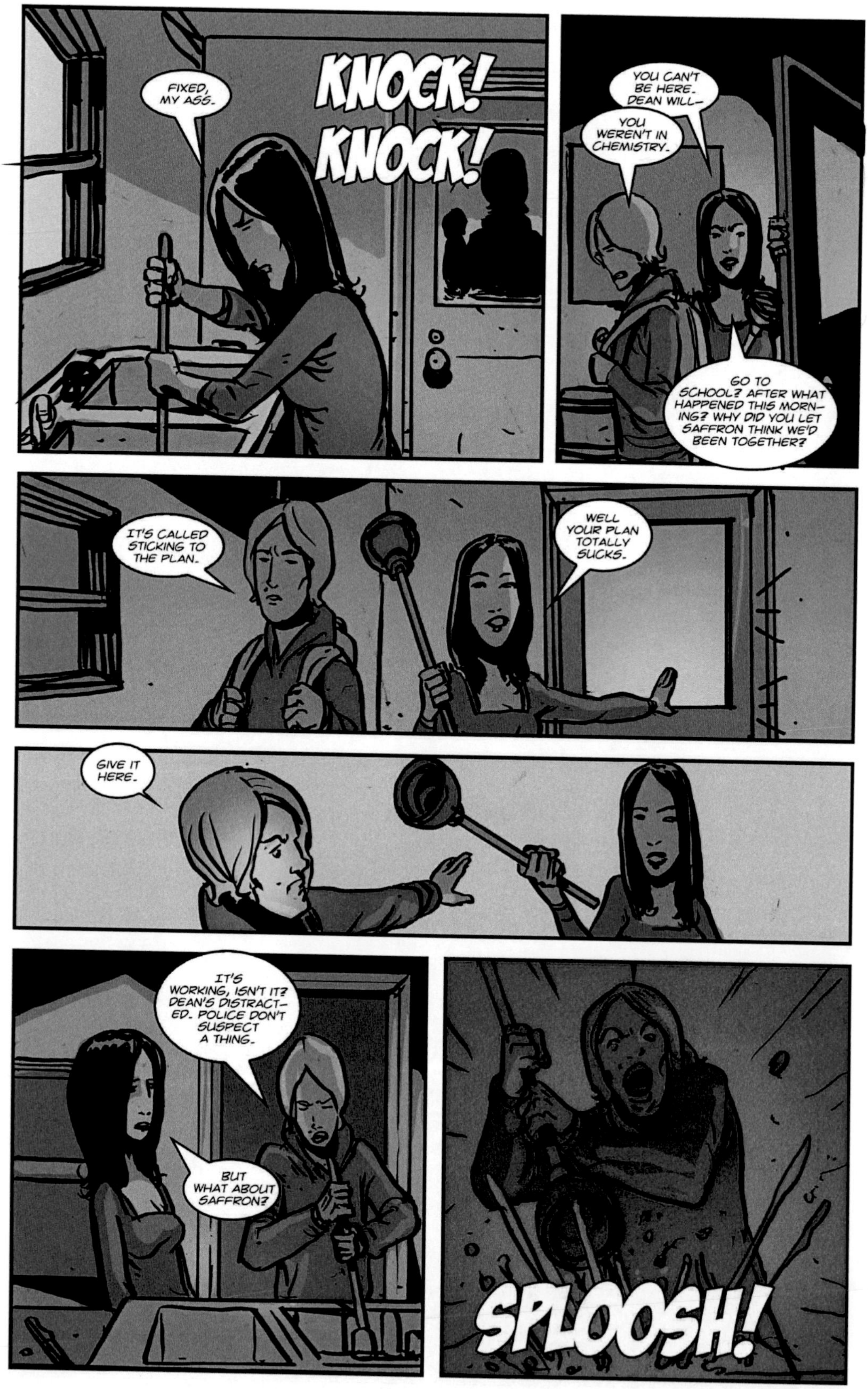
FIXED, MY ASS.
KNOCK! KNOCK!
YOU CAN'T BE HERE. DEAN WILL–
YOU WEREN'T IN CHEMISTRY.
GO TO SCHOOL? AFTER WHAT HAPPENED THIS MORNING? WHY DID YOU LET SAFFRON THINK WE'D BEEN TOGETHER?
IT'S CALLED STICKING TO THE PLAN.
WELL YOUR PLAN TOTALLY SUCKS.
GIVE IT HERE.
IT'S WORKING, ISN'T IT? DEAN'S DISTRACTED. POLICE DON'T SUSPECT A THING.
BUT WHAT ABOUT SAFFRON?
SPLOOSH!

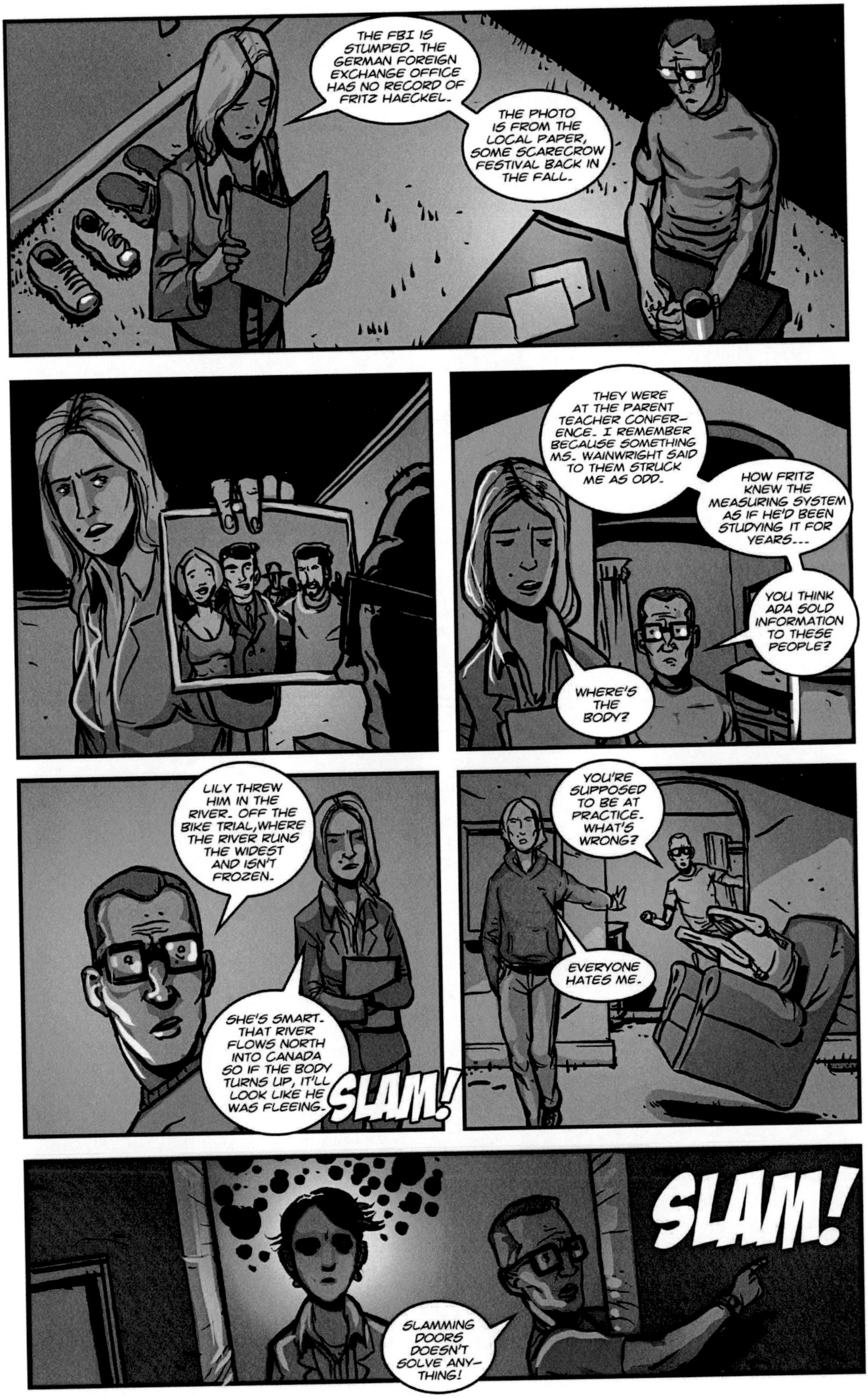
THE FBI IS STUMPED. THE GERMAN FOREIGN EXCHANGE OFFICE HAS NO RECORD OF FRITZ HAECKEL.
THE PHOTO IS FROM THE LOCAL PAPER, SOME SCARECROW FESTIVAL BACK IN THE FALL.
THEY WERE AT THE PARENT TEACHER CONFER-ENCE. I REMEMBER BECAUSE SOMETHING MS. WAINWRIGHT SAID TO THEM STRUCK ME AS ODD.
HOW FRITZ KNEW THE MEASURING SYSTEM AS IF HE'D BEEN STUDYING IT FOR YEARS...
YOU THINK ADA SOLD INFORMATION TO THESE PEOPLE?
WHERE'S THE BODY?
LILY THREW HIM IN THE RIVER. OFF THE BIKE TRIAL, WHERE THE RIVER RUNS THE WIDEST AND ISN'T FROZEN.
SHE'S SMART. THAT RIVER FLOWS NORTH INTO CANADA SO IF THE BODY TURNS UP, IT'LL LOOK LIKE HE WAS FLEEING.
SLAM!
YOU'RE SUPPOSED TO BE AT PRACTICE. WHAT'S WRONG?
EVERYONE HATES ME.
SLAM!
SLAMMING DOORS DOESN'T SOLVE ANY-THING!

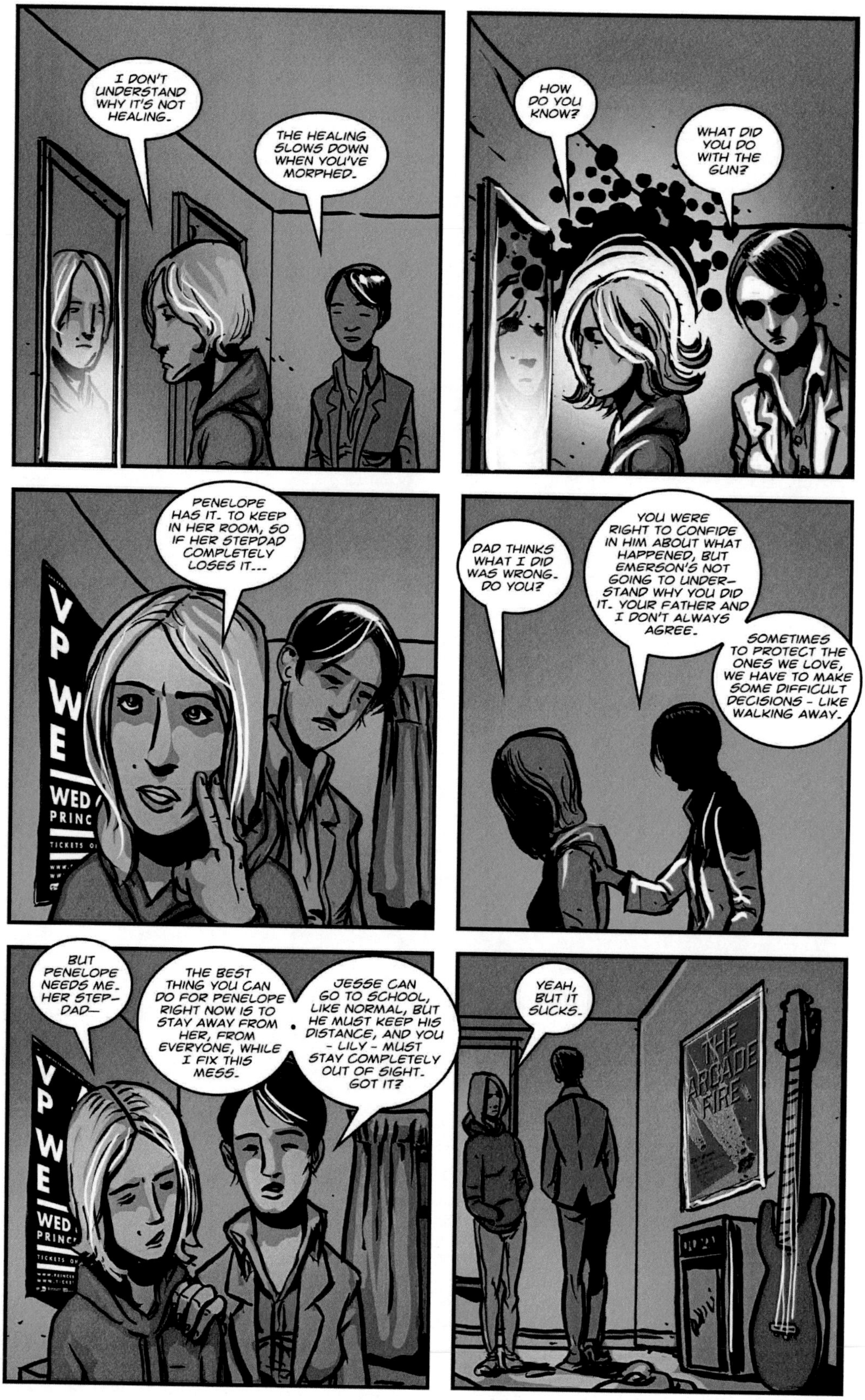
I DON'T UNDERSTAND WHY IT'S NOT HEALING.
THE HEALING SLOWS DOWN WHEN YOU'VE MORPHED.
HOW DO YOU KNOW?
WHAT DID YOU DO WITH THE GUN?
PENELOPE HAS IT. TO KEEP IN HER ROOM, SO IF HER STEPDAD COMPLETELY LOSES IT...
VP WE
WED
PRINC
DAD THINKS WHAT I DID WAS WRONG. DO YOU?
YOU WERE RIGHT TO CONFIDE IN HIM ABOUT WHAT HAPPENED, BUT EMERSON'S NOT GOING TO UNDER-STAND WHY YOU DID IT. YOUR FATHER AND I DON'T ALWAYS AGREE.
SOMETIMES TO PROTECT THE ONES WE LOVE, WE HAVE TO MAKE SOME DIFFICULT DECISIONS - LIKE WALKING AWAY.
BUT PENELOPE NEEDS ME. HER STEP-DAD—
THE BEST THING YOU CAN DO FOR PENELOPE RIGHT NOW IS TO STAY AWAY FROM HER, FROM EVERYONE, WHILE I FIX THIS MESS.
JESSE CAN GO TO SCHOOL, LIKE NORMAL, BUT HE MUST KEEP HIS DISTANCE, AND YOU - LILY - MUST STAY COMPLETELY OUT OF SIGHT. GOT IT?
YEAH, BUT IT SUCKS.
THE ARCADE FIRE

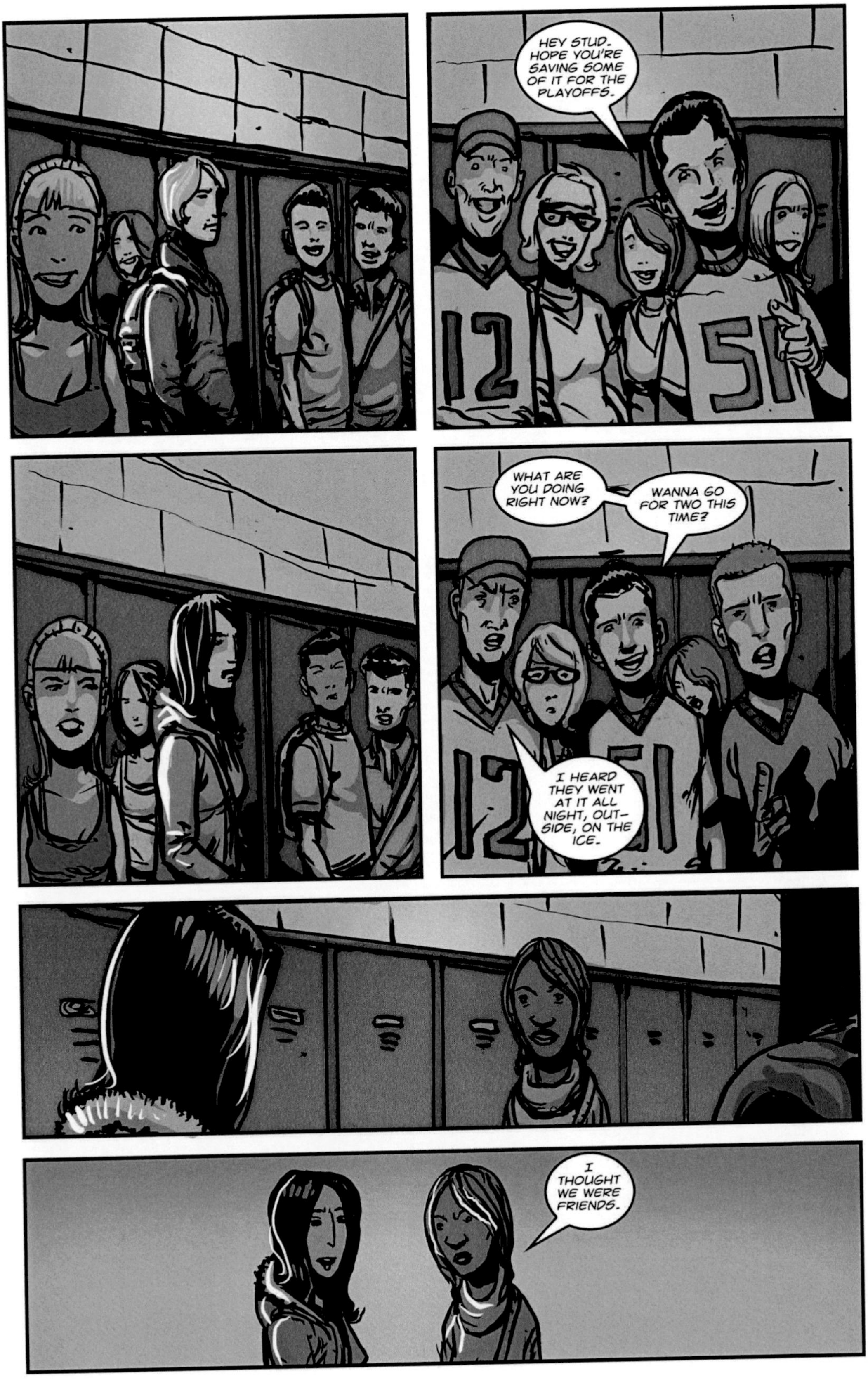
HEY STUD. HOPE YOU'RE SAVING SOME OF IT FOR THE PLAYOFFS.
12
51
WHAT ARE YOU DOING RIGHT NOW?
WANNA GO FOR TWO THIS TIME?
I HEARD THEY WENT AT IT ALL NIGHT, OUT-SIDE, ON THE ICE.
I THOUGHT WE WERE FRIENDS.

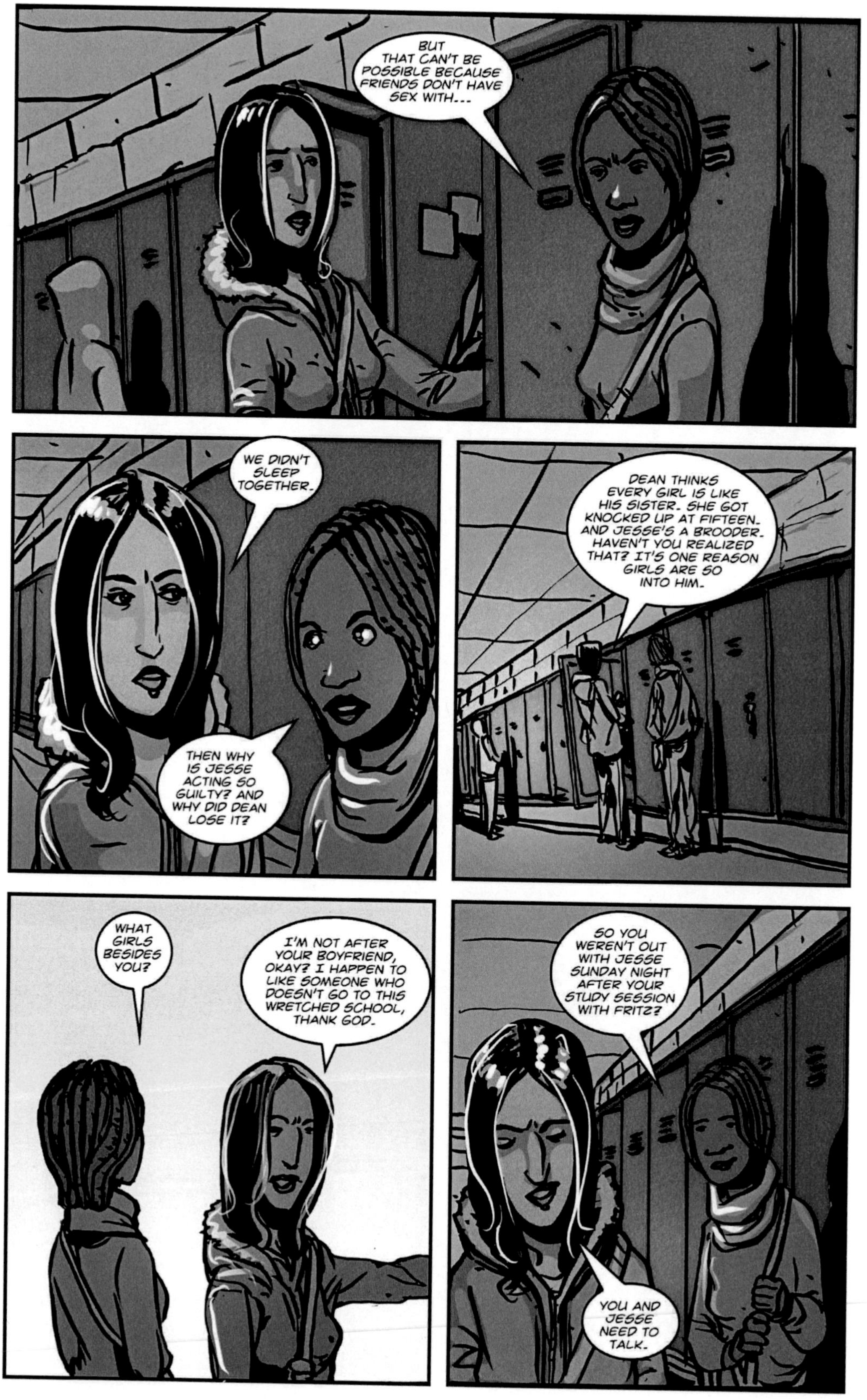
BUT THAT CAN'T BE POSSIBLE BECAUSE FRIENDS DON'T HAVE SEX WITH...
WE DIDN'T SLEEP TOGETHER.
THEN WHY IS JESSE ACTING SO GUILTY? AND WHY DID DEAN LOSE IT?
DEAN THINKS EVERY GIRL IS LIKE HIS SISTER. SHE GOT KNOCKED UP AT FIFTEEN. AND JESSE'S A BROODER. HAVEN'T YOU REALIZED THAT? IT'S ONE REASON GIRLS ARE SO INTO HIM.
WHAT GIRLS BESIDES YOU?
I'M NOT AFTER YOUR BOYFRIEND, OKAY? I HAPPEN TO LIKE SOMEONE WHO DOESN'T GO TO THIS WRETCHED SCHOOL, THANK GOD.
SO YOU WEREN'T OUT WITH JESSE SUNDAY NIGHT AFTER YOUR STUDY SESSION WITH FRITZ?
YOU AND JESSE NEED TO TALK.

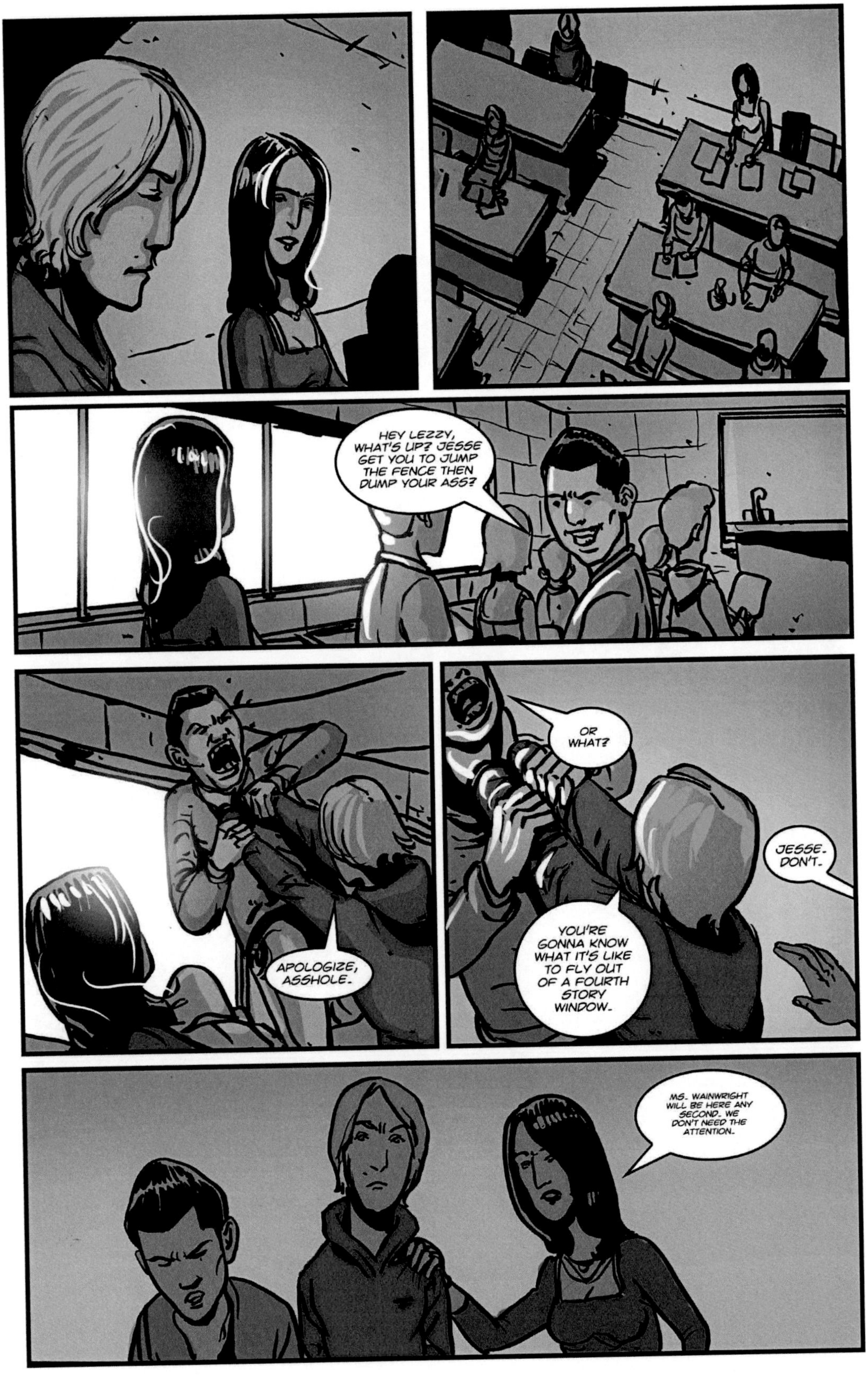
HEY LEZZY, WHAT'S UP? JESSE GET YOU TO JUMP THE FENCE THEN DUMP YOUR ASS?
APOLOGIZE, ASSHOLE.
OR WHAT?
YOU'RE GONNA KNOW WHAT IT'S LIKE TO FLY OUT OF A FOURTH STORY WINDOW.
JESSE. DON'T.
MS. WAINWRIGHT WILL BE HERE ANY SECOND. WE DON'T NEED THE ATTENTION.

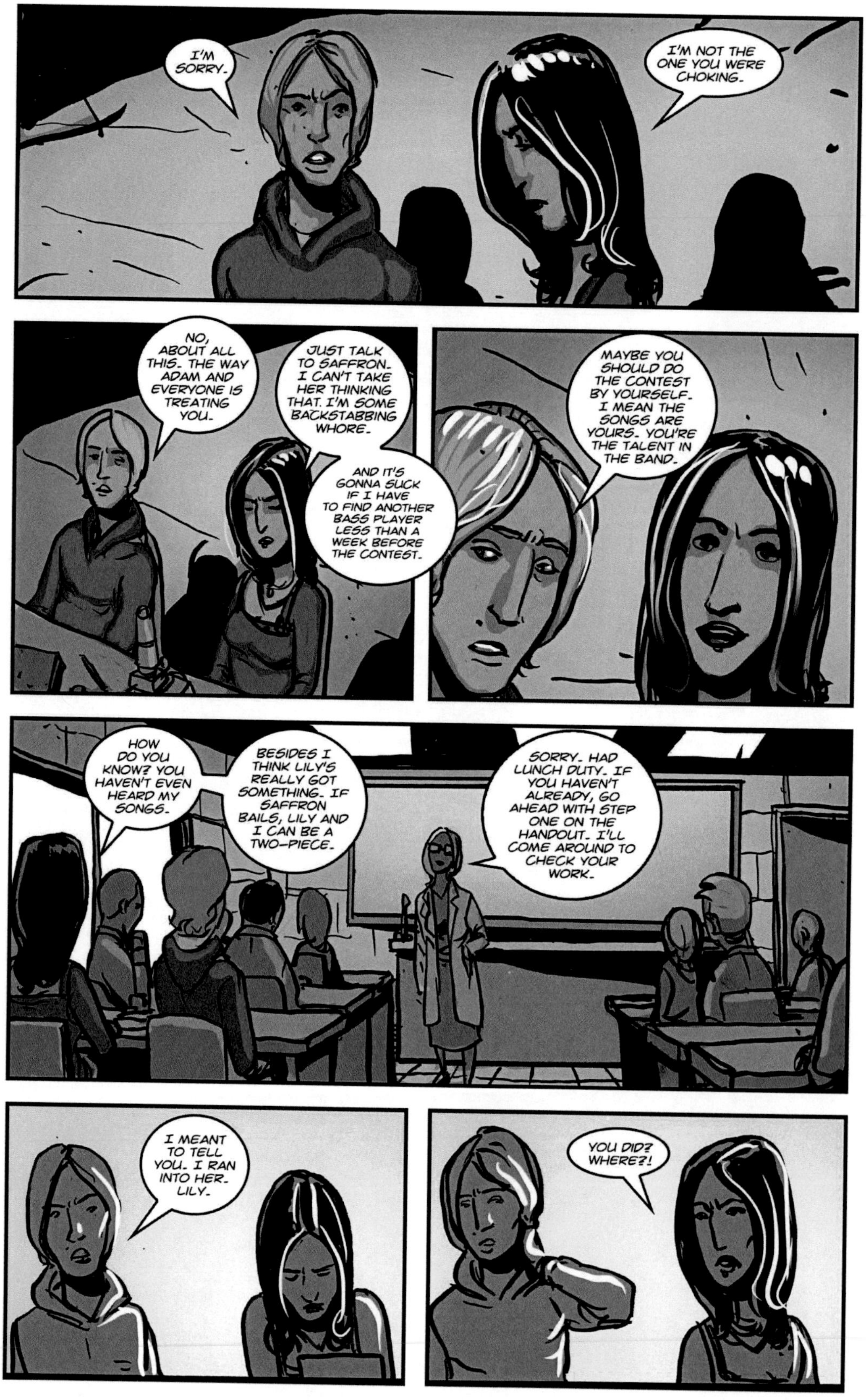
I'M SORRY.
I'M NOT THE ONE YOU WERE CHOKING.
NO, ABOUT ALL THIS. THE WAY ADAM AND EVERYONE IS TREATING YOU.
JUST TALK TO SAFFRON. I CAN'T TAKE HER THINKING THAT. I'M SOME BACKSTABBING WHORE.
AND IT'S GONNA SUCK IF I HAVE TO FIND ANOTHER BASS PLAYER LESS THAN A WEEK BEFORE THE CONTEST.
MAYBE YOU SHOULD DO THE CONTEST BY YOURSELF. I MEAN THE SONGS ARE YOURS. YOU'RE THE TALENT IN THE BAND.
HOW DO YOU KNOW? YOU HAVEN'T EVEN HEARD MY SONGS.
BESIDES I THINK LILY'S REALLY GOT SOMETHING. IF SAFFRON BAILS, LILY AND I CAN BE A TWO-PIECE.
SORRY. HAD LUNCH DUTY. IF YOU HAVEN'T ALREADY, GO AHEAD WITH STEP ONE ON THE HANDOUT. I'LL COME AROUND TO CHECK YOUR WORK.
I MEANT TO TELL YOU. I RAN INTO HER. LILY.
YOU DID? WHERE?!

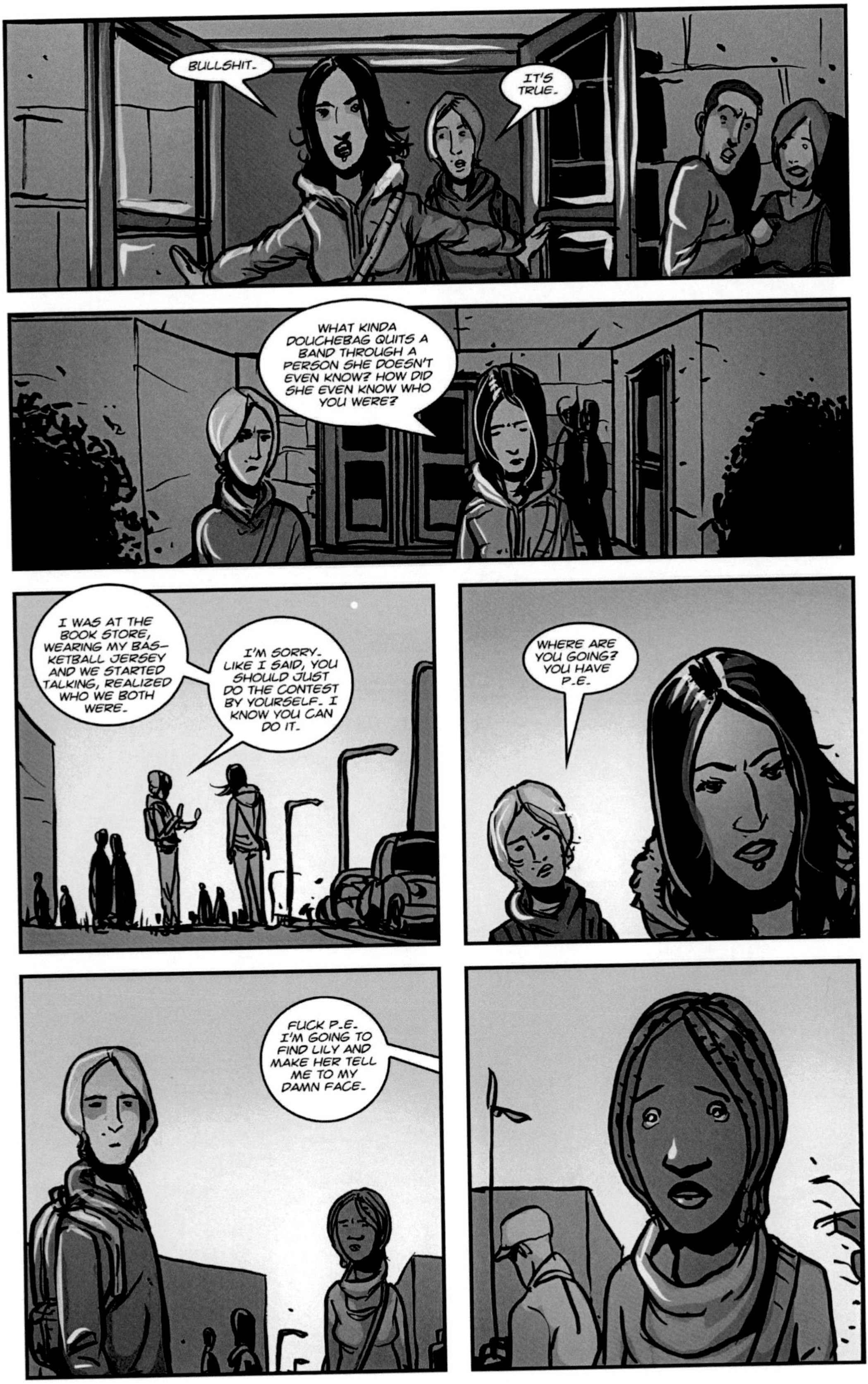
BULLSHIT.
IT'S TRUE.
WHAT KINDA DOUCHEBAG QUITS A BAND THROUGH A PERSON SHE DOESN'T EVEN KNOW? HOW DID SHE EVEN KNOW WHO YOU WERE?
I WAS AT THE BOOK STORE, WEARING MY BAS-KETBALL JERSEY AND WE STARTED TALKING, REALIZED WHO WE BOTH WERE.
I'M SORRY. LIKE I SAID, YOU SHOULD JUST DO THE CONTEST BY YOURSELF. I KNOW YOU CAN DO IT.
WHERE ARE YOU GOING? YOU HAVE P.E.
FUCK P.E. I'M GOING TO FIND LILY AND MAKE HER TELL ME TO MY DAMN FACE.

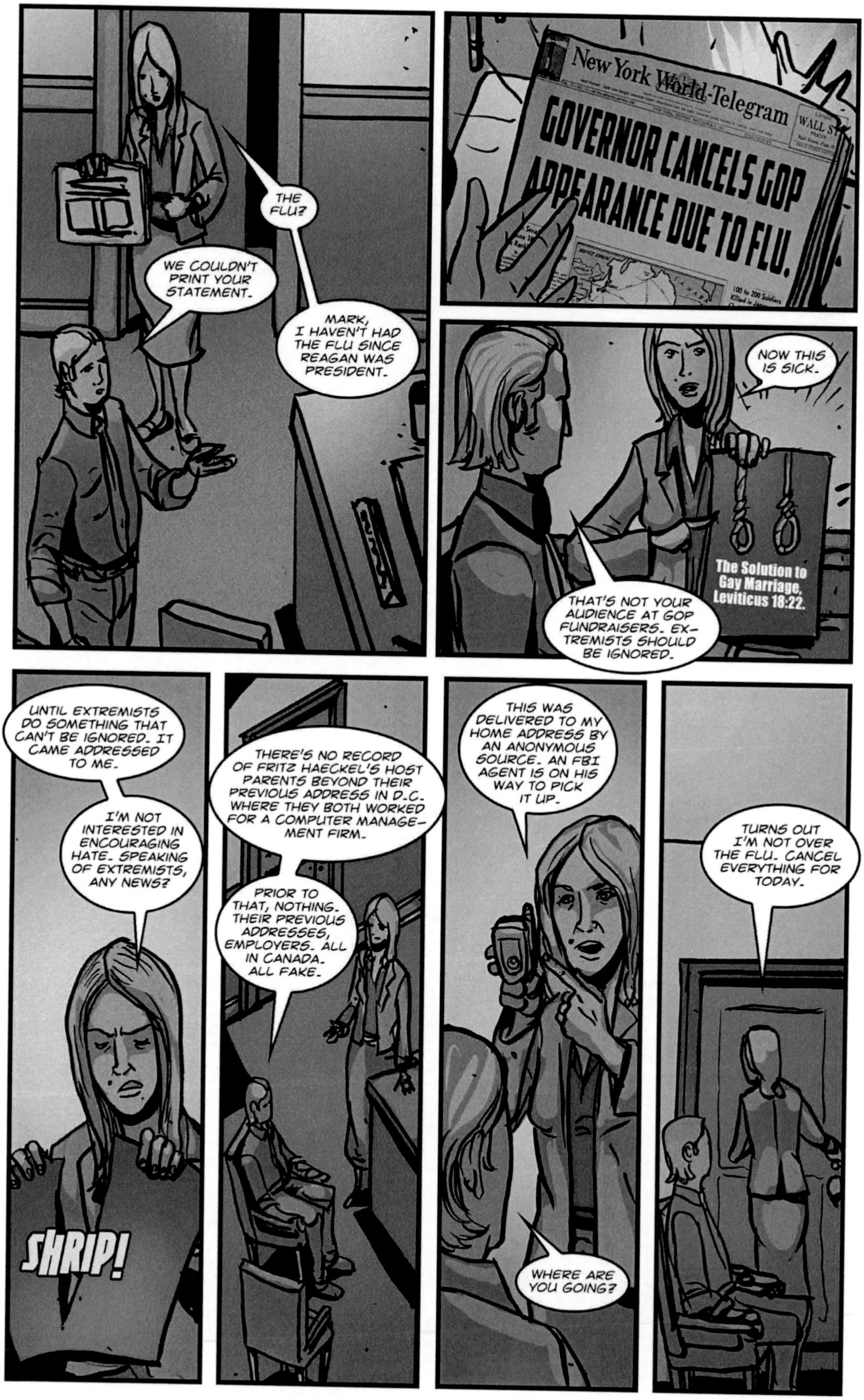
WE COULDN'T PRINT YOUR STATEMENT.
THE FLU?
MARK, I HAVEN'T HAD THE FLU SINCE REAGAN WAS PRESIDENT.
New York World-Telegram
GOVERNOR CANCELS GOP APPEARANCE DUE TO FLU.
NOW THIS IS SICK.
The Solution to Gay Marriage, Leviticus 18:22.
THAT'S NOT YOUR AUDIENCE AT GOP FUNDRAISERS. EXTREMISTS SHOULD BE IGNORED.
UNTIL EXTREMISTS DO SOMETHING THAT CAN'T BE IGNORED. IT CAME ADDRESSED TO ME.
I'M NOT INTERESTED IN ENCOURAGING HATE. SPEAKING OF EXTREMISTS, ANY NEWS?
SHRIP!
THERE'S NO RECORD OF FRITZ HAECKEL'S HOST PARENTS BEYOND THEIR PREVIOUS ADDRESS IN D.C. WHERE THEY BOTH WORKED FOR A COMPUTER MANAGEMENT FIRM.
PRIOR TO THAT, NOTHING. THEIR PREVIOUS ADDRESSES, EMPLOYERS. ALL IN CANADA. ALL FAKE.
THIS WAS DELIVERED TO MY HOME ADDRESS BY AN ANONYMOUS SOURCE. AN FBI AGENT IS ON HIS WAY TO PICK IT UP.
WHERE ARE YOU GOING?
TURNS OUT I'M NOT OVER THE FLU. CANCEL EVERYTHING FOR TODAY.

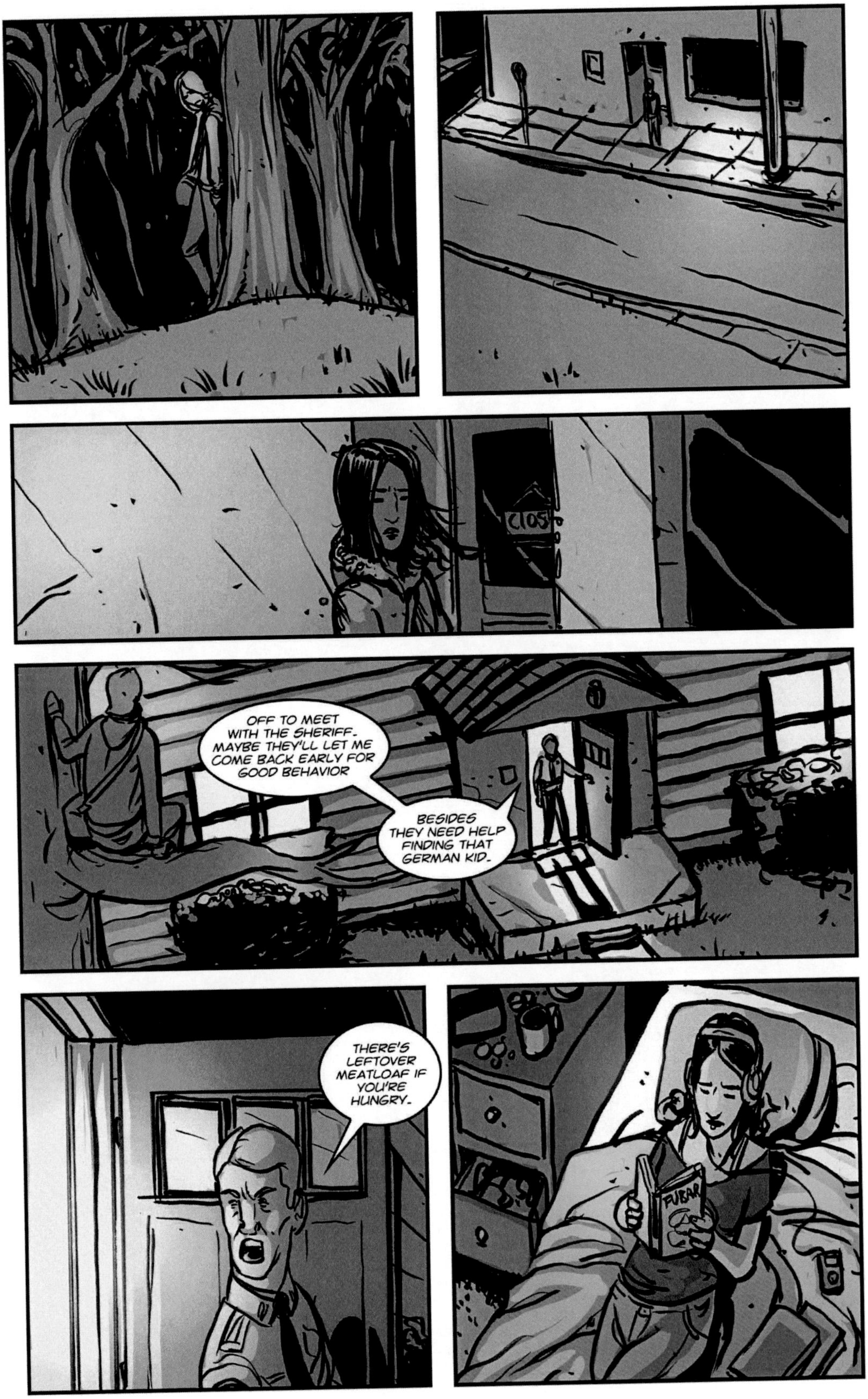
OFF TO MEET WITH THE SHERIFF. MAYBE THEY'LL LET ME COME BACK EARLY FOR GOOD BEHAVIOR
BESIDES THEY NEED HELP FINDING THAT GERMAN KID.
THERE'S LEFTOVER MEATLOAF IF YOU'RE HUNGRY.
FUBAR

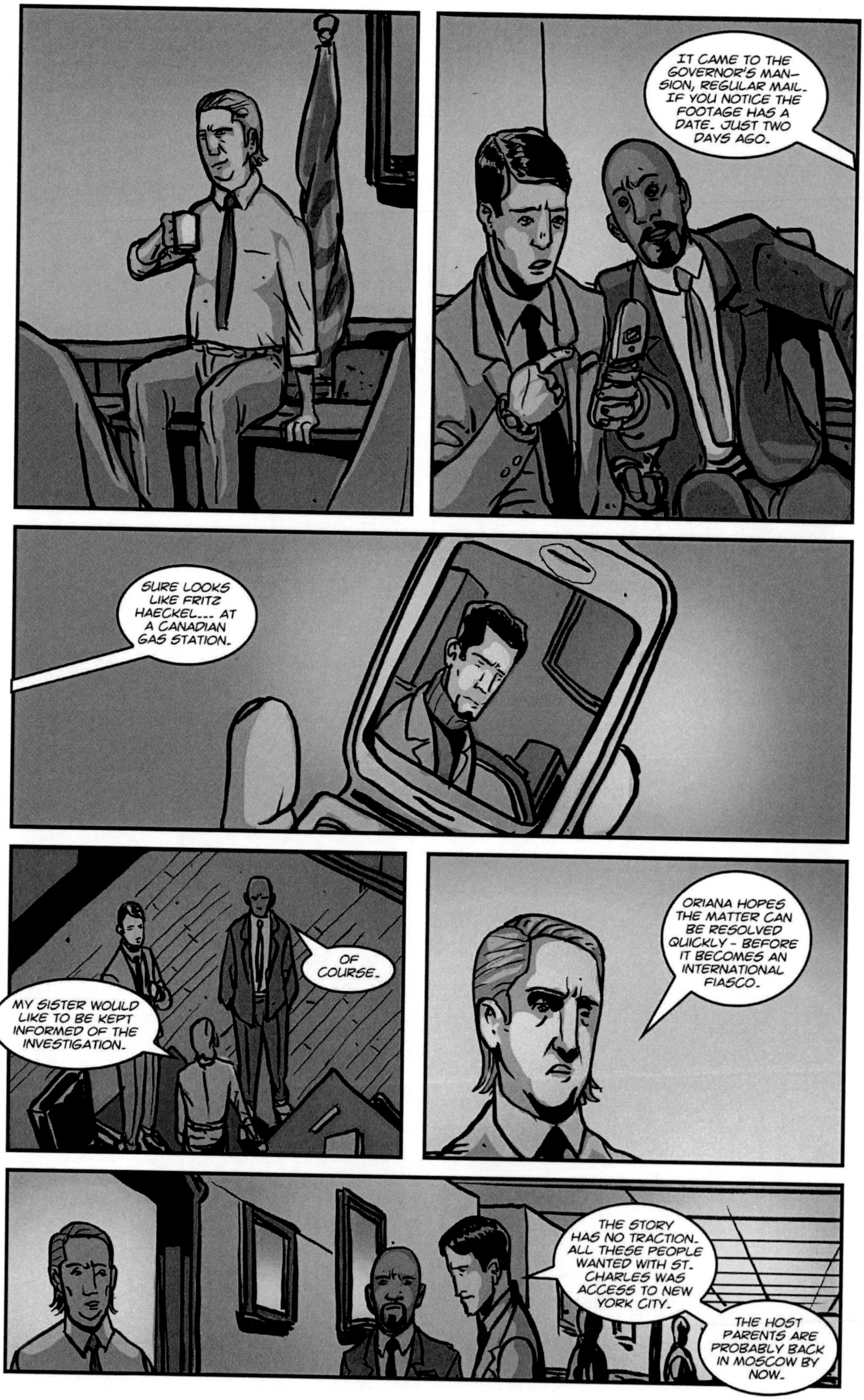
IT CAME TO THE GOVERNOR'S MANSION, REGULAR MAIL. IF YOU NOTICE THE FOOTAGE HAS A DATE. JUST TWO DAYS AGO.
SURE LOOKS LIKE FRITZ HAECKEL... AT A CANADIAN GAS STATION.
MY SISTER WOULD LIKE TO BE KEPT INFORMED OF THE INVESTIGATION.
OF COURSE.
ORIANA HOPES THE MATTER CAN BE RESOLVED QUICKLY - BEFORE IT BECOMES AN INTERNATIONAL FIASCO.
THE STORY HAS NO TRACTION. ALL THESE PEOPLE WANTED WITH ST. CHARLES WAS ACCESS TO NEW YORK CITY.
THE HOST PARENTS ARE PROBABLY BACK IN MOSCOW BY NOW.

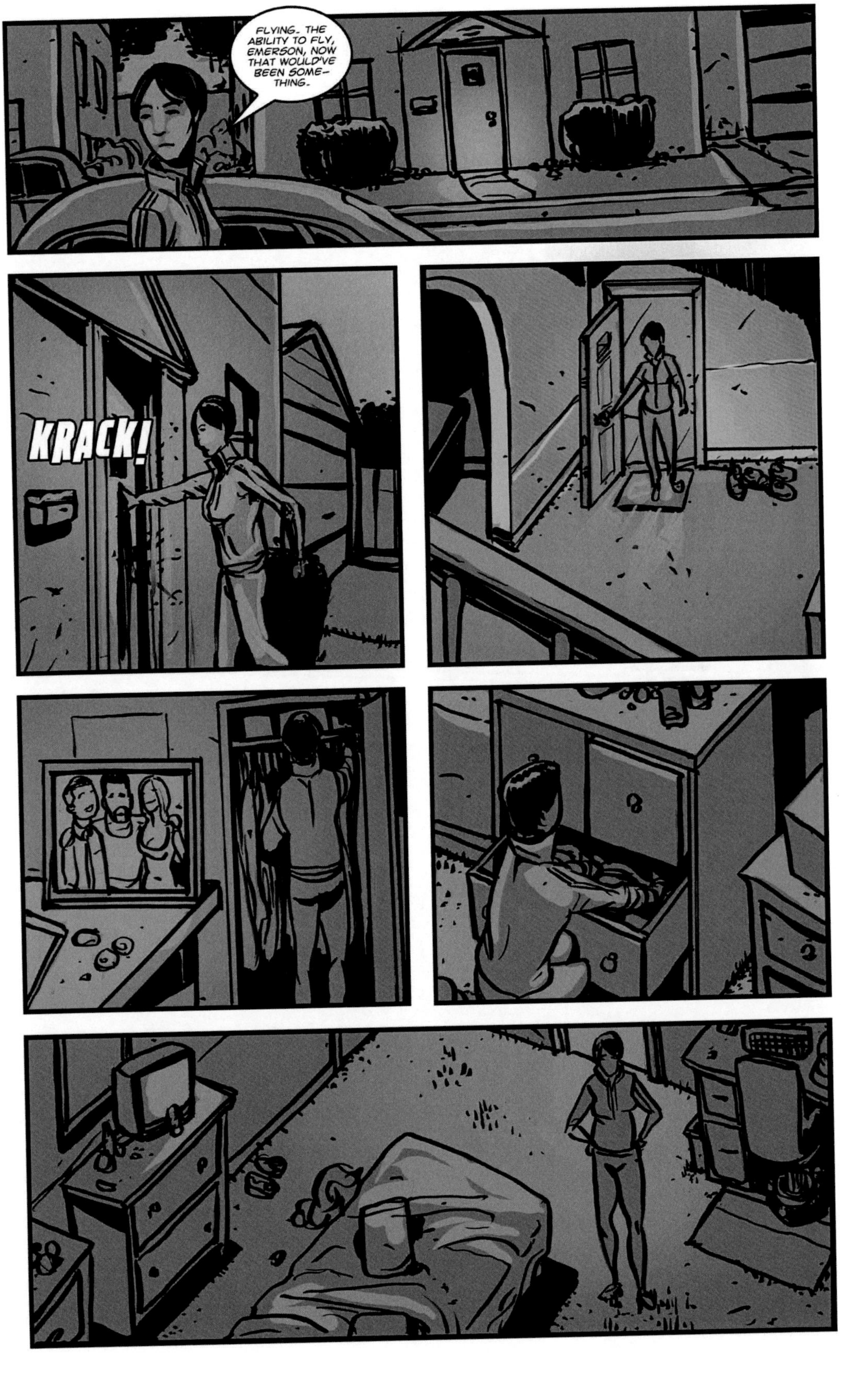
FLYING. THE ABILITY TO FLY, EMERSON, NOW THAT WOULD'VE BEEN SOME-THING.
KRACK!

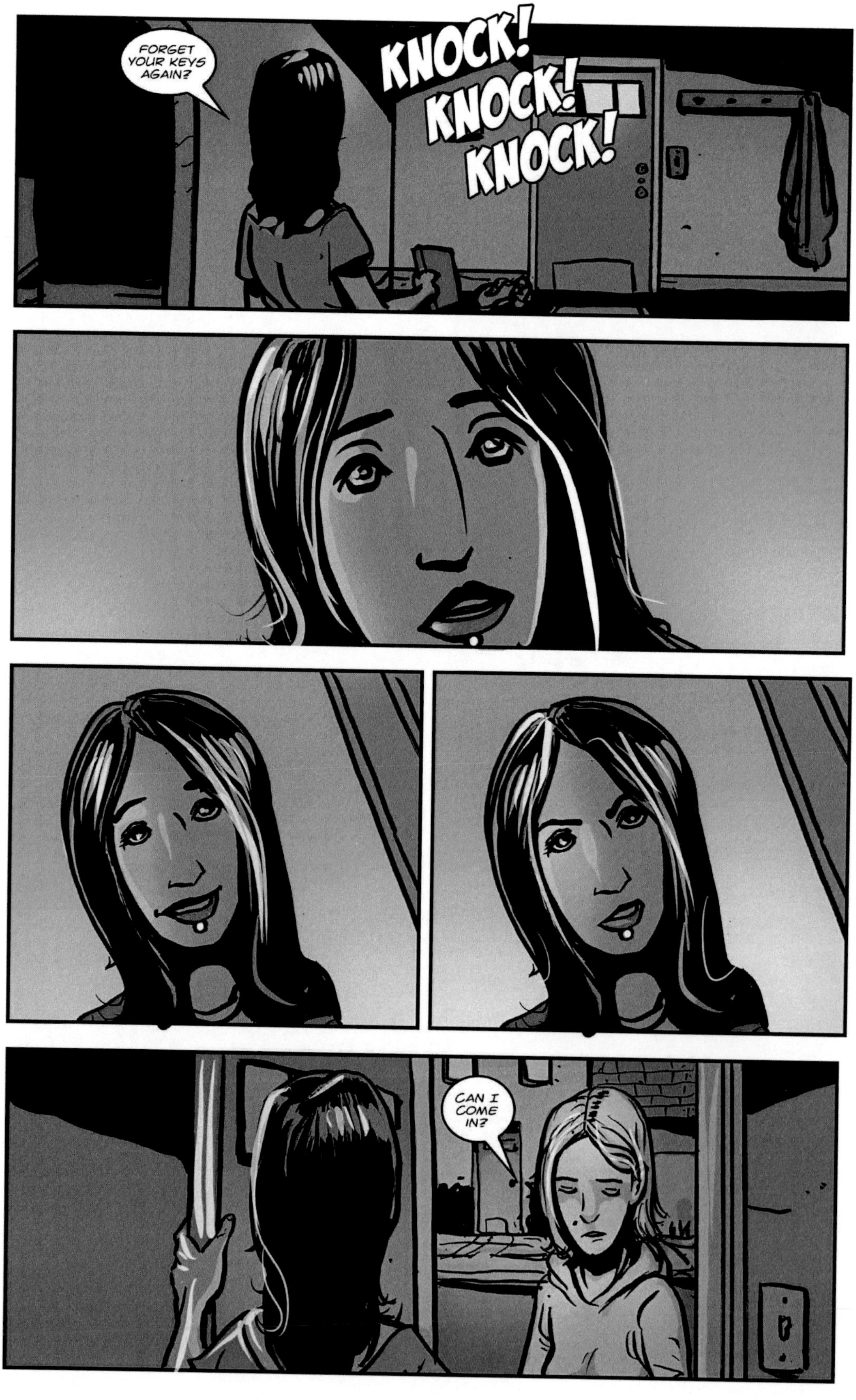
FORGET YOUR KEYS AGAIN?
KNOCK! KNOCK! KNOCK!
CAN I COME IN?

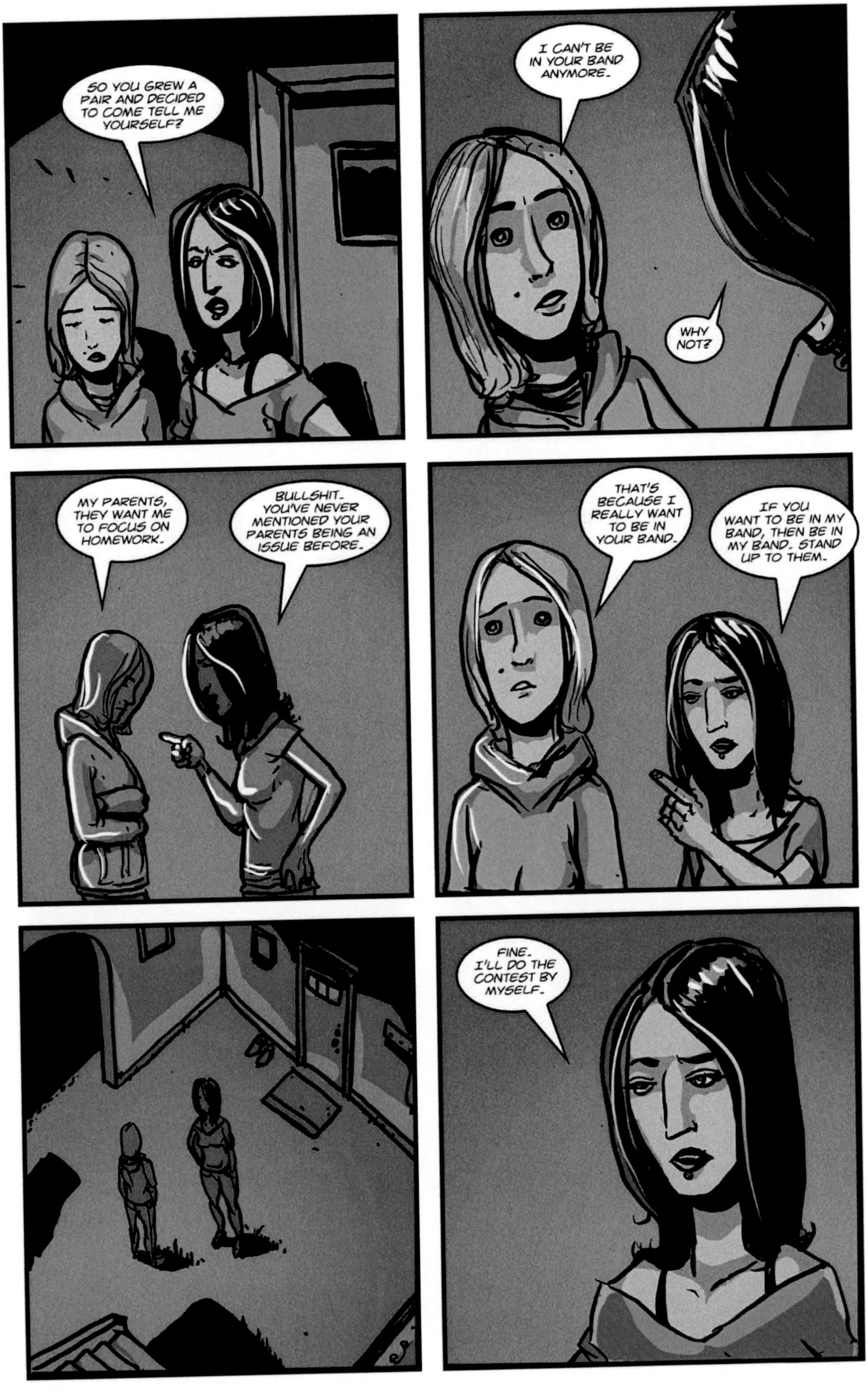
SO YOU GREW A PAIR AND DECIDED TO COME TELL ME YOURSELF?
I CAN'T BE IN YOUR BAND ANYMORE.
WHY NOT?
MY PARENTS, THEY WANT ME TO FOCUS ON HOMEWORK.
BULLSHIT. YOU'VE NEVER MENTIONED YOUR PARENTS BEING AN ISSUE BEFORE.
THAT'S BECAUSE I REALLY WANT TO BE IN YOUR BAND.
IF YOU WANT TO BE IN MY BAND, THEN BE IN MY BAND. STAND UP TO THEM.
FINE. I'LL DO THE CONTEST BY MYSELF.

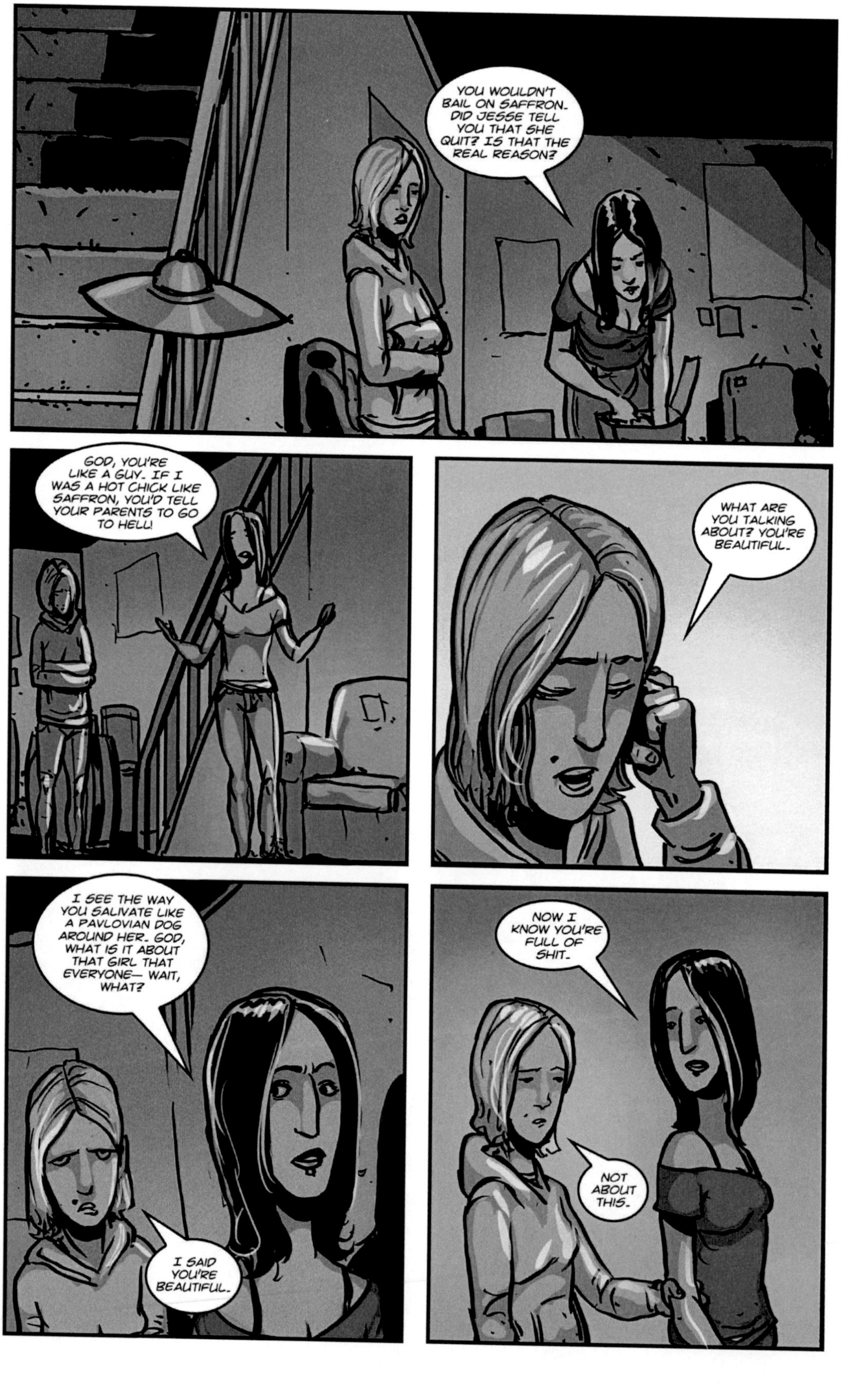
YOU WOULDN'T BAIL ON SAFFRON. DID JESSE TELL YOU THAT SHE QUIT? IS THAT THE REAL REASON?
GOD, YOU'RE LIKE A GUY. IF I WAS A HOT CHICK LIKE SAFFRON, YOU'D TELL YOUR PARENTS TO GO TO HELL!
WHAT ARE YOU TALKING ABOUT? YOU'RE BEAUTIFUL.
I SEE THE WAY YOU SALIVATE LIKE A PAVLOVIAN DOG AROUND HER. GOD, WHAT IS IT ABOUT THAT GIRL THAT EVERYONE— WAIT, WHAT?
I SAID YOU'RE BEAUTIFUL.
NOW I KNOW YOU'RE FULL OF SHIT.
NOT ABOUT THIS.

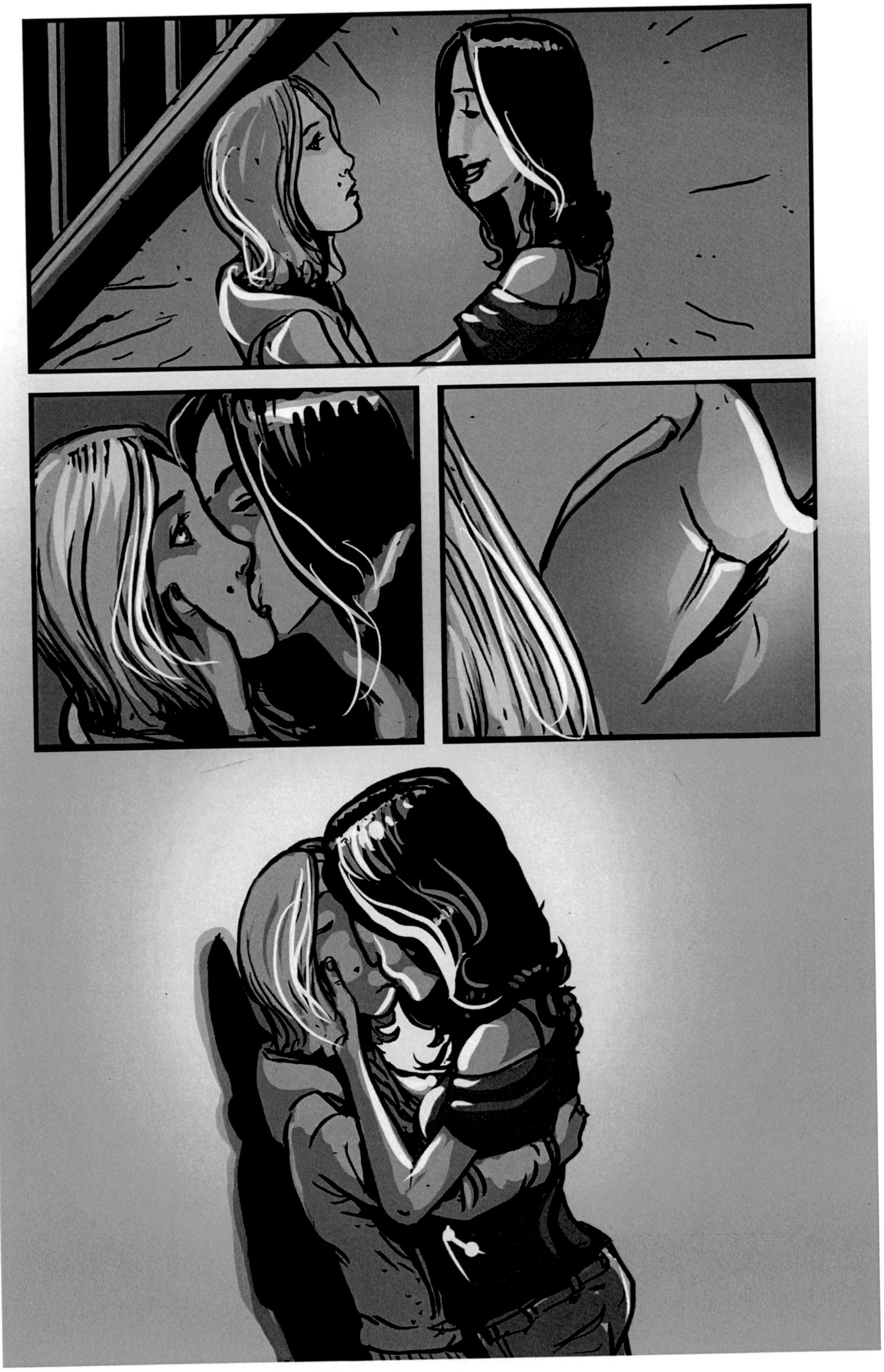

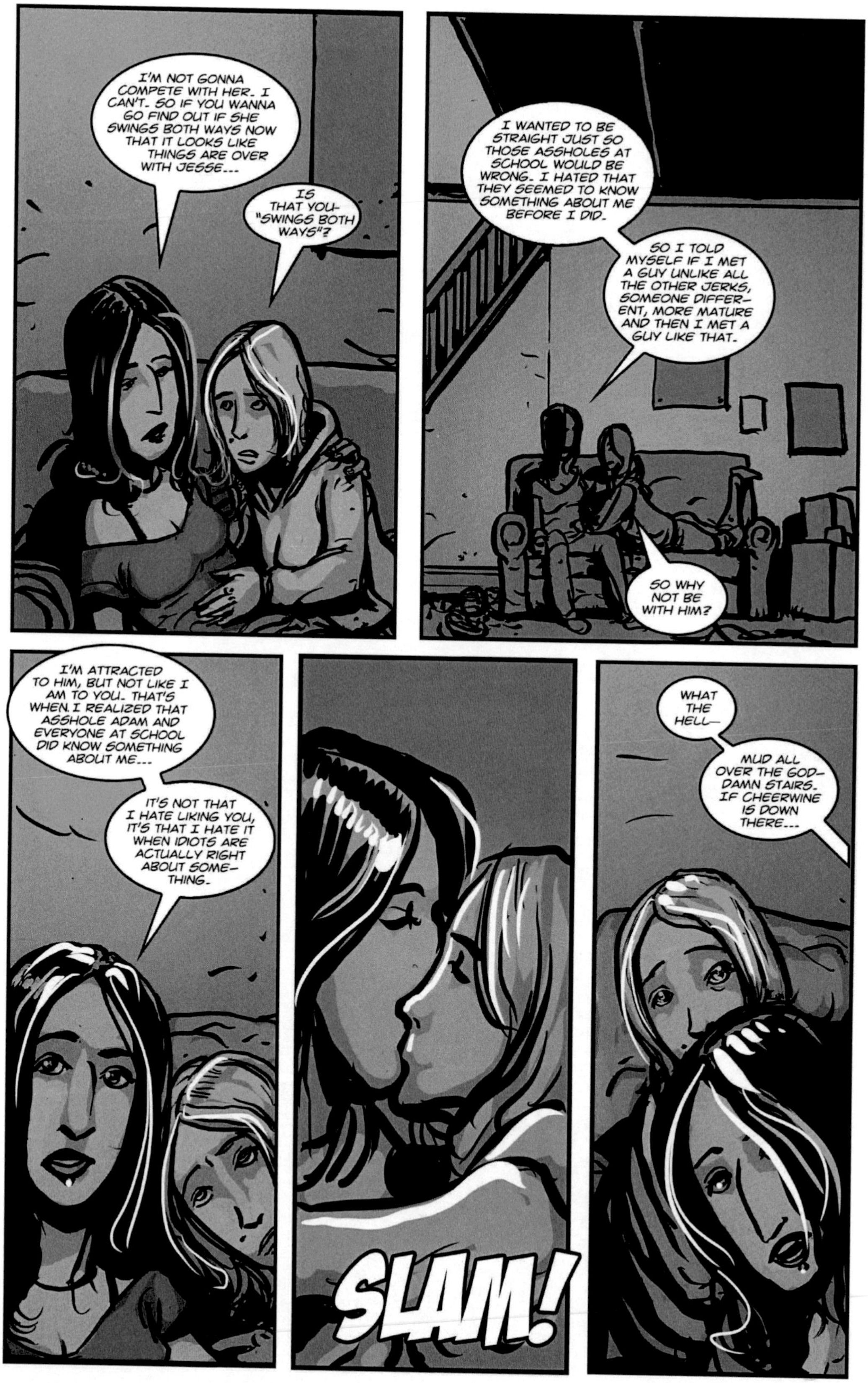
I'M NOT GONNA COMPETE WITH HER. I CAN'T. SO IF YOU WANNA GO FIND OUT IF SHE SWINGS BOTH WAYS NOW THAT IT LOOKS LIKE THINGS ARE OVER WITH JESSE...
IS THAT YOU- "SWINGS BOTH WAYS"?
I WANTED TO BE STRAIGHT JUST SO THOSE ASSHOLES AT SCHOOL WOULD BE WRONG. I HATED THAT THEY SEEMED TO KNOW SOMETHING ABOUT ME BEFORE I DID.
SO I TOLD MYSELF IF I MET A GUY UNLIKE ALL THE OTHER JERKS, SOMEONE DIFFERENT, MORE MATURE AND THEN I MET A GUY LIKE THAT.
SO WHY NOT BE WITH HIM?
I'M ATTRACTED TO HIM, BUT NOT LIKE I AM TO YOU. THAT'S WHEN. I REALIZED THAT ASSHOLE ADAM AND EVERYONE AT SCHOOL DID KNOW SOMETHING ABOUT ME...
IT'S NOT THAT I HATE LIKING YOU, IT'S THAT I HATE IT WHEN IDIOTS ARE ACTUALLY RIGHT ABOUT SOMETHING.
SLAM!
WHAT THE HELL-
MUD ALL OVER THE GOD-DAMN STAIRS. IF CHEERWINE IS DOWN THERE...

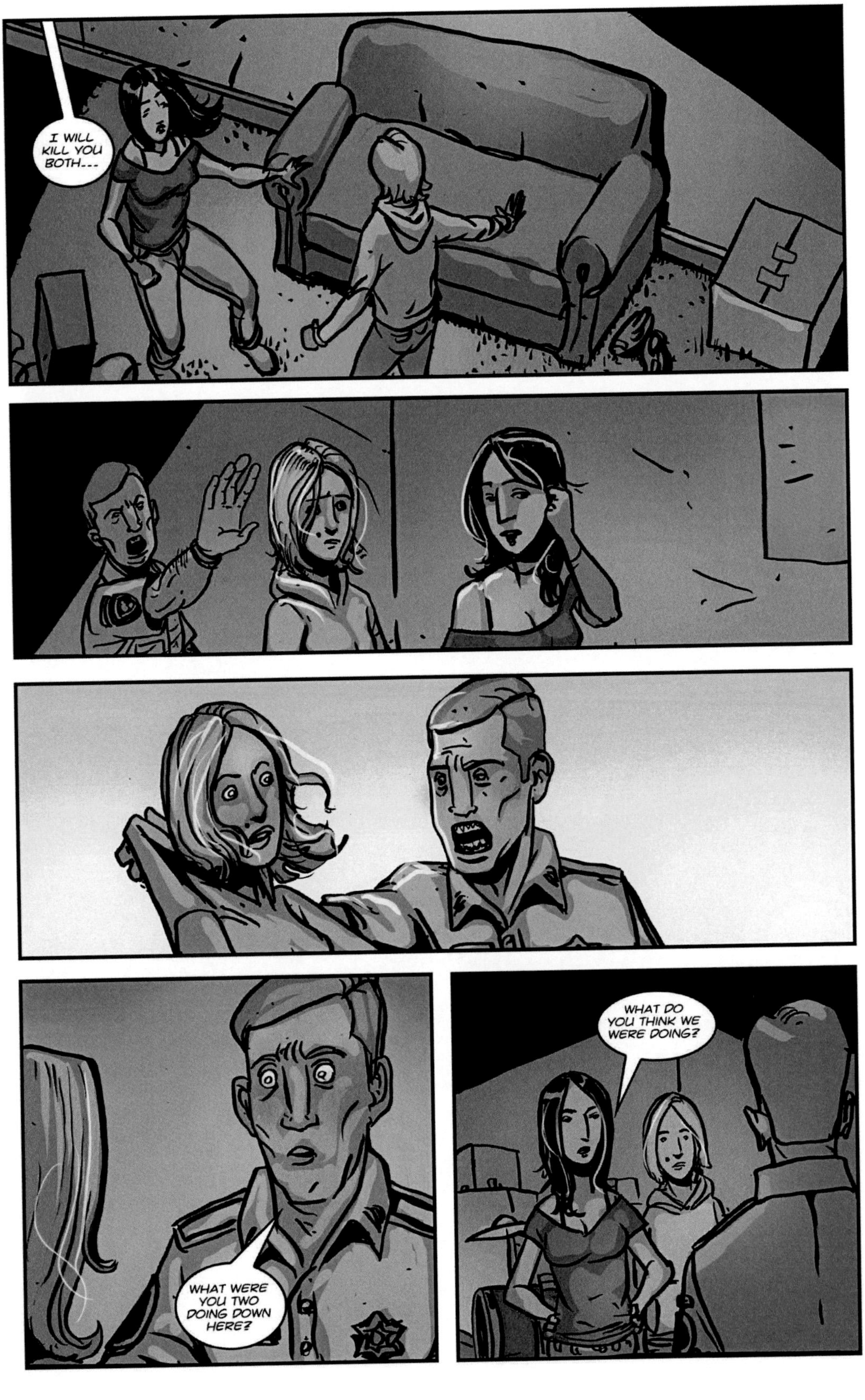
I WILL KILL YOU BOTH...
WHAT WERE YOU TWO DOING DOWN HERE?
WHAT DO YOU THINK WE WERE DOING?

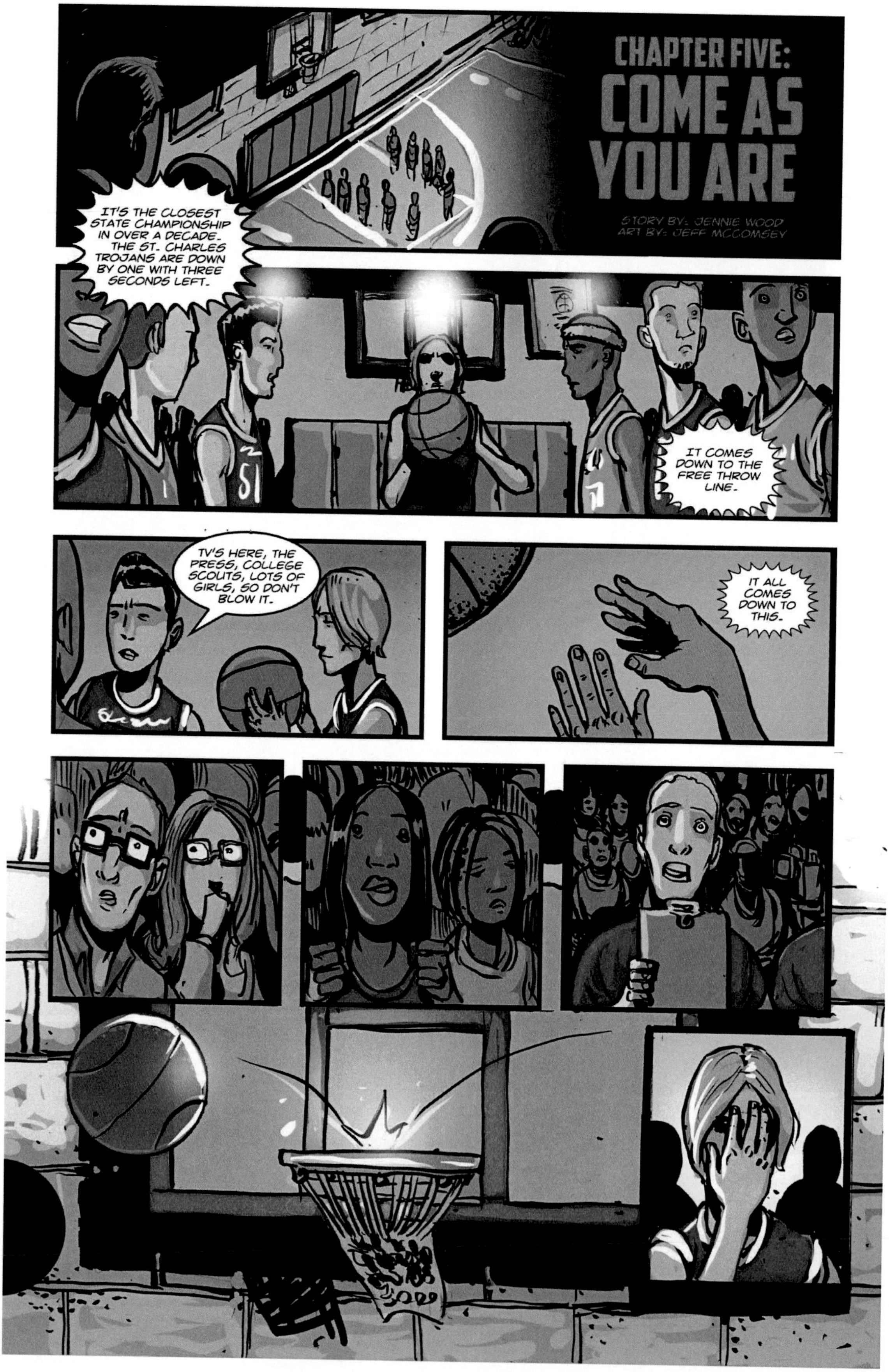
CHAPTER FIVE:
COME AS YOU ARE
STORY BY: JENNIE WOOD
ART BY: JEFF MCCOMSEY
IT'S THE CLOSEST STATE CHAMPIONSHIP IN OVER A DECADE. THE ST. CHARLES TROJANS ARE DOWN BY ONE WITH THREE SECONDS LEFT.
IT COMES DOWN TO THE FREE THROW LINE.
TV'S HERE, THE PRESS, COLLEGE SCOUTS, LOTS OF GIRLS, SO DON'T BLOW IT.
IT ALL COMES DOWN TO THIS.

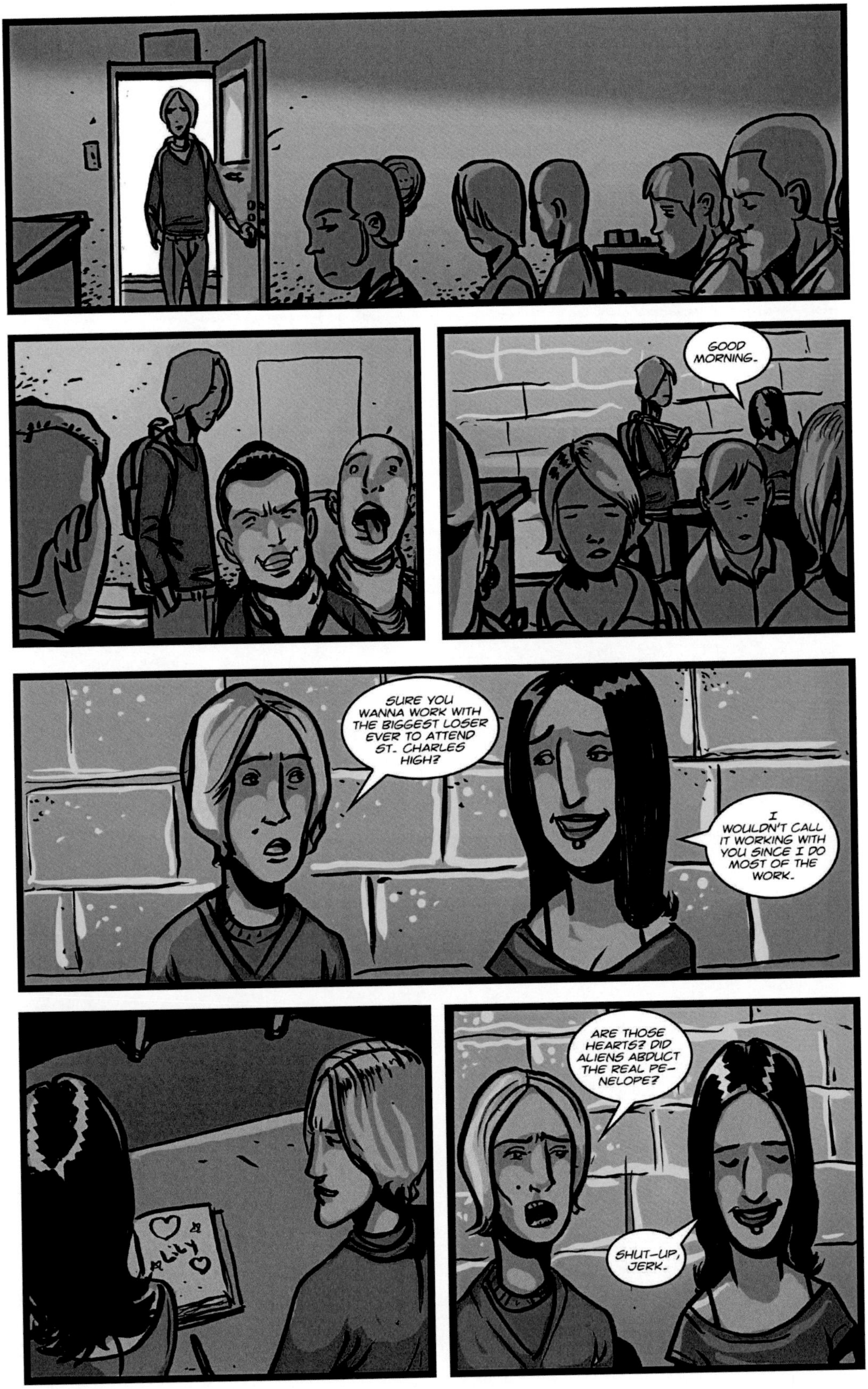
GOOD MORNING.
SURE YOU WANNA WORK WITH THE BIGGEST LOSER EVER TO ATTEND ST. CHARLES HIGH?
I WOULDN'T CALL IT WORKING WITH YOU SINCE I DO MOST OF THE WORK.
Lily
ARE THOSE HEARTS? DID ALIENS ABDUCT THE REAL PE-NELOPE?
SHUT-UP, JERK.

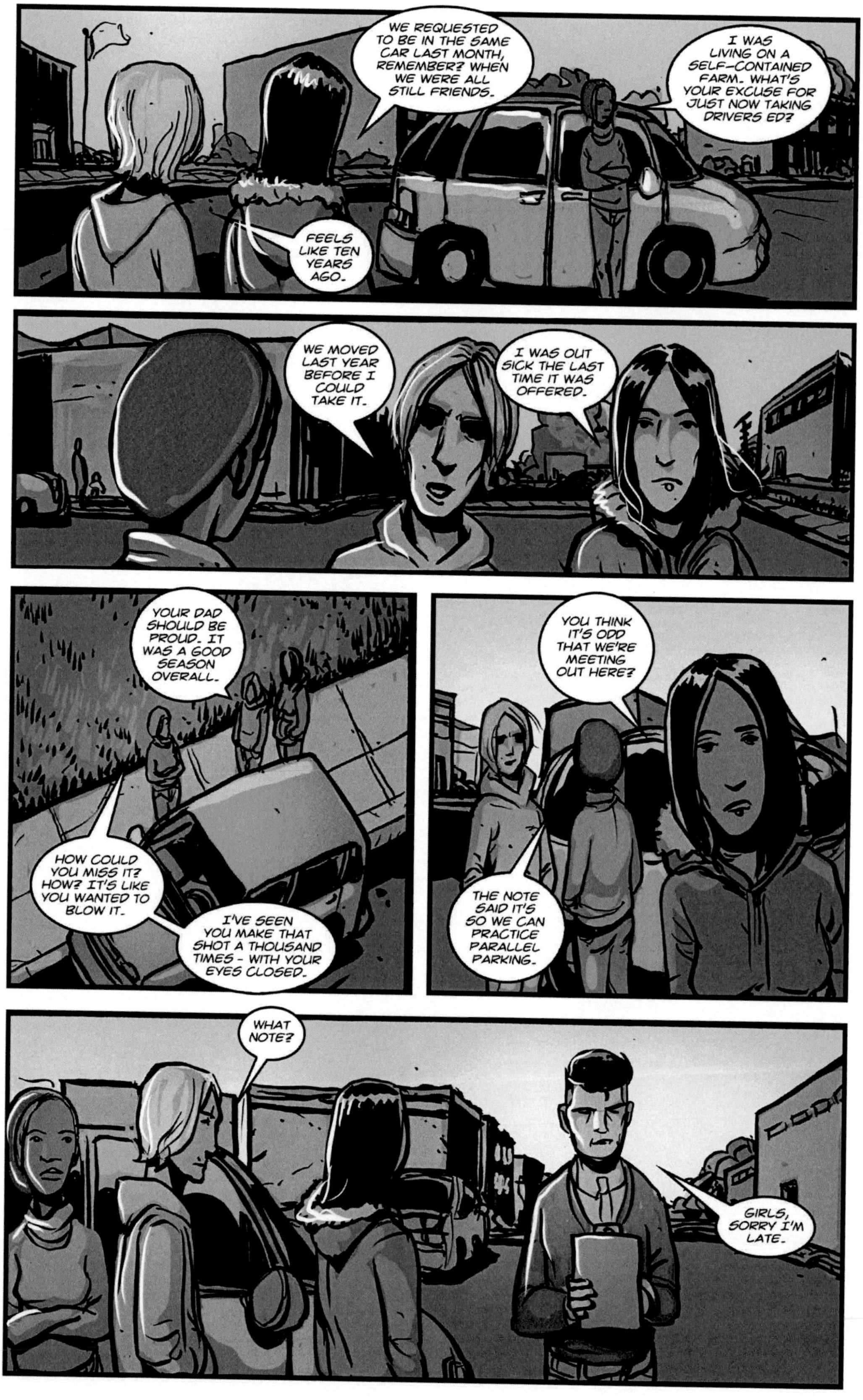
WE REQUESTED TO BE IN THE SAME CAR LAST MONTH, REMEMBER? WHEN WE WERE ALL STILL FRIENDS.
I WAS LIVING ON A SELF-CONTAINED FARM. WHAT'S YOUR EXCUSE FOR JUST NOW TAKING DRIVERS ED?
FEELS LIKE TEN YEARS AGO.
WE MOVED LAST YEAR BEFORE I COULD TAKE IT.
I WAS OUT SICK THE LAST TIME IT WAS OFFERED.
YOUR DAD SHOULD BE PROUD. IT WAS A GOOD SEASON OVERALL.
HOW COULD YOU MISS IT? HOW? IT'S LIKE YOU WANTED TO BLOW IT.
I'VE SEEN YOU MAKE THAT SHOT A THOUSAND TIMES - WITH YOUR EYES CLOSED.
YOU THINK IT'S ODD THAT WE'RE MEETING OUT HERE?
THE NOTE SAID IT'S SO WE CAN PRACTICE PARALLEL PARKING.
WHAT NOTE?
GIRLS, SORRY I'M LATE.

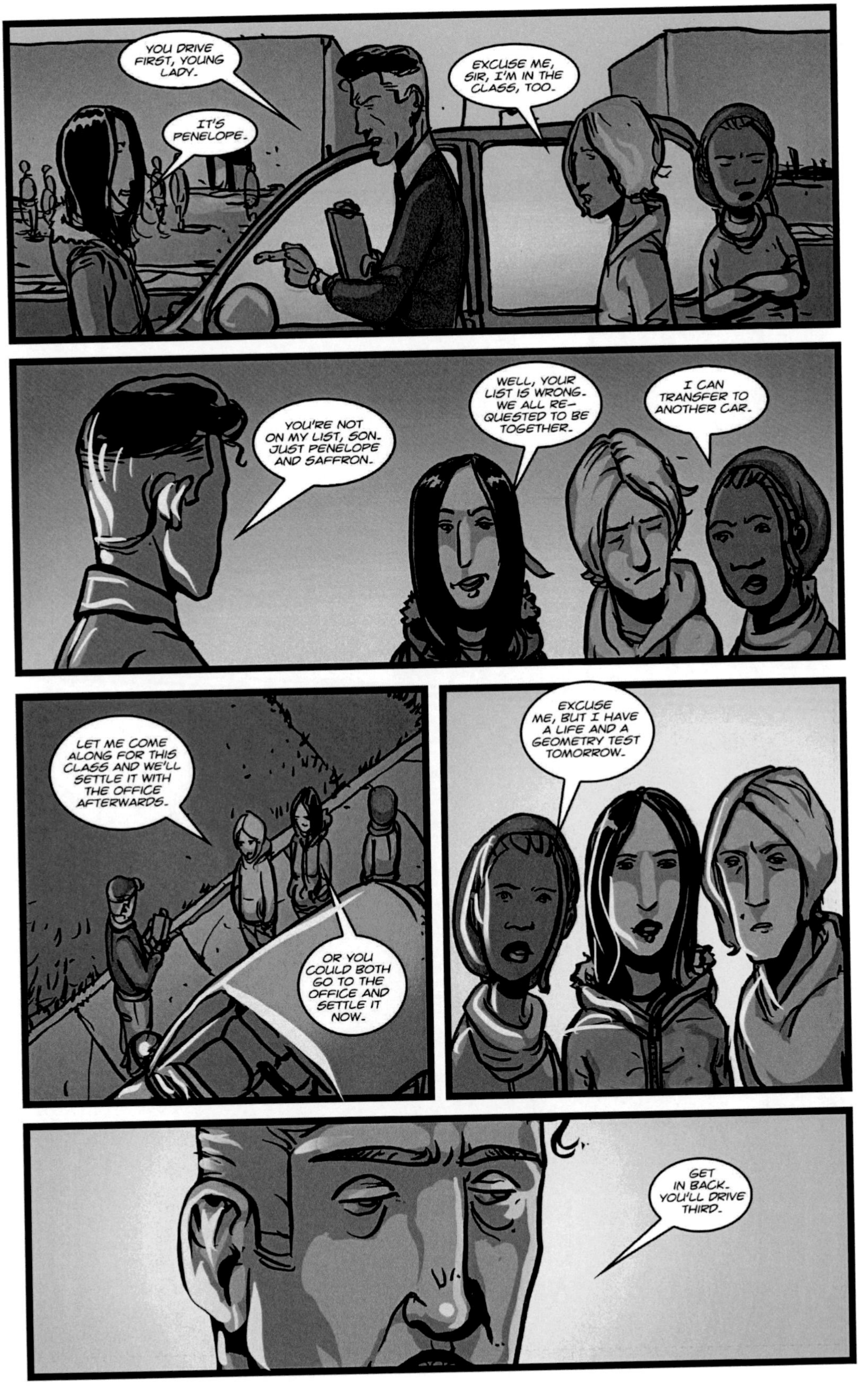
YOU DRIVE FIRST, YOUNG LADY.
IT'S PENELOPE.
EXCUSE ME, SIR, I'M IN THE CLASS, TOO.
YOU'RE NOT ON MY LIST, SON. JUST PENELOPE AND SAFFRON.
WELL, YOUR LIST IS WRONG. WE ALL RE-QUESTED TO BE TOGETHER.
I CAN TRANSFER TO ANOTHER CAR.
LET ME COME ALONG FOR THIS CLASS AND WE'LL SETTLE IT WITH THE OFFICE AFTERWARDS.
OR YOU COULD BOTH GO TO THE OFFICE AND SETTLE IT NOW.
EXCUSE ME, BUT I HAVE A LIFE AND A GEOMETRY TEST TOMORROW.
GET IN BACK. YOU'LL DRIVE THIRD.

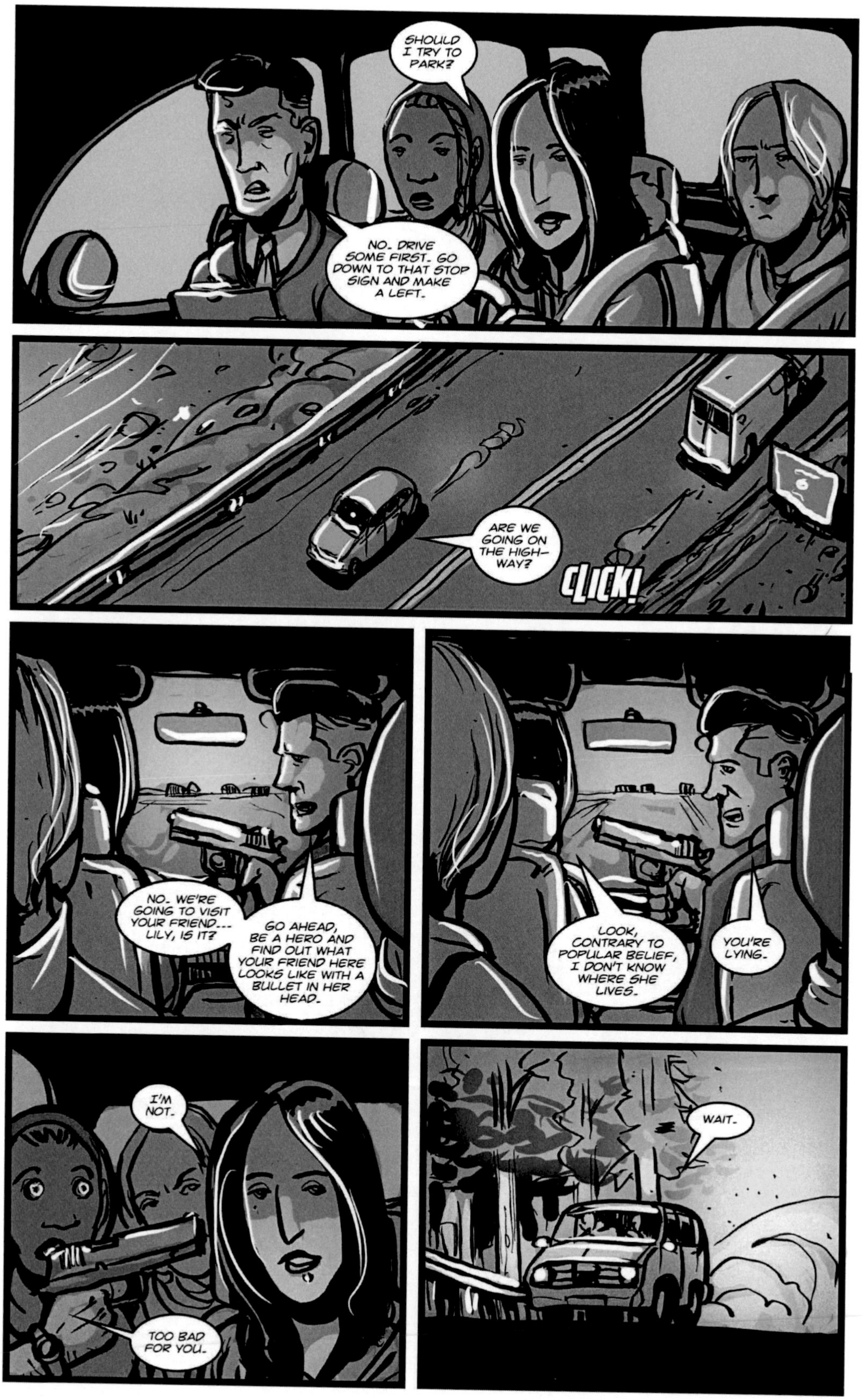

SHOULD I TRY TO PARK?
NO. DRIVE SOME FIRST. GO DOWN TO THAT STOP SIGN AND MAKE A LEFT.
ARE WE GOING ON THE HIGHWAY?
CLICK!
NO. WE'RE GOING TO VISIT YOUR FRIEND... LILY, IS IT?
GO AHEAD, BE A HERO AND FIND OUT WHAT YOUR FRIEND HERE LOOKS LIKE WITH A BULLET IN HER HEAD.
LOOK, CONTRARY TO POPULAR BELIEF, I DON'T KNOW WHERE SHE LIVES.
YOU'RE LYING.
I'M NOT.
TOO BAD FOR YOU.
WAIT.

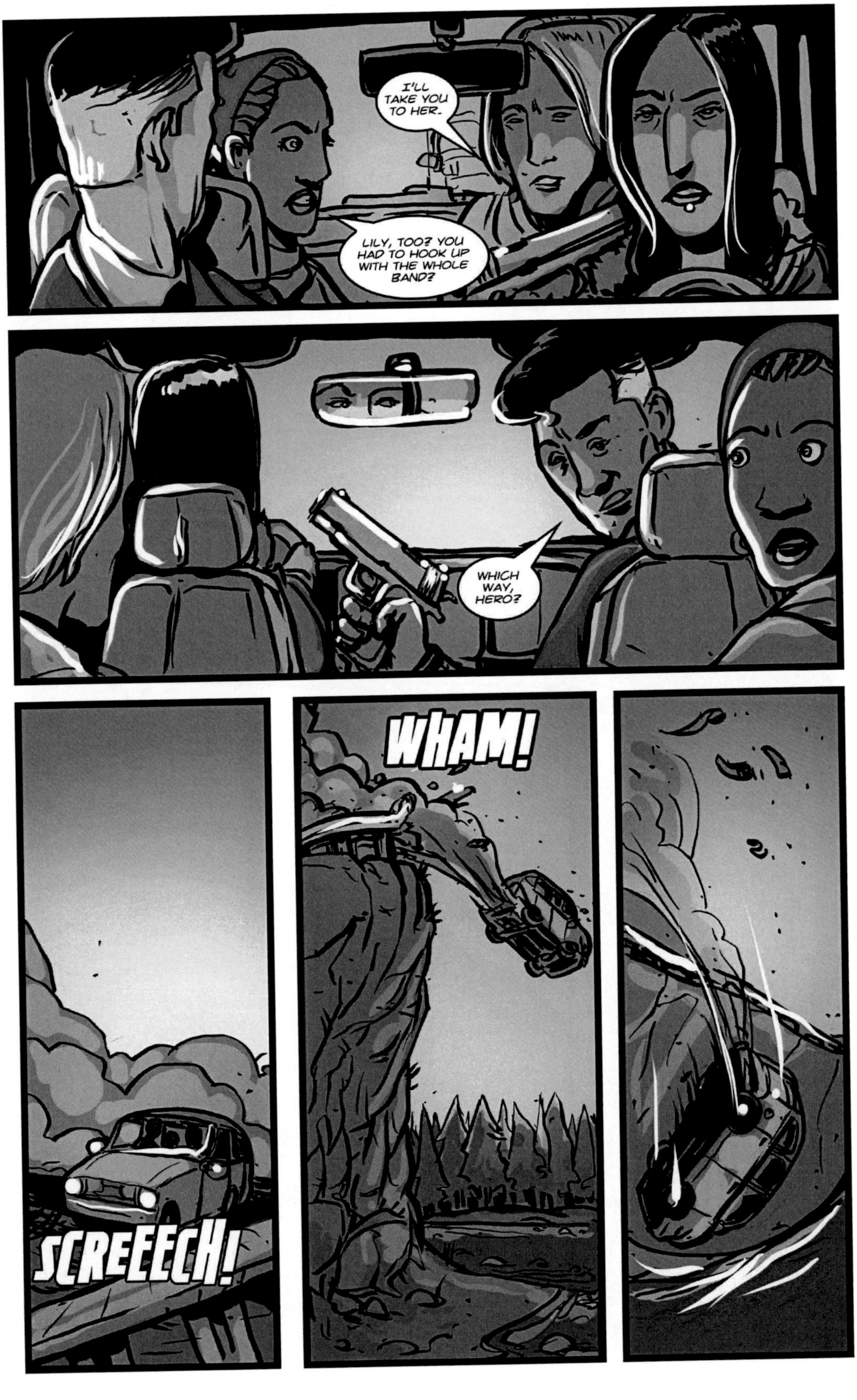
I'LL TAKE YOU TO HER.
LILY, TOO? YOU HAD TO HOOK UP WITH THE WHOLE BAND?
WHICH WAY, HERO?
SCREEECH!
WHAM!

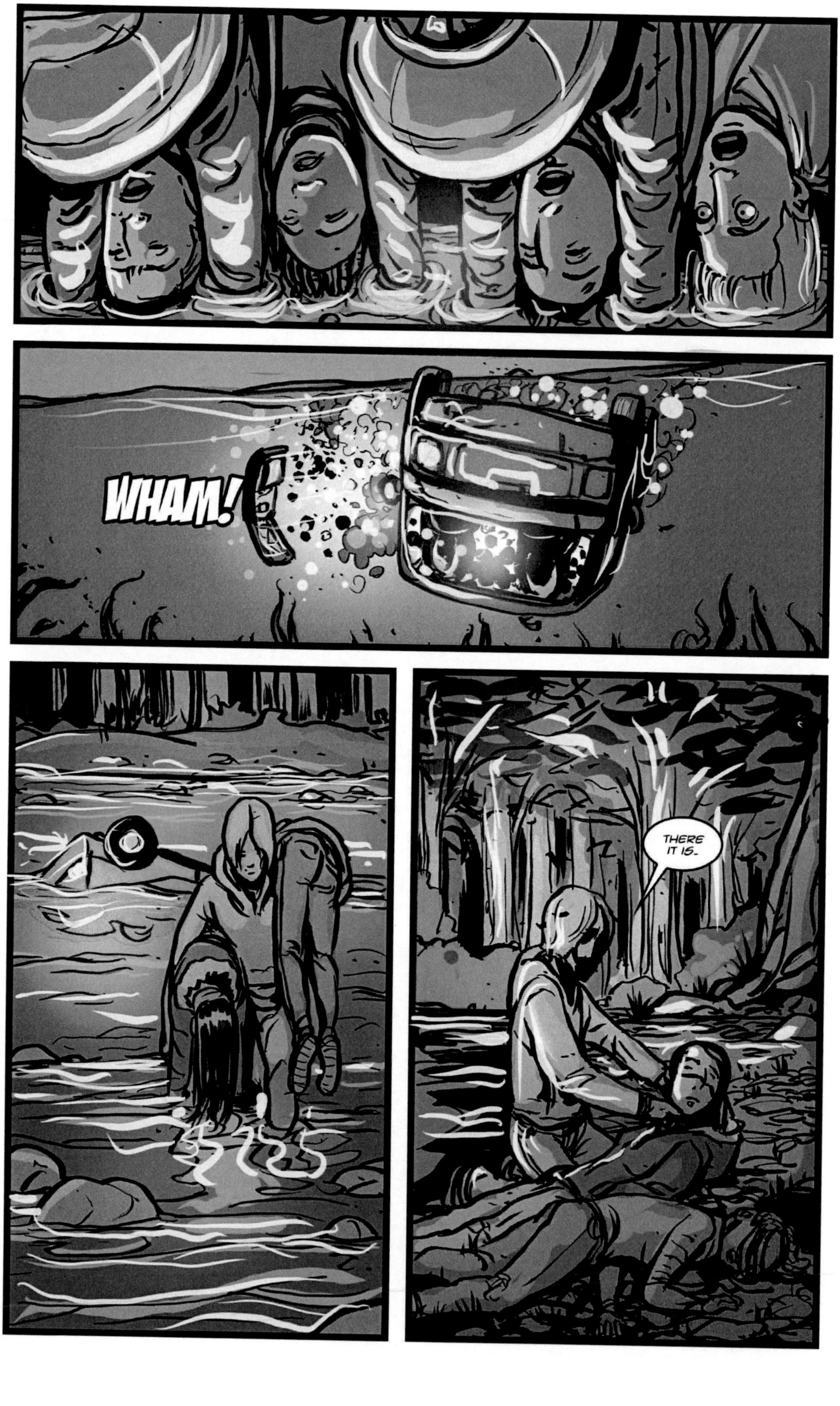
WHAM!
THERE IT IS.

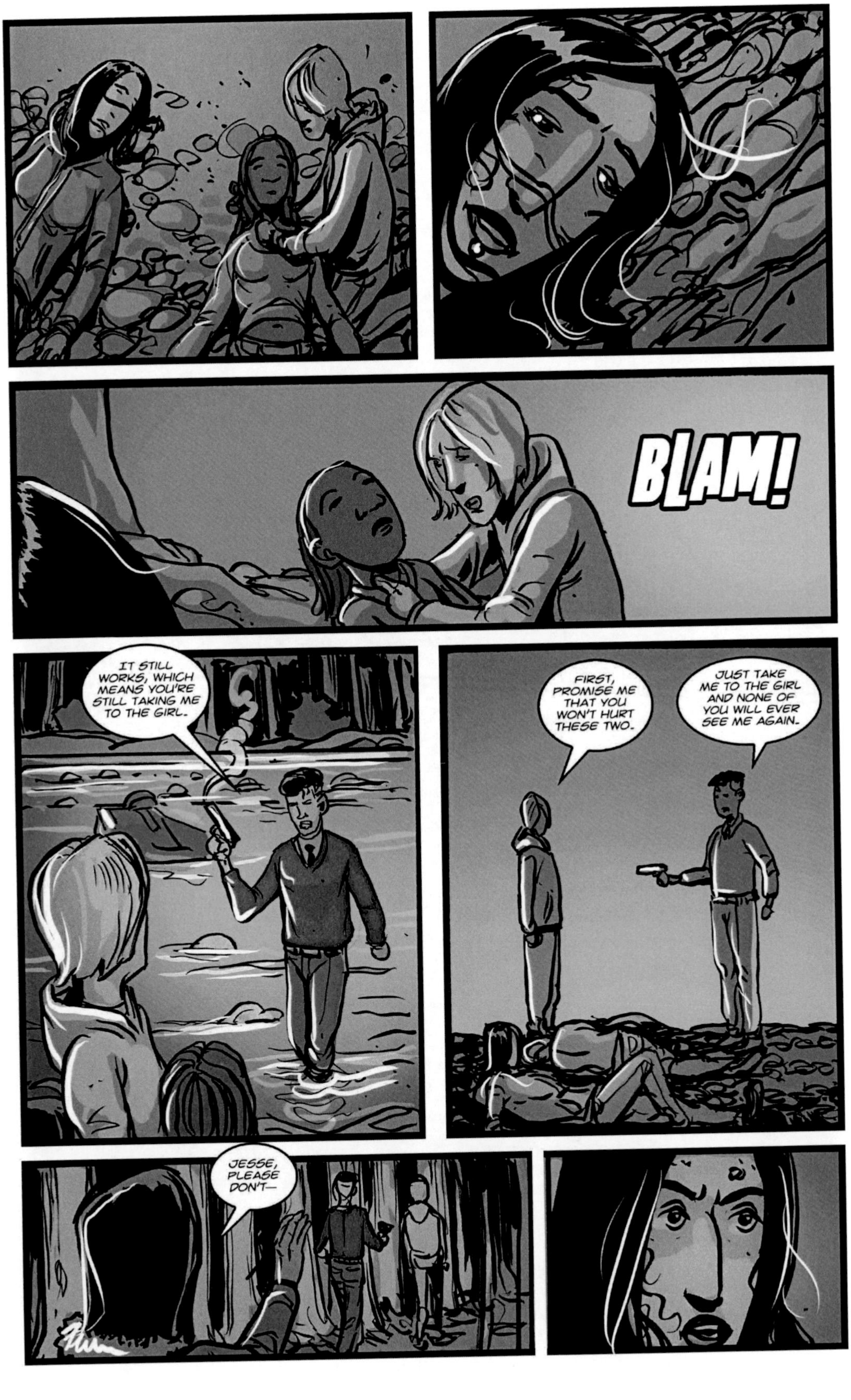
BLAM!
IT STILL WORKS, WHICH MEANS YOU'RE STILL TAKING ME TO THE GIRL.
FIRST, PROMISE ME THAT YOU WON'T HURT THESE TWO.
JUST TAKE ME TO THE GIRL AND NONE OF YOU WILL EVER SEE ME AGAIN.
JESSE, PLEASE DON'T—

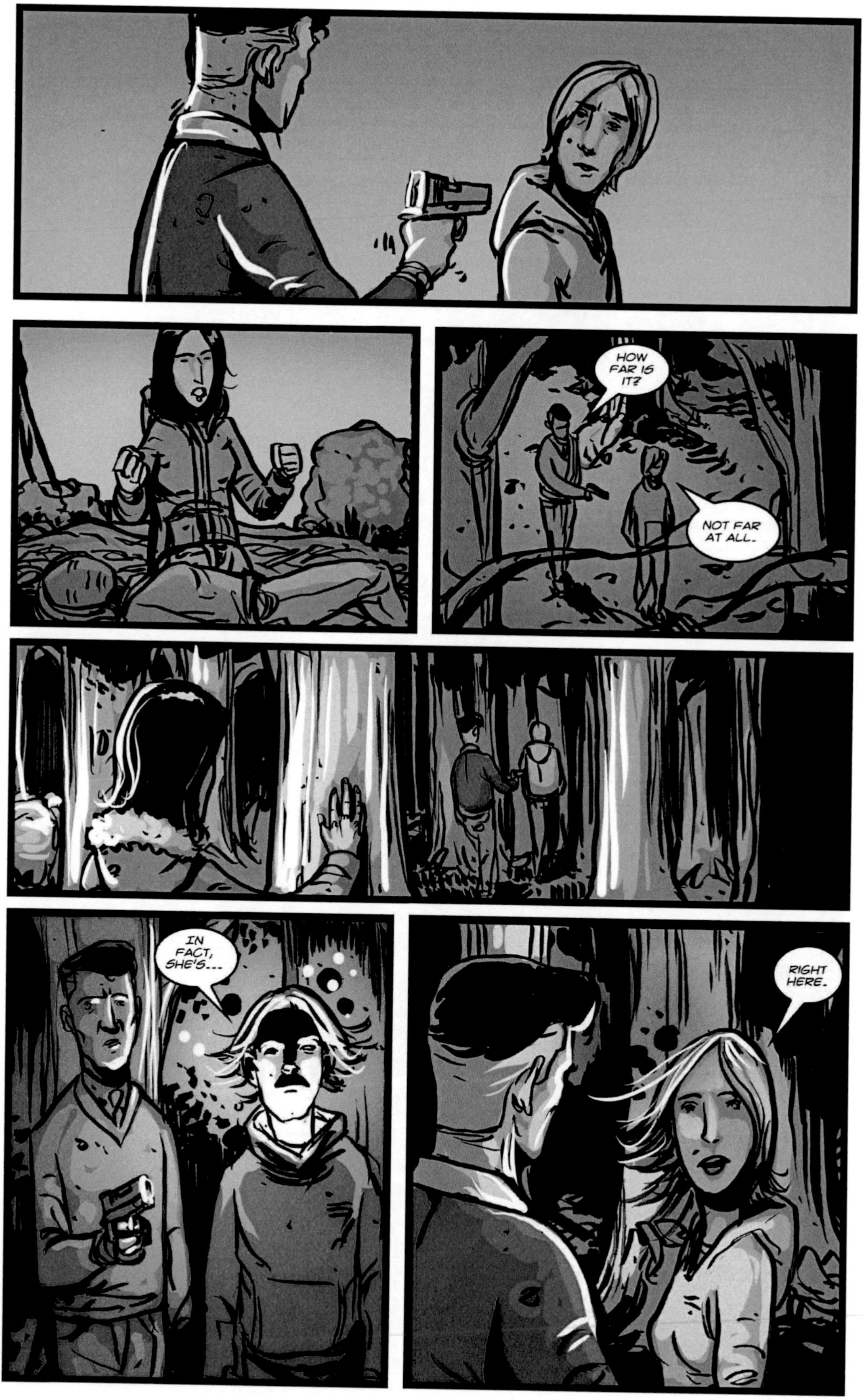
HOW FAR IS IT?
NOT FAR AT ALL.
IN FACT, SHE'S...
RIGHT HERE.

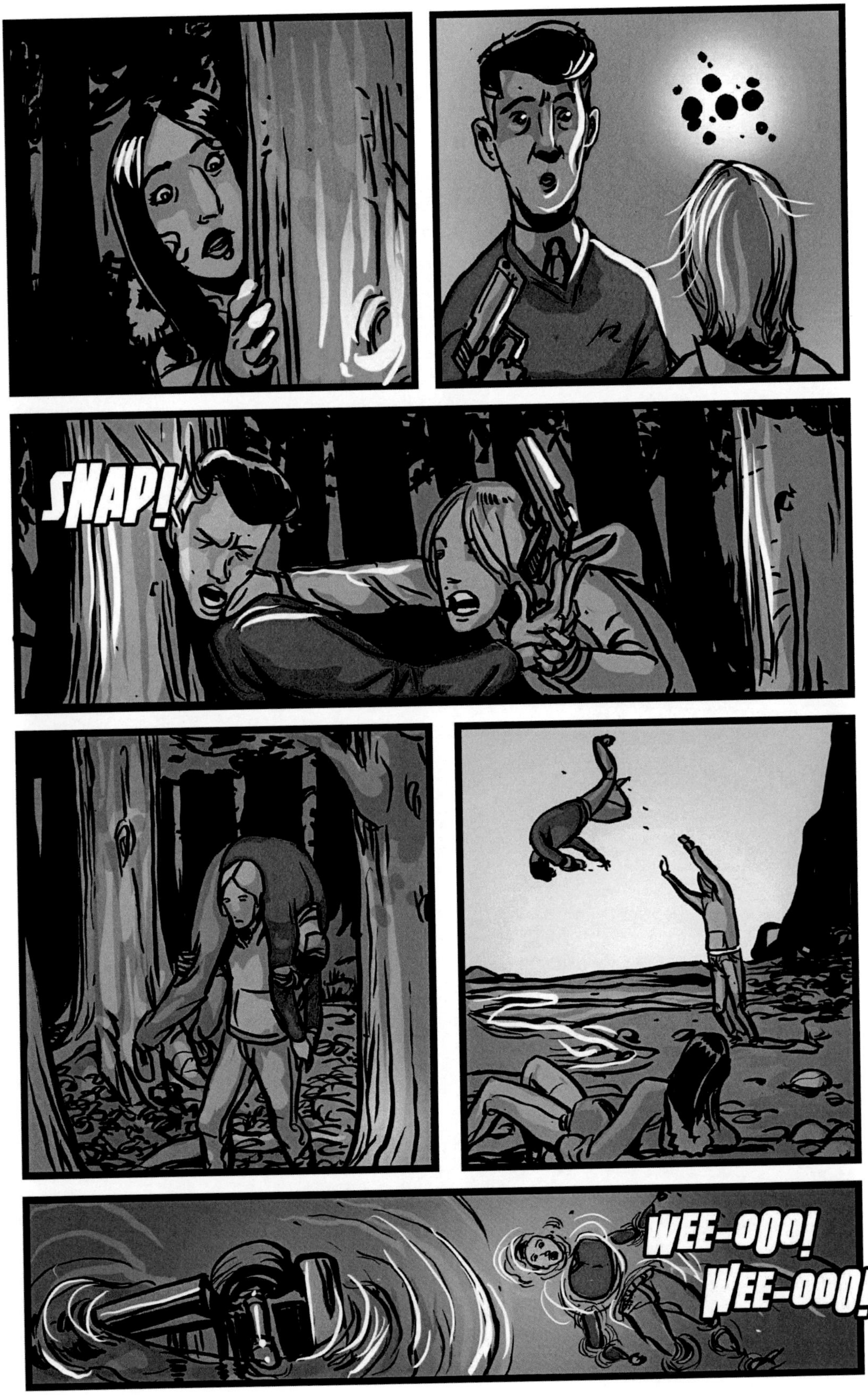
SNAP!
WEE-OOO!
WEE-OOO!

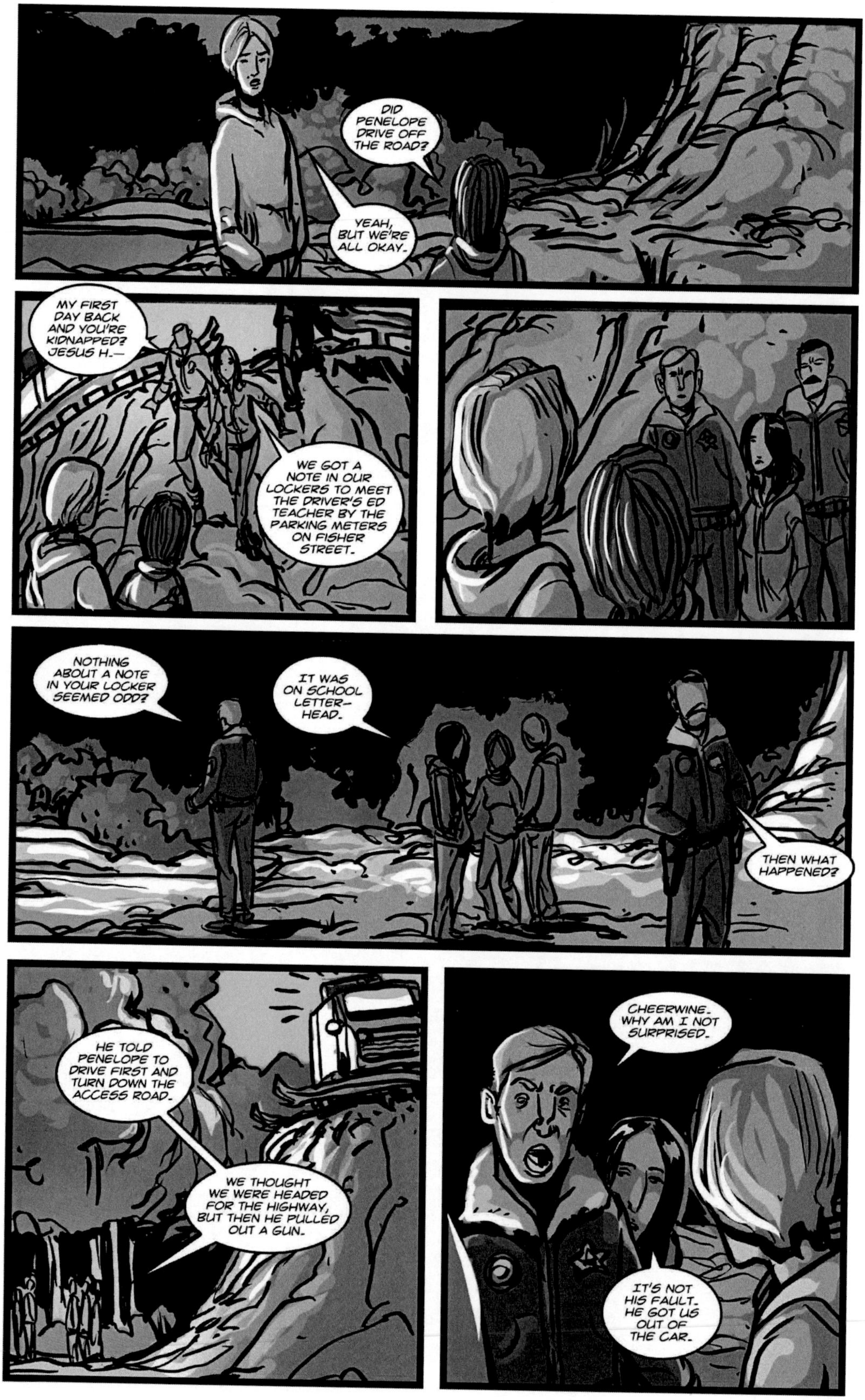
DID PENELOPE DRIVE OFF THE ROAD?
YEAH, BUT WE'RE ALL OKAY.
MY FIRST DAY BACK AND YOU'RE KIDNAPPED? JESUS H.—
WE GOT A NOTE IN OUR LOCKERS TO MEET THE DRIVER'S ED TEACHER BY THE PARKING METERS ON FISHER STREET.
NOTHING ABOUT A NOTE IN YOUR LOCKER SEEMED ODD?
IT WAS ON SCHOOL LETTER-HEAD.
THEN WHAT HAPPENED?
HE TOLD PENELOPE TO DRIVE FIRST AND TURN DOWN THE ACCESS ROAD.
WE THOUGHT WE WERE HEADED FOR THE HIGHWAY, BUT THEN HE PULLED OUT A GUN.
CHEERWINE. WHY AM I NOT SURPRISED.
IT'S NOT HIS FAULT. HE GOT US OUT OF THE CAR.

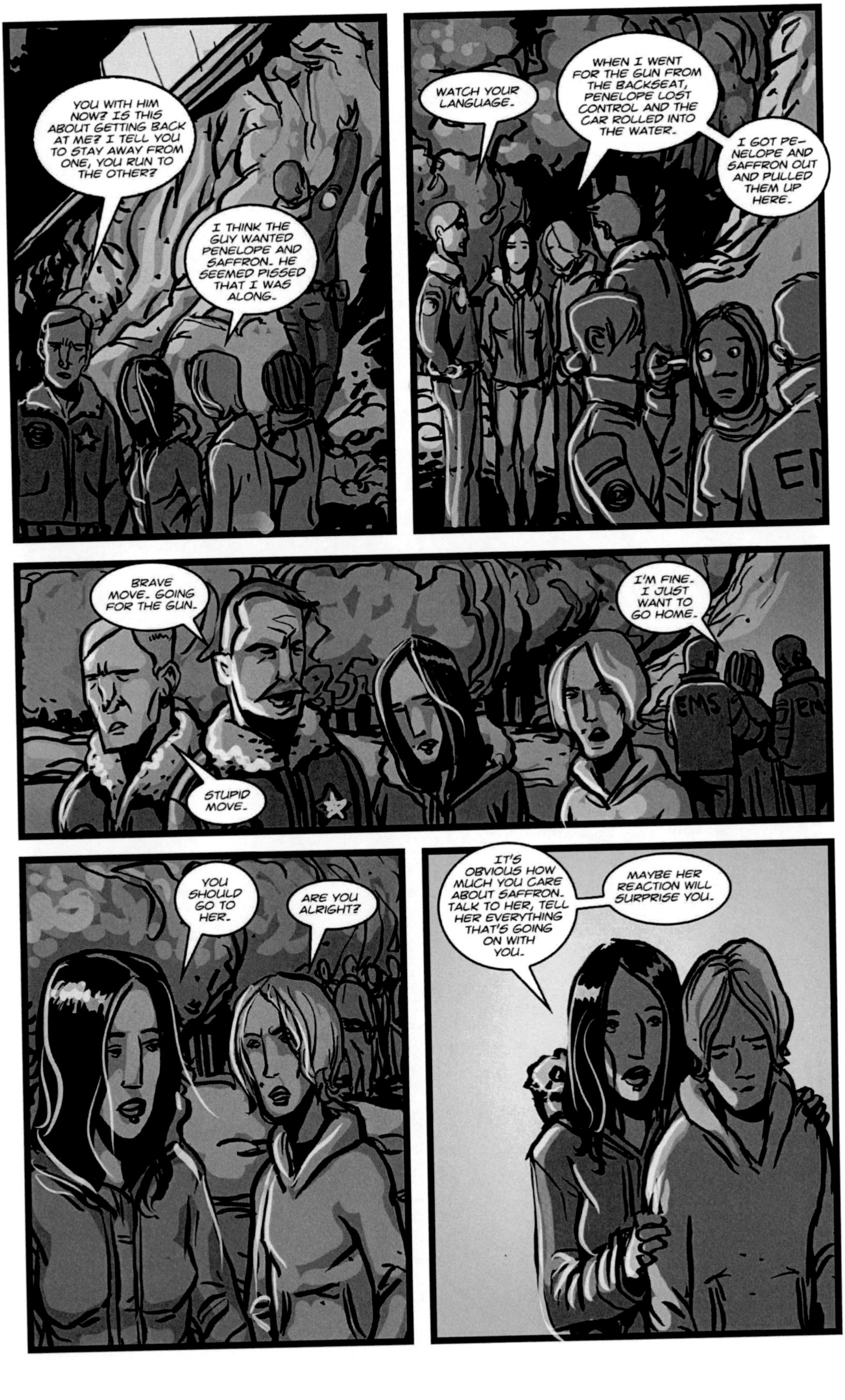
YOU WITH HIM NOW? IS THIS ABOUT GETTING BACK AT ME? I TELL YOU TO STAY AWAY FROM ONE, YOU RUN TO THE OTHER?
I THINK THE GUY WANTED PENELOPE AND SAFFRON. HE SEEMED PISSED THAT I WAS ALONG.
WATCH YOUR LANGUAGE.
WHEN I WENT FOR THE GUN FROM THE BACKSEAT, PENELOPE LOST CONTROL AND THE CAR ROLLED INTO THE WATER.
I GOT PENELOPE AND SAFFRON OUT AND PULLED THEM UP HERE.
BRAVE MOVE. GOING FOR THE GUN.
STUPID MOVE.
I'M FINE. I JUST WANT TO GO HOME.
EMS
YOU SHOULD GO TO HER.
ARE YOU ALRIGHT?
IT'S OBVIOUS HOW MUCH YOU CARE ABOUT SAFFRON. TALK TO HER, TELL HER EVERYTHING THAT'S GOING ON WITH YOU.
MAYBE HER REACTION WILL SURPRISE YOU.

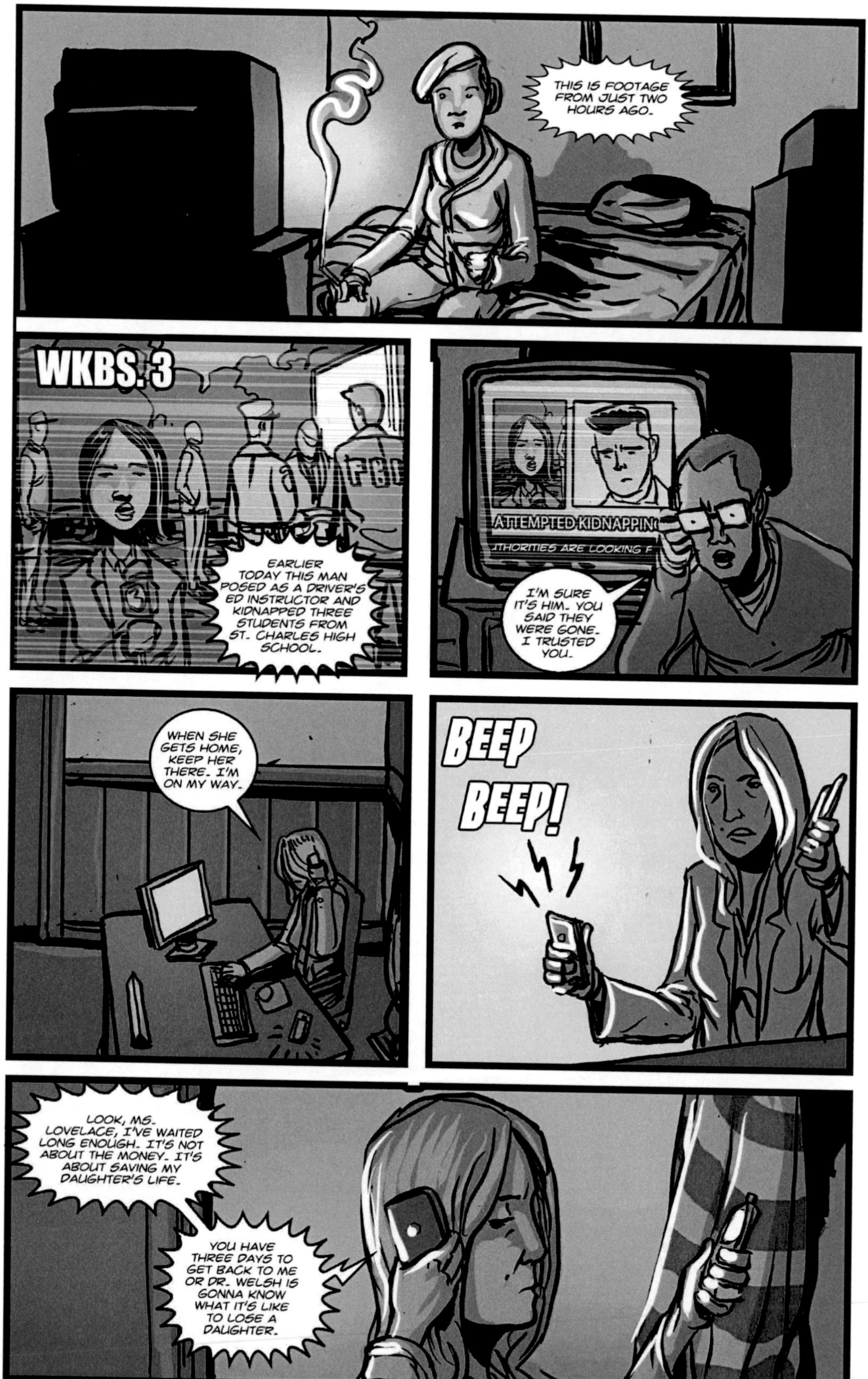
THIS IS FOOTAGE FROM JUST TWO HOURS AGO.
WKBS. 3
EARLIER TODAY THIS MAN POSED AS A DRIVER'S ED INSTRUCTOR AND KIDNAPPED THREE STUDENTS FROM ST. CHARLES HIGH SCHOOL.
ATTEMPTED KIDNAPPING
THORITIES ARE LOOKING F
I'M SURE IT'S HIM. YOU SAID THEY WERE GONE. I TRUSTED YOU.
WHEN SHE GETS HOME, KEEP HER THERE. I'M ON MY WAY.
BEEP
BEEP!
LOOK, MS. LOVELACE, I'VE WAITED LONG ENOUGH. IT'S NOT ABOUT THE MONEY. IT'S ABOUT SAVING MY DAUGHTER'S LIFE.
YOU HAVE THREE DAYS TO GET BACK TO ME OR DR. WELSH IS GONNA KNOW WHAT IT'S LIKE TO LOSE A DAUGHTER.

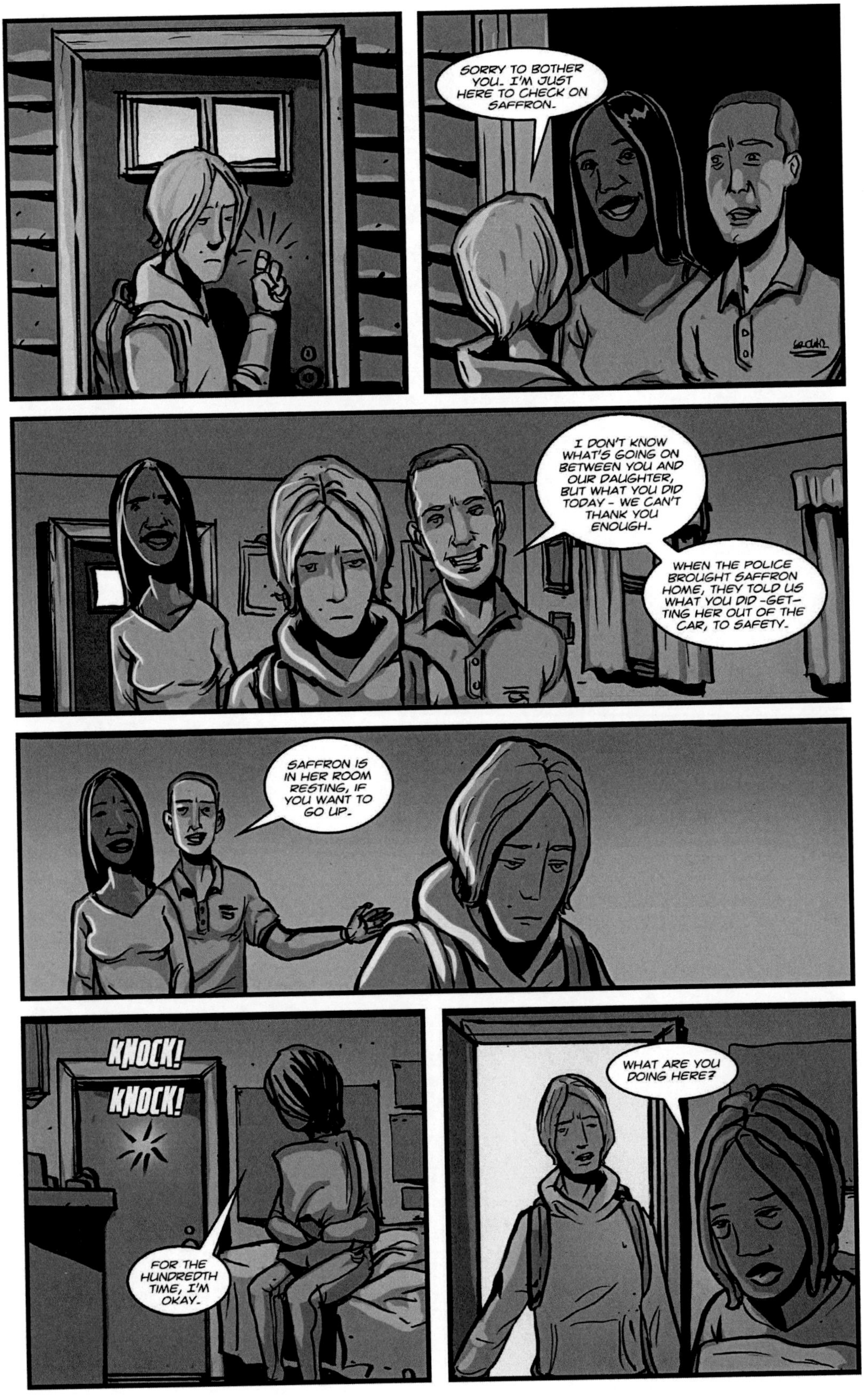
SORRY TO BOTHER YOU. I'M JUST HERE TO CHECK ON SAFFRON.
I DON'T KNOW WHAT'S GOING ON BETWEEN YOU AND OUR DAUGHTER, BUT WHAT YOU DID TODAY - WE CAN'T THANK YOU ENOUGH.
WHEN THE POLICE BROUGHT SAFFRON HOME, THEY TOLD US WHAT YOU DID -GETTING HER OUT OF THE CAR, TO SAFETY.
SAFFRON IS IN HER ROOM RESTING, IF YOU WANT TO GO UP.
KNOCK!
KNOCK!
FOR THE HUNDREDTH TIME, I'M OKAY.
WHAT ARE YOU DOING HERE?

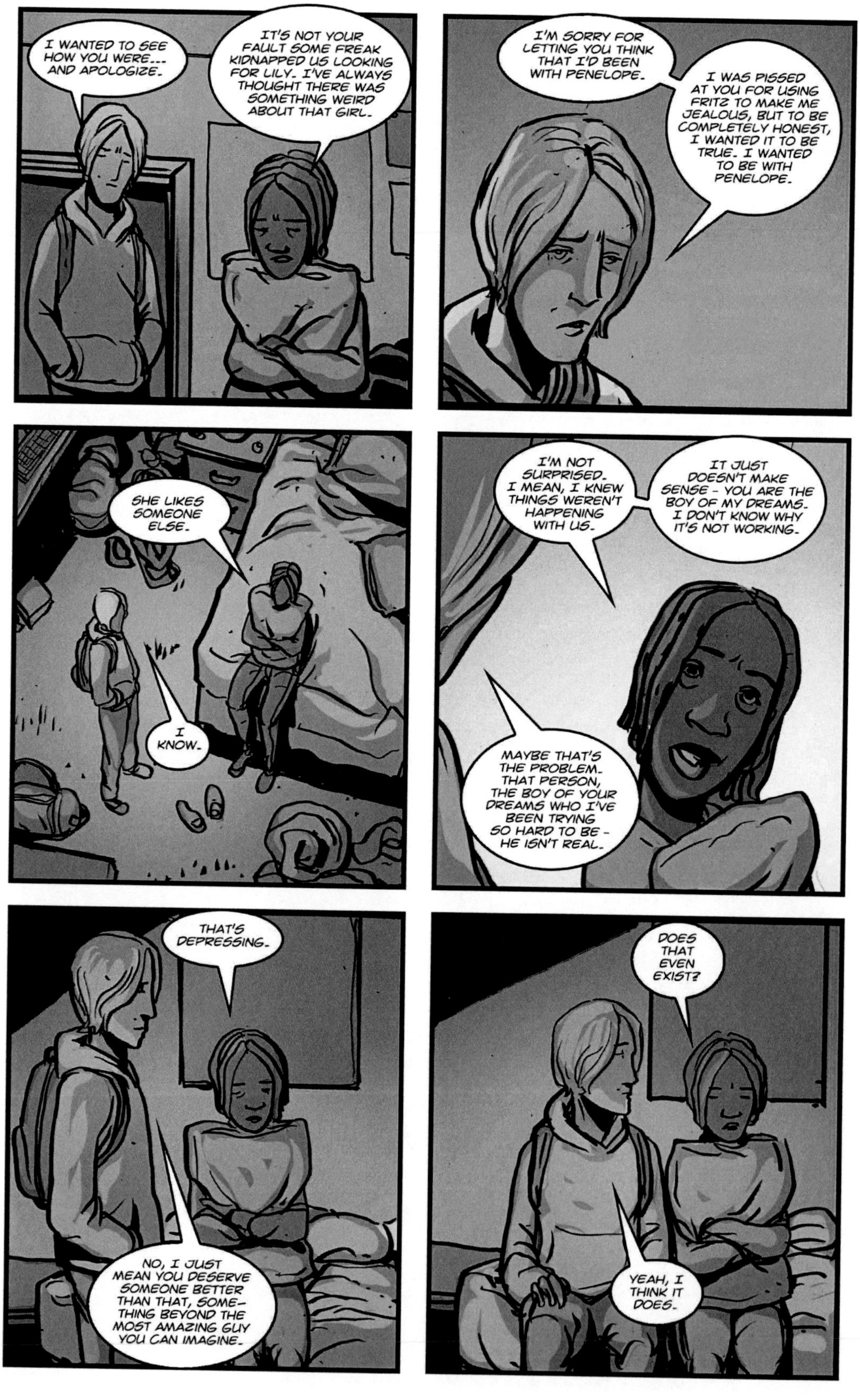
I WANTED TO SEE HOW YOU WERE... AND APOLOGIZE.
IT'S NOT YOUR FAULT SOME FREAK KIDNAPPED US LOOKING FOR LILY. I'VE ALWAYS THOUGHT THERE WAS SOMETHING WEIRD ABOUT THAT GIRL.
I'M SORRY FOR LETTING YOU THINK THAT I'D BEEN WITH PENELOPE.
I WAS PISSED AT YOU FOR USING FRITZ TO MAKE ME JEALOUS, BUT TO BE COMPLETELY HONEST, I WANTED IT TO BE TRUE. I WANTED TO BE WITH PENELOPE.
SHE LIKES SOMEONE ELSE.
I KNOW.
I'M NOT SURPRISED. I MEAN, I KNEW THINGS WEREN'T HAPPENING WITH US.
IT JUST DOESN'T MAKE SENSE - YOU ARE THE BOY OF MY DREAMS. I DON'T KNOW WHY IT'S NOT WORKING.
MAYBE THAT'S THE PROBLEM. THAT PERSON, THE BOY OF YOUR DREAMS WHO I'VE BEEN TRYING SO HARD TO BE - HE ISN'T REAL.
THAT'S DEPRESSING.
NO, I JUST MEAN YOU DESERVE SOMEONE BETTER THAN THAT, SOME-THING BEYOND THE MOST AMAZING GUY YOU CAN IMAGINE.
DOES THAT EVEN EXIST?
YEAH, I THINK IT DOES.

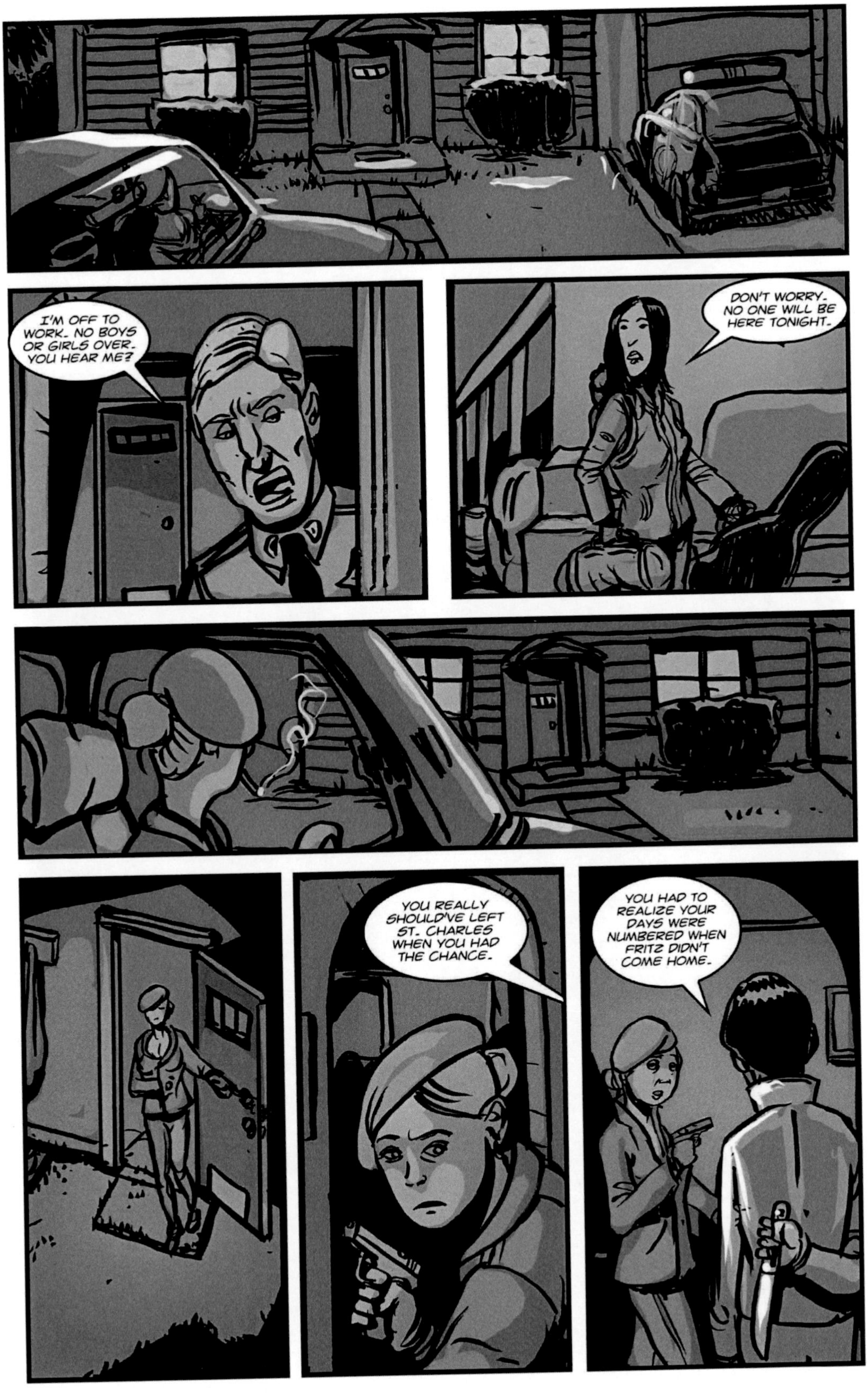
I'M OFF TO WORK. NO BOYS OR GIRLS OVER. YOU HEAR ME?
DON'T WORRY. NO ONE WILL BE HERE TONIGHT.
YOU REALLY SHOULD'VE LEFT ST. CHARLES WHEN YOU HAD THE CHANCE.
YOU HAD TO REALIZE YOUR DAYS WERE NUMBERED WHEN FRITZ DIDN'T COME HOME.

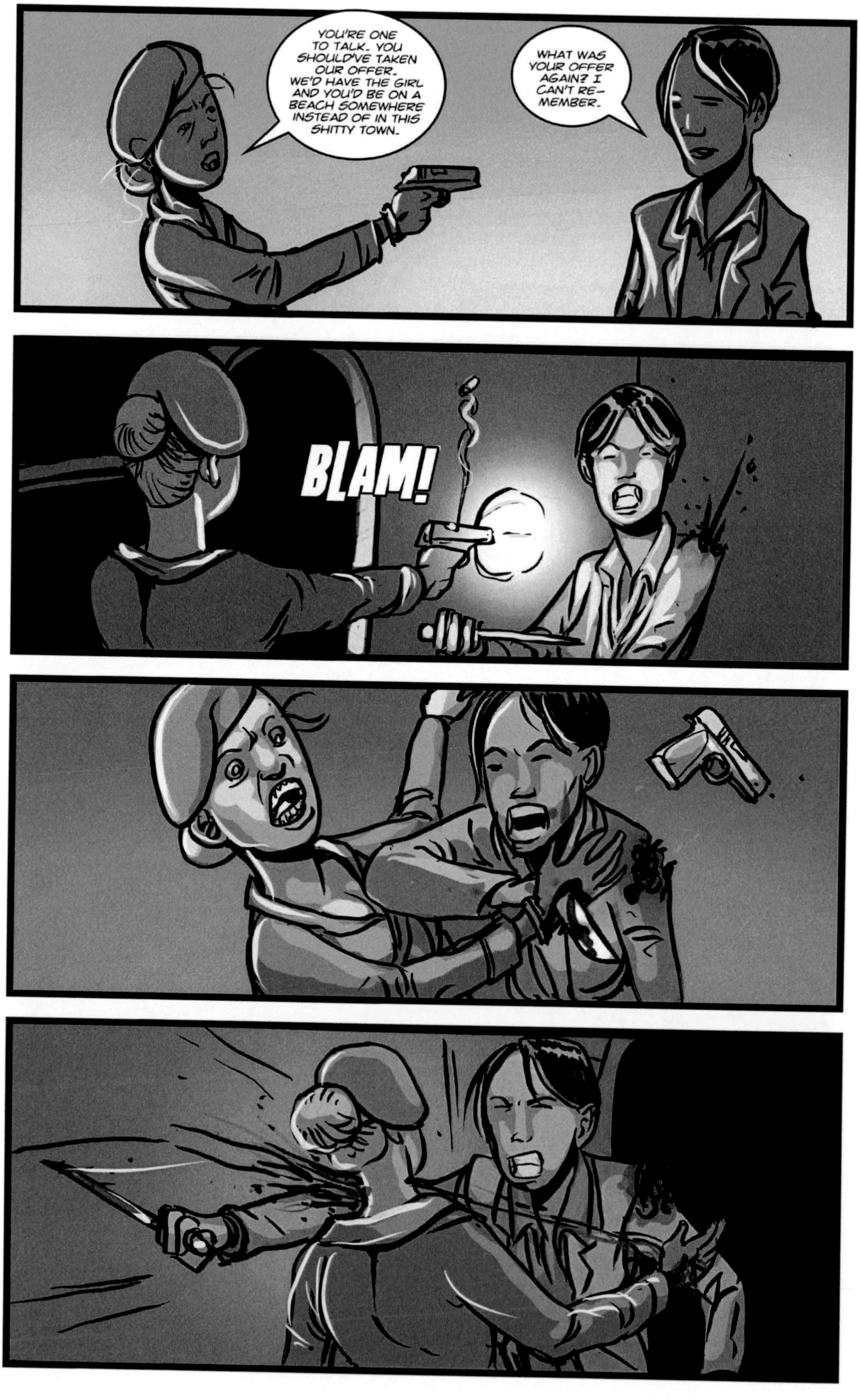
YOU'RE ONE TO TALK. YOU SHOULD'VE TAKEN OUR OFFER. WE'D HAVE THE GIRL AND YOU'D BE ON A BEACH SOMEWHERE INSTEAD OF IN THIS SHITTY TOWN.
WHAT WAS YOUR OFFER AGAIN? I CAN'T RE-MEMBER.
BLAM!

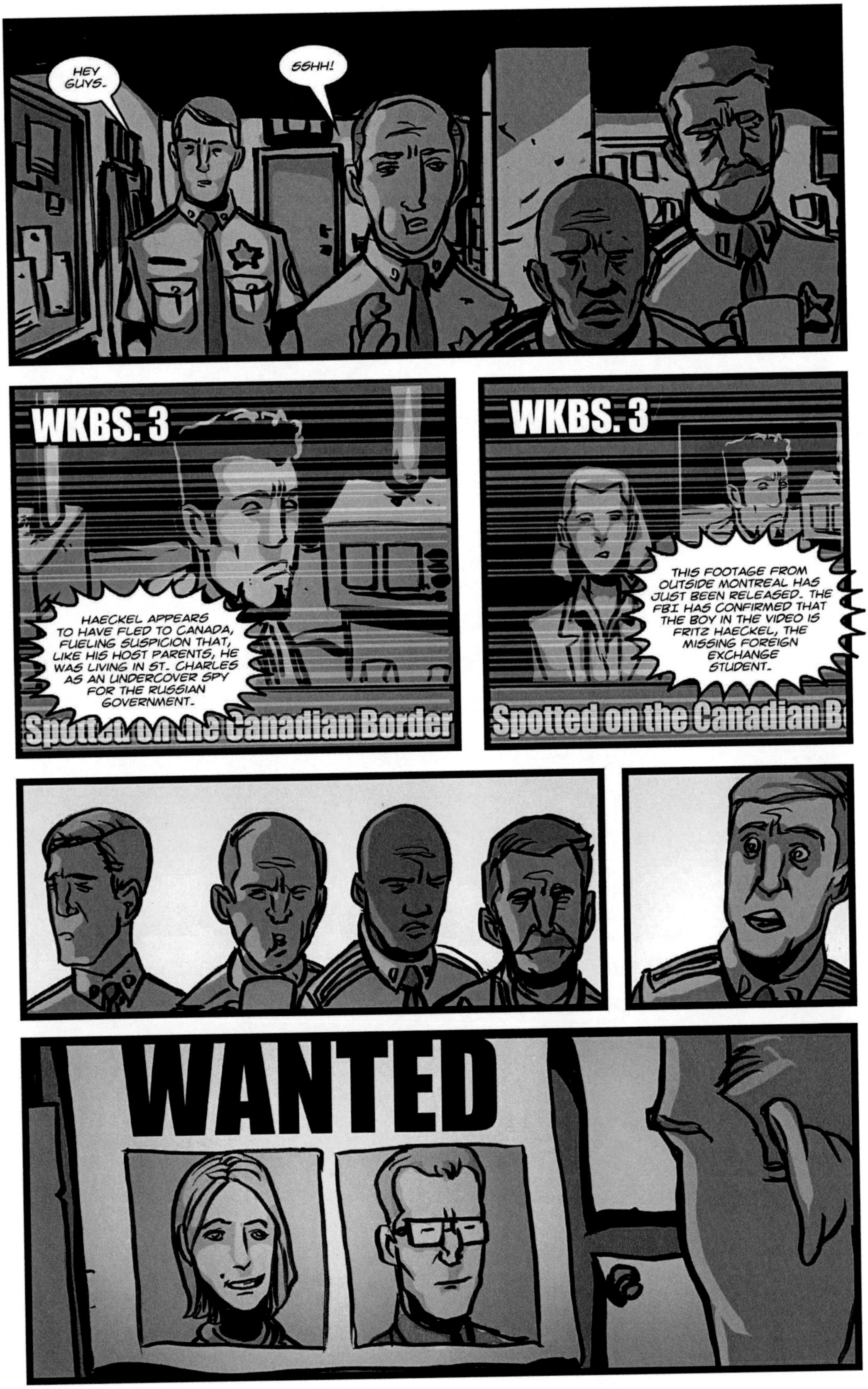
HEY GUYS.
SSHH!
WKBS. 3
HAECKEL APPEARS TO HAVE FLED TO CANADA, FUELING SUSPICION THAT, LIKE HIS HOST PARENTS, HE WAS LIVING IN ST. CHARLES AS AN UNDERCOVER SPY FOR THE RUSSIAN GOVERNMENT.
Spotted on the Canadian Border
WKBS. 3
THIS FOOTAGE FROM OUTSIDE MONTREAL HAS JUST BEEN RELEASED. THE FBI HAS CONFIRMED THAT THE BOY IN THE VIDEO IS FRITZ HAECKEL, THE MISSING FOREIGN EXCHANGE STUDENT.
Spotted on the Canadian B
WANTED

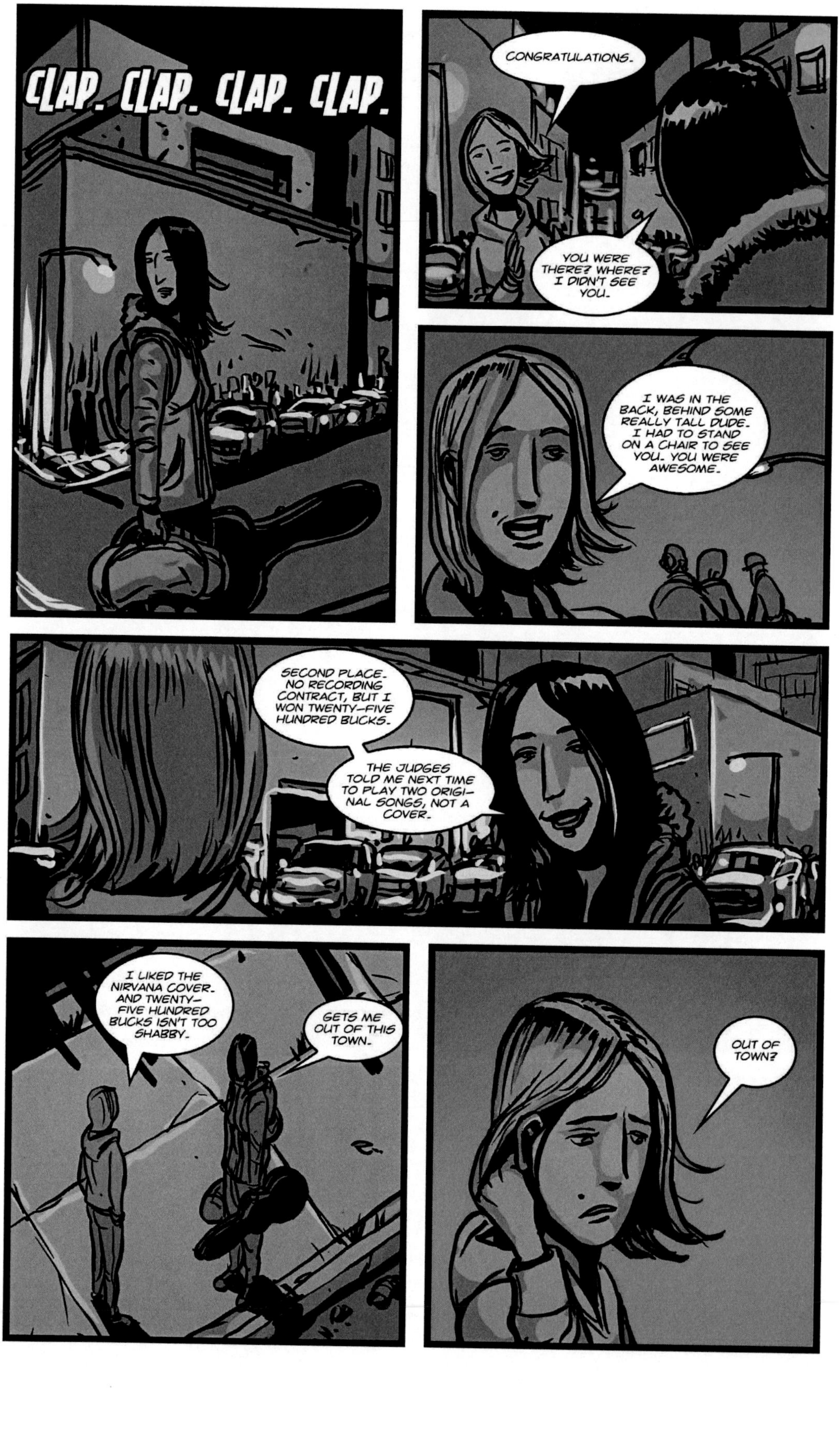
CLAP. CLAP. CLAP. CLAP.
CONGRATULATIONS.
YOU WERE THERE? WHERE? I DIDN'T SEE YOU.
I WAS IN THE BACK, BEHIND SOME REALLY TALL DUDE. I HAD TO STAND ON A CHAIR TO SEE YOU. YOU WERE AWESOME.
SECOND PLACE. NO RECORDING CONTRACT, BUT I WON TWENTY-FIVE HUNDRED BUCKS.
THE JUDGES TOLD ME NEXT TIME TO PLAY TWO ORIGINAL SONGS, NOT A COVER.
I LIKED THE NIRVANA COVER. AND TWENTY-FIVE HUNDRED BUCKS ISN'T TOO SHABBY.
GETS ME OUT OF THIS TOWN.
OUT OF TOWN?

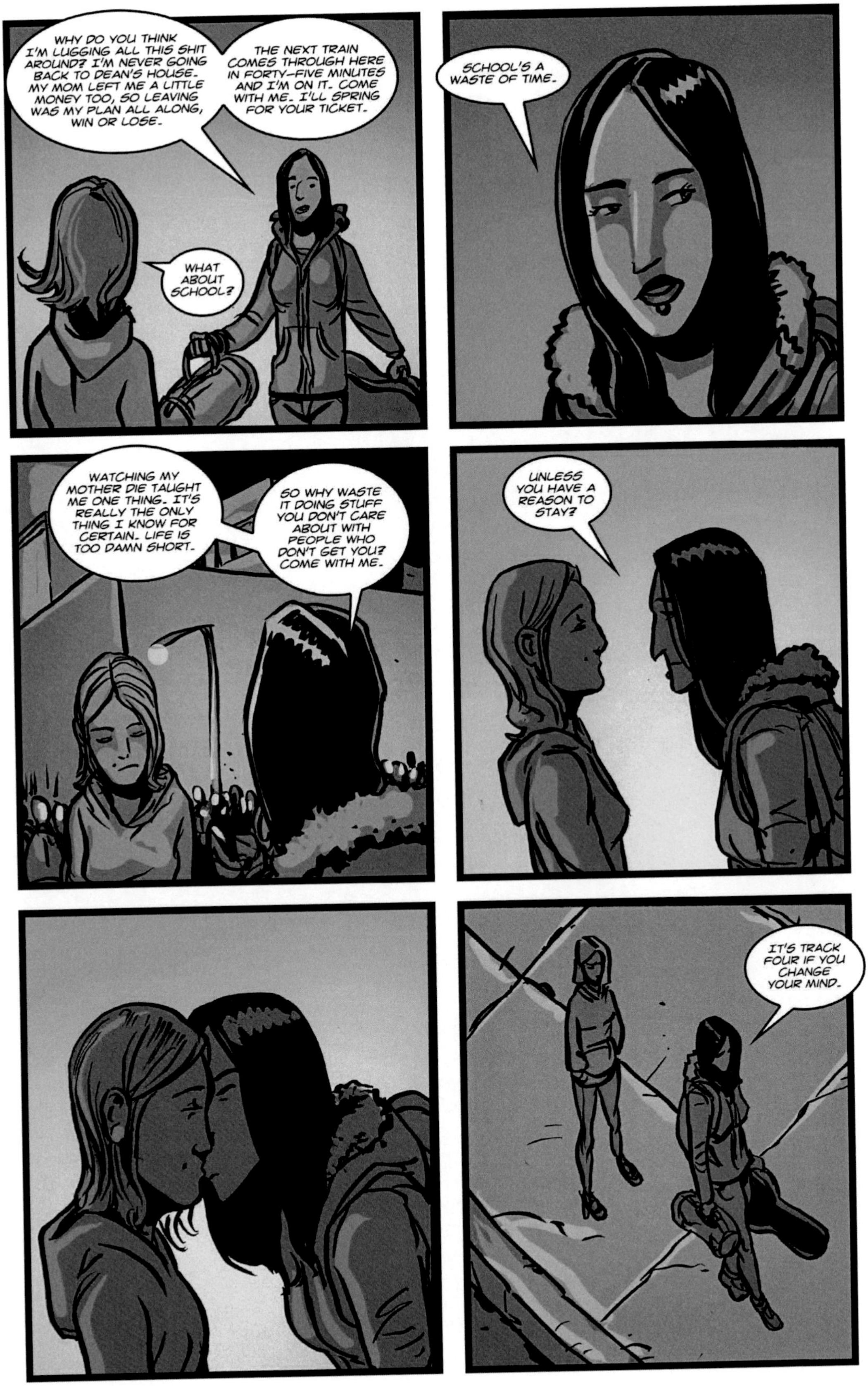
WHY DO YOU THINK I'M LUGGING ALL THIS SHIT AROUND? I'M NEVER GOING BACK TO DEAN'S HOUSE. MY MOM LEFT ME A LITTLE MONEY TOO, SO LEAVING WAS MY PLAN ALL ALONG, WIN OR LOSE.
THE NEXT TRAIN COMES THROUGH HERE IN FORTY-FIVE MINUTES AND I'M ON IT. COME WITH ME. I'LL SPRING FOR YOUR TICKET.
WHAT ABOUT SCHOOL?
SCHOOL'S A WASTE OF TIME.
WATCHING MY MOTHER DIE TAUGHT ME ONE THING. IT'S REALLY THE ONLY THING I KNOW FOR CERTAIN. LIFE IS TOO DAMN SHORT.
SO WHY WASTE IT DOING STUFF YOU DON'T CARE ABOUT WITH PEOPLE WHO DON'T GET YOU? COME WITH ME.
UNLESS YOU HAVE A REASON TO STAY?
IT'S TRACK FOUR IF YOU CHANGE YOUR MIND.

SLAM!

LILY?

WHAT HAPPENED?

SPY MOM IS NO LONGER AN ISSUE.

YOU'RE BLEEDING.

IT'S HEALING.

WHO IS YOUR PATIENT HERE?

ORIANA, LET ME LOOK AT THE WOUND.

I'VE SEEN ADA'S BANK ACCOUNT. YOU'VE PUT OUR DAUGHTER IN DANGER WHILE TRYING TO SAVE STRANGERS. WHO'S THE PATIENT?

ADA MAKES CONTACT WITH THE PATIENTS FIRST. WITHOUT HER, I HAVEN'T BEEN ABLE TO APPROACH THIS ONE.

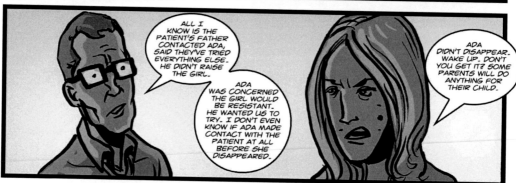

ALL I KNOW IS THE PATIENT'S FATHER CONTACTED ADA, SAID THEY'VE TRIED EVERYTHING ELSE. HE DIDN'T RAISE THE GIRL.

ADA WAS CONCERNED THE GIRL WOULD BE RESISTANT. HE WANTED US TO TRY. I DON'T EVEN KNOW IF ADA MADE CONTACT WITH THE PATIENT AT ALL BEFORE SHE DISAPPEARED.

ADA DIDN'T DISAPPEAR. WAKE UP. DON'T YOU GET IT? SOME PARENTS WILL DO ANYTHING FOR THEIR CHILD.

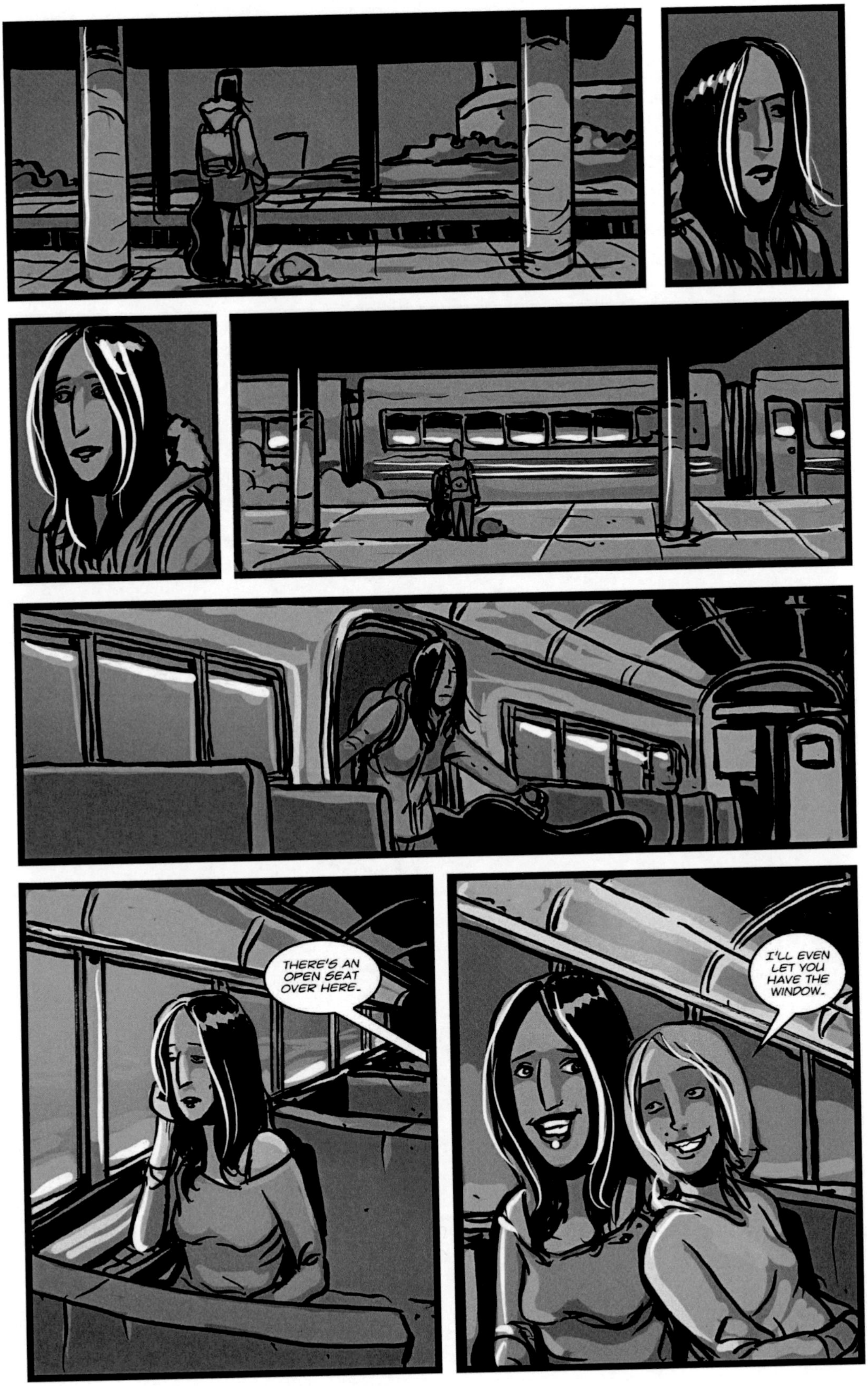
THERE'S AN OPEN SEAT OVER HERE.
I'LL EVEN LET YOU HAVE THE WINDOW.

Jennie Wood is currently revising her first novel, A Boy Like Me. She is also a contributor to the award-winning, New York Times best-selling comic anthology, FUBAR: Empire of the Rising Dead as well as the upcoming FUBAR: American History Z and Vic Boone: Bourbon and Buckshot anthologies. She writes non-fiction features for the educational website, infoplease.com, including a series on transgender-related issues. For more, go to www.jenniewood.com.

Jeff McComsey is the artist on FLUTTER for 215 INK and is Editor in Chief of the World War II zombie anthology and New York Times Best Seller FUBAR, now into its third volume. Primarily Jeff spends his time illustrating funny books and anything else that comes within arm's reach. When he's not chained to his desk drawing pages, he's chained to his desk... drawing pages. You can see more of his work at:
mccomseycomix.wordpress.com